SKIER FLINGS COOL SPRAY ON JACKSON LAKE, WYOMING; JAMES W. ELDER
OVERLEAF: DUNE BUGS ROMP AT CAPE COD, MASSACHUSETTS; B. ANTHONY STEWART, NATIONAL GEOGRAPHIC STAFF

VACATIONLAND U.S.A.

VACATIONLAND

U.S.A.

NATIONAL GEOGRAPHIC SOCIETY

VACATIONLAND U.S.A.
A volume in the World in Color Library prepared by the
NATIONAL GEOGRAPHIC BOOK SERVICE,
Merle Severy, Chief

Published by the National Geographic Society
MELVIN M. PAYNE, President
MELVILLE BELL GROSVENOR, Editor-in-Chief
FREDERICK G. VOSBURGH, Editor

This book was created under the guidance of
FRANC SHOR by the following staff:

MERLE SEVERY, *Editor*

SEYMOUR L. FISHBEIN, *Managing Editor*

THOMAS B. ALLEN, *Project Editor*

CHARLES O. HYMAN, *Art Director*

DAVID H. McCUEN, *Picture Editor*

ROSS BENNETT, WILLIAM CHILDRESS,
DAVID F. ROBINSON, *Editor-Writers*

WILHELM R. SAAKE, *Production Manager*

WILLIAM W. SMITH, *Engraving and Printing*

JAN NAGEL CLARKSON, MARY SWAIN HOOVER, *Research*

EDWARD MARTIN WILSON, *Design*

ROBERT J. VILSECK, *Production;* JOHN R. METCALFE, *Engraving*

DIANE S. MARTON, CAROL M. McNAMARA,
JOY SPALDING RABIN, BARBARA G. STEWART,
ALVIN L. TICE, MOLLY WOODS, *Assistants*

JOHN D. GARST, BOBBY G. CROCKETT, *Maps*

WERNER JANNEY, *Style*

ANNE K. McCAIN, TONI WARNER, *Index*

Contributions by

Russell Bourne, Thomas Y. Canby, Dean Conger, Dick Durrance II, W. E. Garrett, Ralph Gray, Jay Johnston, Anne Dirkes Kobor, Samuel W. Matthews, Arthur P. Miller, Jr., George F. Mobley, Albert Moldvay, John J. Putman, Verla Lee Smith, James L. Stanfield, B. Anthony Stewart, and Peter T. White of the National Geographic staff; Chris Allen, Wayne Barrett, James A. Cox, Charles W. Ebersole, Paul Engle, Colin Fletcher, John Fulton, C. David Hiser, Bern Keating, David Kennedy, Robert W. Madden, Robert M. McClung, Charles E. Mohr, Martin Rogers, Peg Zecher, and others

500 illustrations in color, 18 maps

First printing 325,000 copies

Standard Book Number 87044-083-7
Library of Congress Catalog Card Number 79-112905

Right: Highroads to adventure like the Natchez Trace Parkway braid Vacationland U.S.A.; Charles Harbutt, Magnum

Foreword

Standing on deck in mask, wet suit, and flippers, a heavy tank strapped on my back, I anxiously watched my companions add weights to my belt. As if I didn't already have enough on to make me sink like a stone!

"Good heavens," I thought, "they're trying to drown me."

With family and friends, I had sailed my yawl *White Mist* up the Hudson, off to explore northeastern America by water. Lake Champlain offered unexpected adventure: a chance to join in a search for sunken Revolutionary War ships. I am not a strong swimmer; besides, I had never mastered scuba-diving. But the desire to find something new won out, and I followed the experts over the side.

Strange. Instead of plummeting to the bottom, I felt an extraordinary lightness, and I could breathe quite normally. It seemed so effortless to descend and rise. A wondrous realm opened before my eyes.

Yes, I had the thrill of surfacing with a plank pried from an old wreck. From 1776? No, but I treasure the joy of that quest, and the discovery that at 67 I was still ready for the challenge of a new vacation adventure.

Challenge. Quest. Discovery. Joy. No longer are most Americans content to vacation in a hammock. Forty million a year pitch a tent or park a trailer at one of the Nation's 500,000 campsites. Millions more fill the seasons with hiking, biking, spelunking, trail-riding, canoeing, bird-watching, clambaking, skiing. But then, we've always been a nation of doers. We had to make our own life on the frontier, had to entertain ourselves. We learned and grew by taking on new challenges. Restless, curious, we were ever eager to see what lay beyond the horizon.

Our Space Age vacations reflect that tradition. Pioneers opened the spacious West with their house on wheels, the prairie schooner. Today we're rediscovering the land in camper, trailer, or motor home. And, just as astronauts on the moon look back to earth with new perspective, this change of scene enables us to examine our own lives with fresh eyes. Pit your wits against a trout in a sparkling mountain stream and cares fall away. Relaxed, re-created through challenging activity, I've often come up with solutions to problems that had plagued me.

A do-it-together vacation is an investment in family strength—and in America's future. I've found that hiking,

climbing, horseback riding in the Tetons provide a shared experience and open young eyes to nature's wonders. Let the boys set up camp for the night. Let the girls do the cooking. It channels young energies, gives the children a lifelong interest in their land.

We're a nation of city dwellers—70 percent of our population squeezed onto less than 2 percent of our land. But the wilderness stands there waiting. For each of our more than 200 million citizens, America has set aside an acre or more of public playland, much of it surprisingly accessible. A national forest, a wildlife refuge, or one of 3,000 state park areas may lie at your doorstep. Our Interstate Highway System speeds you to distant places you had to mount an expedition to get to a few years ago.

You can put your boat in recently created Lake Powell, cruise and water-ski amid the grandeur of Glen Canyon, as I have, and visit Rainbow Bridge, that incredible arch of stone soaring higher than the U. S. Capitol dome. Such opportunities exemplify a new concept in our National Park System—recreation areas to challenge the athletic, and to take pressure off the crowded national parks.

Vacationland U.S.A. portrays the wealth of holiday dividends to be gained in these and other areas across the continent. A million miles of rewarding research over the past 12 months converge in this book to present a year-round

A skiing family swings down Aspen's slopes; Dick Durrance II, National Geographic photographer

Houseboat ramblers find the good life on the Mississippi; Albert Moldvay, National Geographic staff

panorama of fun-filled, purposeful pursuits, from snowmobiling in New Hampshire to surfing in Hawaii. Just as National Geographic staff men, their families, and other contributors experienced its adventures, so may you and your family—this year and for years to come.

How would you like to have a cabin by a wilderness lake in Alaska? Or ride with the cowhands at your vacation home on the range? Or raft the rapids in mile-deep Grand Canyon? Or laze along on a Mississippi houseboat? Or scale Mount Rainier?

In these pages we show you how. Nor did we forget that Junior wants to go to the moon, that Sis has stars in her eyes. We've included a tour of John F. Kennedy Space Center, a Hollywood studio, Disneyland. The whole family will relish a swing through San Francisco, Mystic Seaport, San Antonio at fiesta time, candlelit Williamsburg at Christmas. America reveals other faces in Pennsylvania Dutch country, in Cajun country amid the Louisiana bayous, in the Ozarks, where mountain folk weave and whittle, in Indian country, where tribesmen dance for rain.

Our choice is wide. We can clack up a crazy little mountain-goat railroad to the top of Mount Washington, glide past alligators in Okefenokee Swamp, savor the quiet joys of hunting sea shells, explore ghost towns of the Old West, witness the Made in U.S.A. skills that can fashion a Louisville Slugger or 76 trombones. America in all its wondrous variety beckons. Let's go—for the time of our lives!

Melville Bell Grosvenor

CONTENTS

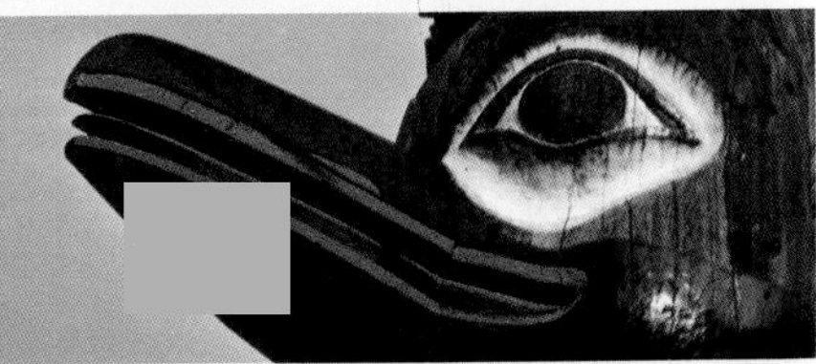

...And the Pursuit of Happiness

WE HOLD THIS TRUTH TO BE SELF-EVIDENT, THAT LEISURE LEAVENS LIFE. SO TAKE OFF! MEASURE YOUR LEISURE IN DAYS OR MONTHS BUT WRAP IT IN EXCITEMENT, SPICE IT WITH CHALLENGE, FUN, ADVENTURE. BEGIN WITH A QUESTING SPIRIT, END WITH THE DISCOVERY THAT HERE IN AMERICA THERE'S WORLD ENOUGH—AND TIME.

Breaker at his heels, a surfer rides the crest of adventure off Higgins Beach in Maine; James R. Holland

Vacation: time to

TAKE OFF

Out in the harbor they wait for us, nodding, impatient to slip the cable and head for the horizon. At the airport they wait, wings spread to gather in the rush of air and freedom. They wait in carports for . . . five o'clock on Friday afternoon . . . school's knell on a day in June . . . the holiday that stretches a weekend . . . the festive week that rings out the old year . . . vacation weeks that promise renewal. Toil has ended, and we must take off. But where to?

Stand by a highway in summer and look east. Here come cars from Ohio, Rhode Island, Georgia. Turn, and you see Utah, California, Wyoming. East waves to West as they pass, each bound for the other's backyard. Floridians pitch a tent in Wisconsin. Alaskans broil on Hawaiian strands just jet-hours from the snows of home. A suburban split-level shrinks to foldaway bunks in a boat or trailer, or just a sleeping bag with a rec room from horizon to horizon. Like Walt Whitman we "take to the open road, healthy, free, the world before me." And like Henry David Thoreau we "come home from far, from adventures . . . and discoveries."

Federal recreation planners in 1965 counted six million of us on skis, twice as many on ice skates, three times that number sledding. And they toted up 451 million picnics! Looking to 1980, they see us spreading 668 million picnics under the skies of Vacationland U.S.A. By then we'll pursue more than 10 billion good times, including 1.67 billion swims, 89 million hikes, 173 million camp-outs, 422 million fishing trips.

Walking and swimming, coming on fast, already top pleasure drives. Still, in 1969, 110 million of us rolled up enough miles to cover 458,000 round trips to the moon. Someday we may vacation there.

JAMES L. STANFIELD, NATIONAL GEOGRAPHIC PHOTOGRAPHER

Patient as pups outside a schoolhouse, craft of the airways, highways, and waterways wait in the shadow of workaday Chicago. Weekends and vacations will scatter them far as families take off in pursuit of fun.

Unwind in a whirl of

EXCITEMENT

DAVID JACKSON. RIGHT: JAMES L. AMOS, NATIONAL GEOGRAPHIC PHOTOGRAPHER

We're a turned-on nation, antennas tuned for excitement. And it comes through loud and clear. We parade with the old circus wagons in Milwaukee, with the Mummers in Philadelphia, with the Rose Bowl Queen in Pasadena. We rock with the jazzmen at Newport, roll into high gear for the 500-mile classic at Indianapolis. We plan and save all year for a jaunt to the Kentucky Derby, or yell ourselves hoarse at hometown trotting tracks, auto rallies, turtle derbies, sled dog races.

Rockets' glare paints the town red as Milwaukee salutes the Fourth of July, and a wild ride in a Chicago amusement park rockets squealing copilots on a flight of thrills.

We plunge into the fantasy world of Disneyland, the swinging world of San Francisco, the with-it world of New York. Give us an amusement park and we'll cheerfully plunk down quarters to be spun, jolted, dizzied, scared out of our wits on a two-minute ride to nowhere—but filled with excitement.

If we can't trek to the stupendous fireworks in Washington, D. C., on the Fourth, we'll head for the nearest patriotic blast-off and crane and cheer long after twilight's last gleaming.

Wild West zest sends us to rodeos and their go-for-broke daredevils, to "frontier" towns and the quick-draw drama of high-noon shootouts.

The new and different excite us. We watch for strange ships with strange flags nosing into New Orleans harbor, threading the St. Lawrence Seaway, entering the Golden Gate. What's newborn at the zoo? We'll go and see—to tune out humdrum and tune in excitement.

Earth, sea, and sky sing a siren song of

CHALLENGE

A sailplaning Texan flirts with thunderclouds, sand sailors race the California wind, and a diver explores the ethereal Eden of a Florida reef.

Last week he sold insurance or managed a restaurant; this week he floats high in a ghostland of cloud and air and sky, hung in the heavens on outthrust wings. Yesterday he branded cattle or roofed a house; today he streaks a mile a minute on seas of sand, lines taut as sinews, sail bulging like hide over the wind's invisible muscle. He delivered your mail, fixed your car, grew your carrots; then he quit your world to challenge one you wonder at, his life belted to his back and his senses flooded with the awesome majesty of the ocean's vestibule.

He's the reacher, the striver, the stretcher of limits, a man ignited by the unspoken dare of a top speed in a record book or a killing curve on a race course. Challenge gnaws at him, taunts him, wrenches him away from his dinner table to blacken his hands in the garage and maybe squeeze another spurt of acceleration out of that beautiful, beautiful carburetor. Challenge wakes him in the night to leaf through visions of fields far below and a blossom of nylon above and a tiny target he almost landed on but missed when a gust caught his chute. It goads him to sea for tarpon, to desert for hot-air ballooning, to mountainside for bobsledding, to river and inlet for outboard racing, to seaside scarp for an exalting plunge and a clean slice into the waves below.

Many try the things he does. Couples go snorkeling, housewives fly, whole families ski. But he does his thing to the hilt. Hang the expense, brave the risk, push the limit. Sixty miles an hour across the sand? Try for 62!

He's a rare breed, cares little that one man envies him, another brands him fool: "You'd never get *me* to try that!"

Never? Never to ride the dizzy crest of challenge, to plumb new depths in strange seas, to tease gravity and sail like a bird on the unseen swells of a crisp, clean ocean of air? Never say never.

JERRY GREENBERG. UPPER: THOMAS NEBBIA.
OPPOSITE: SANDOR ALDOTT

Turn off the highway, turn on the FUN

Circle your town on a map; make the radius an easy half-day's drive. What a world of fun awaits you in that circle! Trout streams you never waded . . . trails you never hiked . . . places you know only as a blur on turnpike exit signs . . . swimming spots where life tips upside down just for the fun of it . . . lakes your map doesn't mention. Lake-makers fill hundreds of new ones every year; they help prevent floods, improve farmlands—and refresh vacationists.

If your road forks, follow Robert Frost: "I took the one less traveled by, and that has made all the difference." Take your time down the super-byways, time enough to pause at hamlets where kids will sell you lemonade on the lawn, where the auctioneer at the firehouse will sell you anything. You may find a church supper that leaves you gasping "Amen!" Or an Old Home Week or town centennial, complete with vintage cars, swaggering bands, and men sporting beards they've curried for months.

Look for a farmer who'll sell you all the apples or berries you can pick—or pumpkins that make neat jack-o'-lanterns. Come summer, you could spend a spell down on the farm; thousands of farmers and ranchers welcome city guests.

Nearly three out of four of us herd in cities. Often when the countryside calls we herd in traffic inching toward beach or mountain or forest. Ever think of breaking away to where you can get out and walk—or bike? Rack bikes on car top or trunk and find country lanes with picture-postcard scenes enlivened by the music of wind hum and insect fiddling.

We've come a long way since Puritans scorned play as a "mispense of time" and Virginians in 1619 outlawed idleness. But we still talk grimly about "the leisure problem." Watch kids solve it; they're untutored masters of the art of fun. A child's hand turns a stick into a pirate's sword; his magic molds men out of snow, swells puddles to seas, hills to Everests.

Alas, maturity. Too often his elders make of hills a strip mine; too often they stain the clouds with dust and smoke. Now we hear the cry of the imperiled land, and we band to save what we could never replace. Where's the fun in a bulldozed meadow, a chain-sawed glade? Conservationists could use another voice. Let's make it ours—to keep the freshness in our circle of fun.

ROBERT W. MADDEN

A country lane for peaceful pedaling, a swimmin' hole for kicking up your heels: Funspots like these in rural New England entice travelers off the busy pikes.

Wild time: a family

ADVENTURE

"I'm holding on tight, Dad. Don't worry!" Dad grabs a safety line, squints through the spray, one eye on the riot of white water, the other on the kids, his mind full of father-thoughts: *Seems like only*

yesterday they were too scared to ride the merry-go-round. Now look at them! The glorified inner tube bucks and bounces—and bears them to adventure. It could be a rattling, steam-snorting old train . . . a hike around a volcano's rim . . . a crawl through a cavern of wonders . . . a muleback ride on the switchback trail down into Grand Canyon. Grab hold of adventure: it binds a family together.

GEORGE F. MOBLEY, NATIONAL GEOGRAPHIC PHOTOGRAPHER

Buoyant spirits light the faces of foam-flung adventurers on the rapid transit of Wyoming's Shoshone River.

EMORY KRISTOF AND (ABOVE) DICK DURRANCE II, NATIONAL GEOGRAPHIC PHOTOGRAPHERS. ABOVE RIGHT: THOMAS NEBBIA. OPPOSITE: ROBERT W. MADDEN

In a spacious land, a bounty of beauty awaits all who

QUEST

"Spring entices, summer makes you welcome, autumn gives you a lingering farewell.... Winter provides the testing months," wrote Edwin Way Teale, who pursued the seasons across the face of America. He clocked the speed of greening spring: 15 miles a day northward, 100 feet a day up a mountain. Some take the measure of a year in calendar leaves; others celebrate its turnings, questing for a place to be, a thing to do that somehow blows the dust out of the corners of life.

You can ride out to the promise of spring, a good horse between your heels. Or romp across hot rippled dunes, trailing laughter like a scarf. Glide into autumn through the small infinity of a misted lake. Or chase winter down the sunstruck snow, flinging frozen billows at the trees.

Cameo moments, ardently sought, long remembered: a downhill run at Aspen, Colorado ... the seas of sand in California's Imperial Valley ... mirrored morning in Virginia's Hungry Mother State Park ... the freshness of a Massachusetts meadow.

Vacation's lasting joy: the thrill of

DISCOVERY

One man walks the boardwalk. Another strolls the sand. One sees snack stands. The other sees a sea shell—and marvels. What a masterpiece this tiny sculpture is to the inquiring mind that seeks it out, to the curious hand that picks it up, to the imagination that wanders its whorls and ridges, wondering that such sublime architecture should mansion so lowly a creature.

Flowers abound; in myriad kinds they paint the brown earth. We look on them, but do we see? "We must look a long time," said Thoreau, "before we can see." Bend close to a sunflower. The butterfly looting its honeypots pollenates not a bloom but a whole bouquet of flowerlets. Those on the rim flare into bright petals; those in the center produce nectar and seeds. A simple discovery—and yet we have learned something wondrous, something new under the sun.

Our desk lamps, traffic lights, and neon signs too often eclipse the sun. We stare so long at paper white and asphalt black that we may never notice how the antic ocean tints the underbellies of her clouds. We swallow water weary with chemicals and perhaps never know the tang of a palmful dipped from a virgin creek. Benumbed by a flickering screen, we forget the sprites that dance in a campfire. Bemused by the racket of our progress, we forget the hymn of wind in the pines.

Vacation is a time to discover, a time to wash the mind's windows, to climb from the rut and find re-creation. We return younger than when we left. And richer. For souvenirs, a shell, a stone, a pine cone. For a lifetime, memories of an adventure, a quest, a discovery. For our children, a new resolve that the world we give them will be fresh with excitement, charged with challenge, filled with fun.

PAUL A. ZAHL AND (OPPOSITE) OTIS IMBODEN, BOTH NATIONAL GEOGRAPHIC STAFF

A Monarch butterfly feasts on the nectar in the sun-seeking eye of a sunflower in the Adirondacks; young eyes and minds dwell on the splendors of an underwater realm off a Florida key.

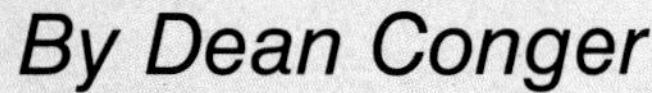

By Dean Conger

A LANDLUBBER FAMILY SIGNS ABOARD, ROLLICKING TO THE NEW VACATION CHANTEY:

We're Off to Sea

Bound for blue-water adventure, a schooner cruises off Maine where Yankee clippers sailed; James R. Holland

B. ANTHONY STEWART AND (OPPOSITE) DEAN CONGER, BOTH NATIONAL GEOGRAPHIC STAFF

BARNACLED AS NEPTUNE'S FOREHEAD, Pemaquid Point raises its 140-year-old lighthouse, beacon for the oilskinned crew of Eastward *exploring Maine's coast under sail.*

Ram Island Lighthouse stood somewhere ahead, swallowed in a fog that obliterated sea and sky. Sailing along in a faint whistle of a wind, we peered past the bowsprit into the swirling grayness.

"A real pea-souper," commented our skipper, Roger Duncan. Beneath the water-beaded hood of his oilskins, he looked tense but confident.

Earlier I had watched him pencil a zigzag course on his chart, jotting a compass bearing and time estimate for each leg. And as each marker or buoy emerged from the gloom and vanished with our wake, I was amazed at Roger's navigation by dead reckoning. With clock and compass he brought us unerringly to each checkpoint. But where was that lighthouse?

A fishing boat loomed out of the fog, startling us. I grabbed the foghorn and gave a loud blast. The muffled chugging receded. Ominous silence. And still no lighthouse.

Then came the sound of surf. Waves crashing on rocks. At the same time I heard a bell.

"Ram Island," announced the skipper with a grin. There stood the lighthouse, shackled to the rocks like Prometheus. A 36-foot stone tower topped by a searching beam.

Roger spun the wheel and set a new course eastward. "Let me know who sees a white bell in about ten minutes," he said. And five day-old sailors strained eyes forward.

Months before, in the comfort of our home in suburban Washington, D. C., my wife Lee and I and our three boys had set our minds on a sailing vacation. A lake? No, we

wanted the tang of salt spray, the sea's challenge. White sails on blue water . . . historic coves to explore . . . quaint village shops piled high with forgotten treasures from the attics of time. Gull cry, spruce smell, lobster fresh from the sea and blueberry pie. We would settle for nothing less than a legend-steeped coast populated with windjammer men straight out of Winslow Homer. Yes . . . Maine, the rockbound coast of Maine, John Greenleaf Whittier's "hundred-harbored Maine."

"If you have to ask what it costs to run a yacht, you can't afford one," J. P. Morgan had snorted. But we did ask, and found that we could vacation aboard a yacht for little more than motels and restaurants would cost us ashore. We lined up *Eastward,* a classic 32-foot Friendship sloop, gaff-rigged and clipper-bowed, and a skipper who knew the Maine coast (it winds 3,478 miles to span 228 as the gull flies!) like the back of his bronzed hand. July at long last rolled around, and in high spirits off we went to Boothbay Harbor to adventure 10 days "before the mast."

No one had said anything about fog—at least a clammy, all-embracing fog like this. It hid the hillside houses, made wraiths of main-street shoppers, set lobstermen to chores ashore or yarning around potbellied stoves in harborside sheds.

Our skipper, lean of limb, sharp of nose, spare of speech, had already placed our duffel bags on the bunks in *Eastward's* cabin. He had stowed the food—bacon and butter next to the hull where water temperature would keep them sweet, beverage cans cooling in the bilges beneath the floorboards. With quizzical eye he studied his crew: Lee and I self-conscious in our new oilskins; Chris 8, Kurt 10, and Eric 11—none of us knowing a buoy from a lobster pot.

JAMES R. HOLLAND. DEAN CONGER (LEFT) AND B. ANTHONY STEWART (OPPOSITE), BOTH NATIONAL GEOGRAPHIC STAFF

"I think we can make it to Christmas Cove," he said. "Shall we give it a try?"

The boys were raring to go. Why not, I shrugged.

"Good," the skipper said. And he was down the slippery, seaweed-hung ladder, bounding nimbly onto the deck.

I walked back up the pier to get my final load of gear. Gulls jeered from perches on the pilings. A wharfside whittler watched me pick up my packages and said, "You goin' out in this soup?"

"Why, yes," I answered, my confidence ebbing with the outbound tide. "Captain Duncan said. . . ."

"Oh. You're with Duncan, are you? Sure. He'd go."

Ghosting past the rocky foot of Ram Island Lighthouse, we entered open waters of the Gulf of Maine. No longer did the coast's hundreds of curiously named islands or glaciated peninsulas shelter us. Rearing, then rolling slowly down, we felt as if we were riding the backs of an endless school of whales. "It's Nova Scotia next if we miss this buoy," Roger said with a twinkle. "Nearest land is only 127 feet away—but it's straight down."

"Tell me! Tell me!" the bell rang out. It rode the swells

HALF LAND, HALF WATER, THIS SPRUCE-SPIKED REALM NURTURES *hardy folk famed for individuality, rock-ribbed honesty, salty humor—and cussedness. Where the rest of the country refers to north on the map as "up," Maine Yankees persist in "going down east," remembering days when their ships sailed upwind to Boston and coasted home before southwesterlies on a "downhill run." And the term Down East stuck for the magic coast of Maine.*

Along this shore the love of sail lingers—expressed in a full-rigged weathervane (far left), or found in the shelter of Tenant's Harbor (left), where Eastward *let down her sails among gleaming yachts, windjammers jammed with vacationists off for a week wherever the wind wills, and rust-streaked lobster boats.*

The welcome's warm here and elsewhere—not that the tide of summer migrants will change locals by so much as a gnat's eyelash. These Yankee traders will sell you their wooden lobster buoys as antiques, and switch to more durable plastic. The color of a buoy (above) identifies its owner's traps. Pirating of his pots, like horse stealing out West, makes a man so mad he's "swole up like a sculpin."

B. ANTHONY STEWART, ROBERT E. GILKA (OPPOSITE UPPER), AND DEAN CONGER (LOWER), ALL NATIONAL GEOGRAPHIC STAFF

grandly, tossing its head and tolling its rhythmic message. The sea around it shivered; dark patterns swept across the surface. "Look at those cat's-paws," Roger called. "There's wind coming. Give me a hand with the sails, boys, and we'll see what *Eastward* will do."

I turned the wheel as Roger instructed. *Eastward* responded like a dignified horse, rounding slowly, holding her head nearer the wind. The boys took lines off the cleats and, on command, heaved on this one and that. The heavy blocks squeaked; the freshening wind bellied the mainsail, topsail, staysail, and jib. *Eastward* came alive, no longer rolling now but leaping forward under the press of sail.

I felt exhilaration at the wheel. Lee leaned back contentedly against the cabin. The boys, proud of their seamen's role, trailed fingers in the water.

We anchored for the night in Christmas Cove, a favorite with mariners. Capt. John Smith explored this part of Maine in 1614 "to take Whales and make tryalls of a Myne of Gold and Copper." Failing in these pursuits, he set his men

CRUSTY CHAMP OF MAINE, THE LOBSTER *blushes at a banquet in his honor. He has made mouths water round these parts since Indians feasted on lobster and clams steamed over hot rocks and seaweed. English colonists found profits in lobstering; Maine men still do, air-shipping* Homarus americanus *to tables coast to coast. Bluish green in the trap, the cannibalistic crustacean turns red when cooked.*

Bathers turn blue if they overdo in the chill Atlantic; but Acadia National Park's beaches are bully for basking—and girl-watching. The Congers found warm ponds there, and this sunset from atop Cadillac Mountain, first point on our East Coast to catch the sunrise.

44

DEAN CONGER, NATIONAL GEOGRAPHIC STAFF

LIKE HOMECOMING SWALLOWS, Friendship sloops flock to their namesake port in July. As No. 44 sweeps in, eyes scan the clipper bow, a hallmark of the famed lobstering craft designed in the 1880's. Beamy, deep-keeled, she'd stand up to a nor'easter; in light airs gaff rig and topsails spread a cloud of canvas. On wintry days one crewman huddled below and watched the other's face; when his nose turned white, they changed places.

Then came engines, decline, discovery by sportsmen. Derelicts were spruced up, new ones like Eastward *built, and Friendship saw a classic reborn.*

to fishing. Here our boys gleefully caught four fish and cleaned them—then stood by in amazement when gulls swooped in and brazenly stole them! Well, we'd have fillet of mackerel another night—and delicious, too. This first evening Roger prepared a hearty stew, and as we basked in the warmth from the coal-burning galley stove, it seemed at last we had a vacation going for us.

Later that night I wasn't so sure.

I awoke to the sound of feet padding overhead. The clanking of anchor chain told me we were about to move—and in a hurry. I emerged from the cabin into blustery blackness. Rain stung my face. Wind and sea were rising. *Eastward* pitched, halyards slatting against her mast.

Again the sound of Roger's wet bare feet slapping along the deck. Young Kurt, who had been sleeping in the cockpit underneath a leaking canvas cover, was unceremoniously lifted off the engine hatch and dumped in a damp corner. The electric starter tormented the engine; reluctantly the spark plugs began to fire.

The skipper, in wind-whipped pajamas, saw me and called out, "Anchor fouled. We were dragging!"

Slowly, ever so slowly, we moved ahead. When we had pulled out of danger, Roger cut the engine and dashed forward. Splash! Anchor and chain went over the side. "Guess we'll be all right now. The anchor's dug in and is holding," the skipper reported, and clambered back into his sleeping bag.

Funny way to spend a vacation, I thought as I pulled the blankets up over my ears.

DEAN CONGER AND (OPPOSITE) M. LEON LOPEZ, BOTH NATIONAL GEOGRAPHIC STAFF

CAPTAIN OF UNCHARTED DREAMS, HELMSMAN ON ADVENTURE'S course, Eric Conger scans the main with eyes no longer bounded by suburbia. "Better than any roller coaster," Eric exclaimed as Eastward *climbed one wave and careened off the next.*

He clambered up headlands to peer at the bones of ships wrecked in raging surf, dug clams and saw them transformed into chowder, and gorged on wild raspberries. "This is living!" he concluded.

The lighthouse below ushered Eastward *into Northeast Harbor at Mount Desert Island, named for its "bare and rocky summits" by the French explorer Champlain in 1604. Artists discovered the area in the 1840's. Rockefellers and Morgans, Pews and Cadwalladers arrived with yachts, servants, stables of horses to rusticate in palatial summer "cottages" around Bar Harbor. Today Acadia National Park, sharing more than half the island, opens spectacular vistas to visitors the year round.*

When the gods bring clear skies to Maine, you're almost blinded when you come up on deck in the morning. The sharp angles and fresh colors of Maine painters like John Marin and Andrew Wyeth come to mind as you gaze at the glittering pink granite ledges. Islands that you couldn't possibly see for their distance hang right there a few inches above the horizon, mirage-like reflections.

In our 10 days under sail we enjoyed several mornings like this. One began at Camden, surely the loveliest of towns on the sea, with its white clapboard churches towering over elm-shaded streets, its flower baskets blooming on lampposts, and its pleasure fleet bobbing in the hill-girded harbor. We picked out the chubbiest residents of a lobster pound and crossed over to Lasell Island to eat them, boiled over a driftwood fire.

On another morning we walked barefoot in the squishing, gleaming mud of McGlathery Island to dig for clams at low tide. Eric got hit square in the eye by the long-distance squirting champion of all clamdom. But retribution was sweet—Roger's clam chowder topped any we had ever tasted. And at sunset on another glorious day, we looked out to sea from Cadillac Mountain on Mount Desert Island and swore we could see all the way to Ireland.

We put on a good show sailing into Northeast Harbor, fashionable haven at the foot of that mountain. We swept in under full sail, weaving in and about the anchored boats. We dropped topsail, jib topsail, jib, and staysail smartly and coasted up to the only empty mooring, while crews of yachts we passed sang out compliments on our Friendship sloop and seamanship.

Roger had schooled us well. Everyone had his duties, and each of the boys got a chance at the wheel. Were these my rambunctious kids? I wondered as I watched them making splices and working at knots by the hour, learning to tie a bowline, reef knot, sheepshank, and clove hitch. Kurt managed a very good eye splice, while Eric became expert with the oars; at each harbor he ferried us ashore in the "peapod" we towed astern. The skipper's teaching skills came as no surprise; in winter Roger directs the upper grades of a fine New England prep school.

He even persuaded us to start the day with a bracing swim. And Maine's 58° water is great—once you're out of it. Then, while fishing, the boys hauled in two dogfish—small, not man-eaters certainly, but unmistakably sharks—and even Roger couldn't get any of us over the side again.

Our real test came the day we headed out for Monhegan Island. That day didn't dawn. It burst upon us in the form of a northeast storm. The clouds hung so low I couldn't see the tops of what Longfellow called "those lordly pines! Those grand, majestic pines!" As we foamed out of harbor under short sail—main and staysail—I heard Eric yell, "Look at those waves; here comes one!" It was a shout of eagerness, not fear.

"Hard alee," Roger called. "Heads up now, watch that boom." Lee ducked and the boys scrambled for their positions. "Grab your sheet now. Pull her in before she starts to fill! That's it, tie her down." And off we went on the other tack as neatly as if he'd been commanding so many plebes from Annapolis.

But even Roger had his work cut out for him. "It's a confused sea, coming at us from all directions," he apologized when a wave slopped aboard and cold spray blinded us. "It's hard to keep a heading in this."

He rode his seat as if on a bucking bronco. When 30-mile-an-hour gusts hit, he'd fight the wheel with all his might. His eyes kept searching the rain-swept seascape for the island that seemed to have sunk into Davy Jones's locker. He ducked below to check the course and take a reading on the fathometer. "Thought we might be too far northward," he remarked when he emerged reassured.

"LET ME TELL YOU ABOUT THE BIG ONE I JUST SOLD," *says Myrtle Gascoigne, elbow-deep in flotsam and jetsam washed up by history's tides. Travelers on U. S. 1 ring her door chimes in Newcastle, seeking antiques for modern homes. A rosewood clock, Sandwich glass, ceramics, a large framed drawing of a ship's billethead capture their curiosity. Knowing eyes look for makers' marks on pewter, silver, old china; and study mortising and pegging on the underside of tables.*

"Wouldn't give it shed room myself," sniff locals, as they see throwaways go for hard cash. "Tourists must leave their wits t'home," they say, as buyers bid up prices for a grandfather clock, a pine chest, a hobbyhorse at an auction up the road. Hope springs eternal for a Duncan Phyfe chair, a Paul Revere porringer, a pamphlet of Poe's Tamerlane and Other Poems *—a coveted first edition. And what about the time even a queen's belongings went on the block? The guillotine ended plans to spirit Marie Antoinette to America, but tradition says her clothing and gilded mirrors made it to Maine.*

Other collectors search along the shore for treasures when the tide's out. They find symmetry in a sea urchin skeleton, mystery in the wavesounds locked in shells (below).

B. ANTHONY STEWART AND (OPPOSITE) M. LEON LOPEZ, BOTH NATIONAL GEOGRAPHIC STAFF

"SEAGULLS HARANGUING THE SUNRISE," TALL SPARS PIERCING SKY AND SEA, *Pretty Marsh Harbor mirrors its name. Here* Eastward *rendezvoused with Cruising Club of America boats, anchored in "rafts" of from two to a dozen so crews could enjoy a gam, as did whalers at sea. Distant home ports lettered on transoms showed the tide-like pull of Maine once you've got her salt water in your veins. Rockport-born Edna St. Vincent Millay wrote: "I . . . that was happy all day long on the coast of Maine— I have need to hold and handle shells and anchors and ships again!"*

ROBERT E. GILKA AND (OPPOSITE) DEAN CONGER, BOTH NATIONAL GEOGRAPHIC STAFF

When Monhegan pushed above the gray waves, Roger explained that once we came into the lee of the island we'd take down the sails, then motor up the narrow entrance into the anchorage. The bald headlands thrust higher and higher. The time came, but the engine starter whirred and whirred in vain. Roger reset throttle and choke. The starter whirred again, weaker now.

"That's an engine for you," he said bitterly. "We'll sail in."

Without the boys we couldn't have done it. As Roger tacked back and forth in the channel, they helped trim sails, spot buoys, and call out the water's depth from the fathometer. Once, as we closed with the town's granite pier before coming about, I glimpsed a knot of men in slickers watching us. No doubt calculating our chances of making it, I thought. Well, here's where we sink or swim as a family of sailors. Not that swimming was a pleasant prospect, not in that surf. "It's like trying to swim in the foam of an ice-cream soda," Roger had noted. "There just isn't any support to the water with so much air in it."

Now he called above the howling wind. "There are two mooring buoys over there. We'll take the one on the right—it's easier to shoot. If we miss it, *Eastward* goes on the rocks." He turned to me: "I want you to go forward and let down the staysail when I tell you. When you've got it down, take the boathook, reach down with it, and pick up the buoy. Remember, you have just one crack at it."

Alone on the foredeck, I grasped the staysail halyard (I hoped it was the staysail halyard!) and hung on. We bounded across the harbor seemingly in the wrong direction: The mooring buoy was over *there*. Then *Eastward* turned on her heel as if she knew her life depended on it. Her bow slammed up and down into the waves as she faced into the wind.

"Now!" Roger shouted. "The staysail!" I released the halyard and the sail fell flapping to my feet.

"Okay. Now get out there and *pick up that buoy!*"

Forgetting the boathook, I crawled forward and groped into the water. Nothing; too soon. Now I soared into the middle of the sky, now I plunged back into the water. Then the buoy sat there right at my fingertips. I grabbed it. I had it!

Minutes later, when we had furled the sails and gone below to dry out by the cabin stove, I found myself chattering away just as happily as the boys. "How high do you think those waves were?" "Silly of other boats not to sail on a day like this." "What if we had missed the mooring!"

But we hadn't.

By David F. Robinson

GLASSY LAKES, PURLING STREAMS, GREEN-GARBED PEAKS THAT HIDE THE HIGHROADS SET A SYLVAN STAGE FOR

A Camper's Tale

Night fire flames as day's coppery embers cool at Middle Saranac Lake, New York; Martin Rogers

MARTIN ROGERS. BELOW: "ADIRONDACK SCENE (BATKIN'S CLUB)" BY FREDERICK RONDEL, 1856; COURTESY ADIRONDACK MUSEUM

BREAKFAST BY BULL RUSH BAY begins the camping family Robinson's day in the Adirondacks (above), whose rugged peaks Champlain glimpsed in 1609. "Hatirontaks"—"They eat trees"—scoffed Iroquois braves, legend says, at Algonquians who roamed here. In the 1800's came wealthy campers to lounge while guides raised lean-tos, set out venison, trout, and sundry spirits (opposite). Emerson extolled this Eden; Currier & Ives lithographed it; Adirondack Museum now preserves its lore. When timbermen and tourist tides threatened it in the 1890's, New York State set up a parkland—today covering nearly six million acres—to remain "forever wild."

If the skull-splitting thunderclap hadn't jolted me awake, David's yell would have. "Thunderstorm!" came his teen-aged baritone from somewhere down by the lake. I sat up just as lightning caught a snapshot of him, sleeping bag crammed under one arm, his night under the stars abandoned as he raced the first fat drops to the log shelter.

Hard behind him they came, splatting on the roof, hissing on fireplace stones still hot from the evening campfire. For David and me, my wife Pat and 10-year-old Scott, this first night out amid the Adirondack Mountains of upstate New York would end wet and wakeful unless we rigged for a storm—and quickly, warned the rising winds.

We shucked our cocoons and scrambled for the tarpaulins, huge plastic sheets that crackled as the wind helped unfold them. Hasty knots in strands of clothesline soon held them taut across the shelter's open front. Four besprinkled figures repackaged themselves in Dacron and down. Three quickly fell asleep.

Why do we do this? yawned the fourth. Why paddle laden canoes through lake and corkscrew river to match wits with a nightful of thunderbumpers here on the northeast shore of Middle Saranac Lake? Why tent in two feet of New Jersey snow when we could have lounged by the TV at home? Why rough it on the lip of a still-active Hawaiian volcano? Why trailer to a Michigan lake owned by bears and mosquitoes, or shiver through a freak frost on a Virginia ridge, or pack a tot in diapers into the Maine woods, or hold our breath while a Nova Scotia skunk finds his way into our tent and—whew!—out again?

Answers stumbled through my sleep-misted mind: To save motel bills. To work off a few pounds. To aim the boys toward manhood. To get away from it all.

More than that: To get *back* to it all. To meet a storm, a living creature of body and voice and brute force. To watch a temperamental lake change its mood. To learn respect for fellow creatures who camp out summer and winter without all the stuff I think I need. No plastic. No clothesline. No soft, warm sleeping bag.

Sleep closed in while the storm boomed and splashed on the safe side of the plastic.

Dawn brought sun-split clouds, a tranquil lake, and feathers. Scott's sleeping bag, on active duty since World War II, wheezed clouds of down out of a brand-new tear. The breeze saw to it that each of us received a share.

"What a mess!" Pat laughed, fingering the rip to see if it would hold a few stitches. Scott shook his head as he harvested feathers by the combful. David snorted off a downy mustache. "What's for breakfast?" he asked, with

TACITURN TOAD, BUSY WOODPECKER, myriad creatures underfoot and overhead lure nature lovers to Adirondack wilds. Alert ears hear the hermit thrush fluting in the forest; sharp eyes spot grouse, loon, even bobcat. White-tailed deer and black bear still forage, game fish still jump. Moose and elk no longer wade the streams but may one day be reintroduced; their spoor lingers in the names of sky-hued gems like Elk Lake (below), where a lone canoeist glides amid cloud-wreathed peaks on waters that will ride the Hudson to the sea.

the perspective that only an unfed 14-year-old can know. But the idea of food had considerable appeal; in moments we were up, dressed, and at the knots of the tarps.

We unveiled a perfect portrait of the Adirondack Forest Preserve, that huge haven of lake and tree and bird and peak we'd heard so much about on the camper's grapevine. There sprawled our lake, edged in the greens of poplar and pine and framed between stately shafts of birch. Blue mountains admired themselves in its mirror, and something—an otter, we guessed—carved a silvery vee just off our tiny beach. In the days ahead we would awake to many such calendar views, and hike or paddle to many more as we reached into the wilds of this magnificent realm, where for generations men weary of the man-made world have gotten back to nature's.

Over Pat's fabulous flapjacks we swapped ideas for the day's agenda, reveling in choices few can make at home. Swim? Fish? Bird-watch? Explore? Or just loaf? The day itself decided. It was the kind that draws a camper's eye to the horizon. Storms had scrubbed the air so clean the mountains seemed like flat cutouts close

WILLARD PRICE. OPPOSITE: UPPER, MARTIN ROGERS; LOWER, PAUL A. ZAHL, NATIONAL GEOGRAPHIC STAFF

ROOFTOP OF NEW YORK, *Mount Marcy (above) —known by the Indian name* Tahawus, *cloud splitter—summons hardy spirits to its 5,344-foot summit on five trails dotted with open-faced Adirondack lean-tos. Formed of rock more than a billion years old, the Adirondacks rank among earth's oldest peaks, probably rose long before the Alps and Rockies. An agile hiker (opposite) hops the rocks at O K Slip Falls. Not far from here Vice President Teddy Roosevelt, fresh from a Marcy climb, became President in 1901 as William McKinley, shot by an assassin, breathed his last.*

enough to touch. Broken clouds curbed the sun's heat and glare. A perfect day for conquering a mountain.

We could see our goal as we stowed our gear in the two canoes and pushed off into Bull Rush Bay. Ampersand Mountain, small by Adirondack standards, arched its green backbone above the lake's southeast shore, where the trail began. There one of the lake's four shelters waited—we hoped. It's first come, first served in these state-operated facilities, with a limit of three nights' tenancy in any one.

We loafed across the lake, laughing at downy ducklings, slipping up silently on sunning turtles, watching weeds twitch as unseen lunkers finned about in the shallows. Boy Scouts in assorted sizes and bathing outfits roughhoused offshore as we scraped onto the beach. Pup tents clustered by the hut like chicks around a hen. But a bronzed and whiskery scoutmaster bade us move right in; he and his charges would be paddling out to an island as soon as a grillful of hot dogs was done and downed.

"Tomorrow I'll hike out to the highway and bring back a turkey," he said. "Join us for turkey dinner?" Scout hikes have come a long, long way since my days in uniform.

While Pat and David assembled sandwiches, Scott and I trimmed four fallen branches into hiking staffs. After the ritual initialing of each we hit the trail, belts festooned with lunches, canteens, binoculars, and cameras, pockets abulge with bird books and toadstool guides, loins girded with sweat shirts for the cooler air aloft. Rangers at the Ray Brook station had rated Ampersand "a fairly easy three-mile climb." Just right, we thought; we could be down in time for supper.

We strolled along the broad up-and-down trail. Here a woodpecker flashed, there a stand of mushrooms dared us to identify them. In a muddy spot a set of hand-size bear tracks told us whose forest this really was. A mile and a half up the trail we lauded ourselves for having nearly reached the top. A quick sprint should do it.

But who could sprint up a trail suddenly tilted to a staircase angle? Down below we had jabbered volumes; now we spoke in telegrams as we panted upward. The summit

"CLIMBING TAHAWUS" FROM "PICTURESQUE AMERICA," 1874. OPPOSITE: MARTIN ROGERS

BREEZE-COOLED TRAILER BUNKS AWAIT YOUNG ANGLERS IN ARIZONA'S WHITE MOUNTAINS; ROBERT B. WHITAKER. OPPOSITE: TENTER TAKES A CAKE FROM AN OUTDOOR OVEN AT A GASLIT CAMPSITE IN VIRGINIA'S SHENANDOAH VALLEY; BRUCE DALE, NATIONAL GEOGRAPHIC PHOTOGRAPHER

CAMPING AS YOU LIKE IT—TENT, TRAILER, OR ROLLING MOTEL

Americans conquered the wide open spaces with the live-in prairie schooner. Today they're rediscovering the land in the covered wagon's successors—the camping trailer, truck camper, travel trailer, and motor home. Where once only dad and his son the eagle scout backpacked into the forest primeval, now mom and sister Sue harken to the call of the wild. And they take everything with them—even the kitchen sink.

Many of the 40 million seasonal nomads haven't forsaken their old canvas castle. Tents dot the nation's half-million campsites (page 421) in a variety of styles: the wall model, not the easiest to set up but roomy, best for long stops; the exterior-frame umbrella tent; the lightweight Pop Tent (opposite) that goes up in a jiffy and needs no stakes.

The camping trailer gets tenting off the ground (above). Compact, easily towed, it unfolds into a bunkroom for up to eight; some boast crank-up fiberglass roofs and swing-out kitchens. In the truck camper the bedroom rides piggyback on a pickup; mom can turn truck driver for the next leg of the trip if dad goes fishing and catches only a cold. And if they own a luxury travel trailer or a self-propelled motor home he can recuperate in stylish comfort with wall-to-wall carpeting and color TV, even toast his toes before an open fire—indoors. The fireplace has joined the kitchen sink!

should be just ahead, probably behind that rock, that tree. . . .

Shouts and laughter ahead! Must be people at the top. Suddenly here they came, bounding down the trail, a trio of teen-aged boys. "Summit just ahead?" we wheezed.

"Well, it's about three-quarters of a mile"—my heart sank—"after you come to the steep part"—and stopped.

The vote was four to nothing; on rubbery legs we pushed on up nature's staircase. At the "steep part" the stair became a ladder with rungs of root and rock. While our muscles labored, our minds had time aplenty to contemplate a Great Truth we had forgotten: In hiker's parlance, a three-mile climb is just that. If you want to come down again, well, that'll cost you another three miles.

The top at last! On a bald rock dome we stood in silence and traced the round horizon—azure lakes, moth holes in the green felt far below . . . Bull Rush Bay . . . the thread of river linking Middle to Lower Saranac Lake . . . the marina where our mini-bus vacationed. Outboards like water beetles creased Fish Creek Ponds, where tents stand so close their ropes cross and campers relax to the music of motorbikes, portable TV, and the neighbors' dogs. We took seats in this awesome arena and lunched atop the world.

Then someone noticed the sun; it had slid disturbingly close to the horizon. We clicked a few last photographs and plunged into the woods, laboring down ladder and stair as the gathering gloom erased the trail ahead.

"Look," I told my doughty band, "You wait here. I'll run on ahead and come back with the flashlight."

I coaxed leaden legs into a sort of run. Armies of black trees watched me pass; a big one put a kink in the trail. I dodged around it—and slammed everything into reverse.

Hello, bear. Nice bear. Sorry if I disturbed you, bear. Ever see a man tiptoe backward? Watch.

That night by a fire big enough to scare away King Kong, my mate and cubs heard how I stared down a bear that reared up twelve feet tall, all fangs and snarl. And off in the woods I swear I heard a four-foot bear snickering.

One day we chugged across the lake in a rented outboard trailing laden canoes to the shelter on Rices Point. Here, says a plaque, Martha Reben, "who loved the wilderness," camped many times. Pat's brow furrowed. "Reben, Reben. Yes! I read her book, *The Healing Woods*. She came here with tuberculosis and recovered."

"Who wouldn't?" mused David as four sunburned, smoke-perfumed bushwhackers looked and listened and sniffed, addicts all to the world's best medicine.

For us, one of its essential ingredients is fish. Camp

IT'S "CHURCH AHOY" EACH SUNDAY IN THE SUMMER as folk around Upper Saranac Lake wend to worship on tiny Chapel Island. Before highways laced the lake region, people traveled best by boat; builders in 1889 sited their church for easy access. A free ferry keeps pews full in a rustic kirk raised in 1958 after the first one burned.

chores done, we paddled out to see if they were hungry in Hungry Bay. Long shadows floated on the water as the boys yanked in perch and sunnies and Pat's deadly sidearm dropped a treble-hooked spoon into shoreside weeds.

"Let's go over by that little brook," she suggested. "It looks weedier there."

I stroked us over. She flipped the lure in—and the line twanged taut! Her pole doubled over as she played her quarry to the canoe. Suddenly it exploded from the water, a fine, fat northern pike maybe two feet long. The boys wowed and Pat reeled in; I groped for the net—in vain. It waited back at the campsite. The fish wouldn't wait. As it labored alongside I made a frantic grab and almost scooped it into the boat. But something snapped. In a splash it was gone, lure and all.

Pat laughed off my chagrin, pointing out that we ought to be paddling back anyway. As we glided across the bay, we suddenly realized the twilight around us was alive. Bats! Hundreds swirled about, sometimes darting between us. I assured all that they wouldn't crash into us, and paddled a little faster as I wondered to myself if they would. From the shore's safe haven we watched spellbound as a maelstrom of tiny ogres laundered the buggy air.

Next dawn a loon laughed idiotically at the two-legged creature that doused a sleepy face in the lake and shoved off in a canoe. I ignored its bad manners and stroked to the brook. There in the weeds a twin to the lost lure plunked in. The line yanked! Two feet of scrappy northern pike shattered the mirrorlike surface, sounding and leaping. I played it to the net I'd been careful to remember. Fierce eyes in a bullet head glared defiance as I hoisted the prize from its world to mine. Though an autopsy yielded no lost lure, this may well have been the one that got away—once.

One cast, one fish. Adirondack anglers aren't often that lucky, but the fishing is good enough for it to happen to some. And when your catch goes from cove to stove in less than an hour, you find out what flavor is all about.

A dismal drizzle kept us close to camp all that day. I whittled, Pat read. The boys slogged about in boots and flappy ponchos and finally alighted to play checkers with acorn caps on a paper towel. Dinnertime dragged while a steamy fire sputtered through its cooking chore. Day slunk away westward; night oozed in, black and clammy. If spirits stalk the woods, this was their hour.

GORDON W. GAHAN

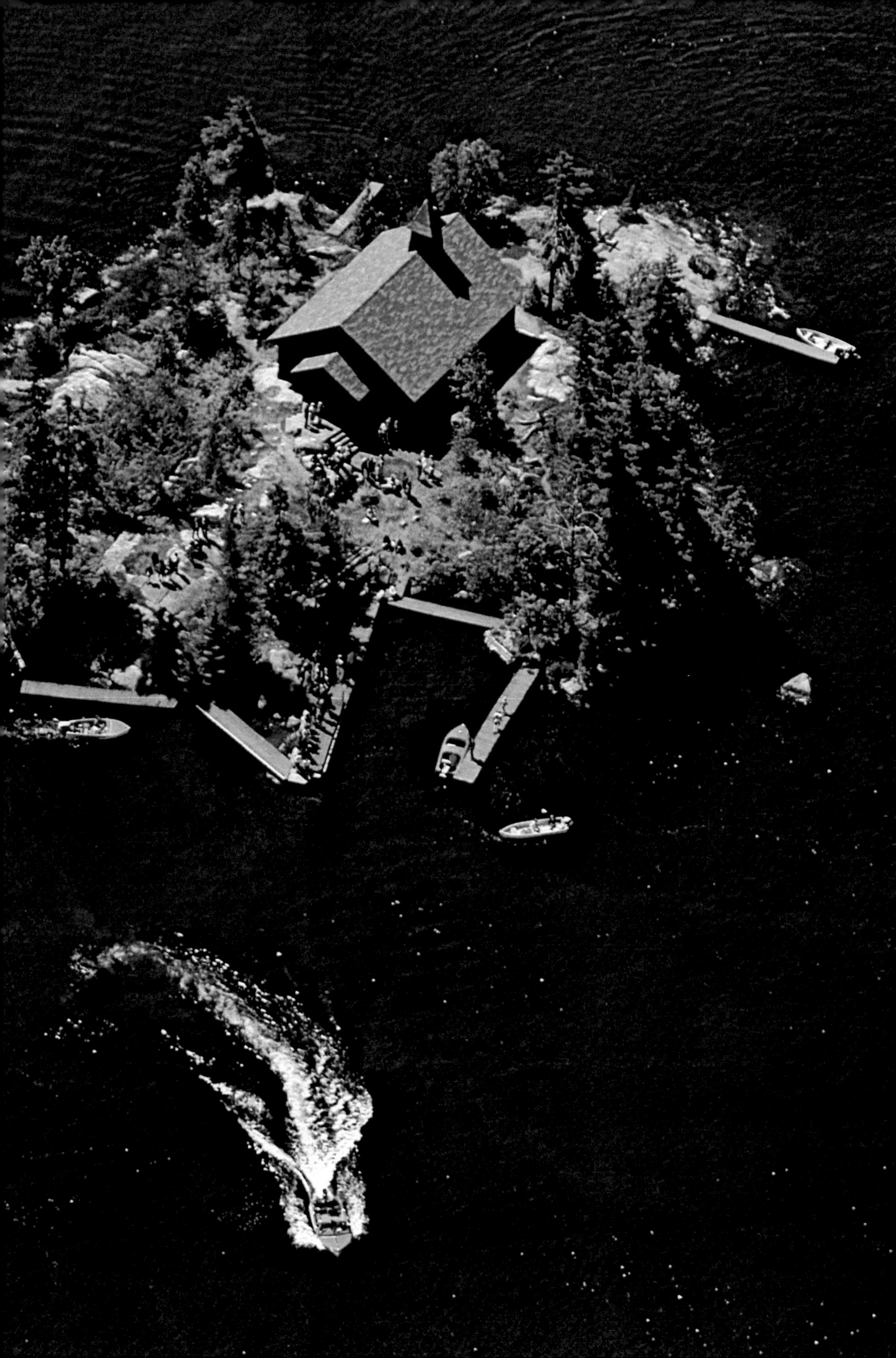

"LONGBOATS ON AN ADIRONDACK LAKE" BY JAMES DAVID SMILLIE, 1874; COURTESY ADIRONDACK MUSEUM. BELOW AND OPPOSITE: MARTIN ROGERS

GIFTS OF THE GLACIERS, TWO THOUSAND LAKES nestle amid Adirondack heights in hollows dammed by ice-borne rocks. Hundreds remain so remote that hatchery fish come in by air. Some hold only trout. Pike, bass, even salmon challenge anglers in others. Pint-size perch gives Robinsons more chuckle than challenge on Middle Saranac (opposite lower). Reels sang when big ones bit.

Boaters long have plied here, first in Indian birch-bark canoes, later in longboats of the 1800's (upper); gunners even paddled out to shoot deer along the shores. "You do all your sporting from your boat," wrote one enthusiast in 1869. "This takes from recreation every trace of toil."

Rivers link the lakes and vein the backwoods. A panful of water from Cold River heads for the dinner pot on a fireplace (below) that warms a shelter. Coals cook best, but if pesky mosquitoes hum, wily woodsmen stoke up smoke.

We knew how to ward them off. Out came the cards for a rollicking round of Old Maid. We males thought it fitting that Pat ended up with the spinster queen in the first hand. Scott dealt another. We played the cards down to four. Then two. Then—none. The queen had vanished!

We never found her. We knew we wouldn't, even while we searched. That's the kind of night it was.

Given a choice, we'd still be on Rices Point. But some of the wildest country in the East lies just south of the Saranacs, and we had promised ourselves a taste of it. Cars, boats, and bikes stay behind; here the hiker reigns, trudging old logging trails with all his needs strapped to his back. Fresh eggs, juicy steaks, and quarts of milk stay behind, too. When ounces count, a man finds he can live quite well on powdered this and freeze-dried that.

"Beef stroganoff," said the fuzzy-chinned young counselor as we sniffed the wisps wafting from his battered pot. That day he and his four campers had trekked the 15 miles to Cold River, where they now occupied one shelter and we the other. A splash of the river's crystal water had transformed a pouchful of what looked like sweepings into the delicacy that scented the evening air.

Our freeze-dried pork chops looked no better—gray, cardboard-like little slabs—until soaked and grilled to a savory brown. We've tasted better chops, but we wouldn't want to carry them 15 miles.

We'd gladly carry fishing gear twice that for another crack at the trout in Cold River. One morning Scott hunkered down atop a midstream rock, set a wriggling worm adrift, and felt excitement he'll remember all his life as he dueled a handsome—and later toothsome—speckled trout. It dimmed the thrill not a bit when passing hikers told of netting 10 apiece on nearby Moose Creek; this one was *his*.

And so was the luck that day. Pat caught two fingerlings and poison ivy. David caught our cork-handled knife half a mile downstream after nudging it off his rock. I caught three crayfish. All through our evening trout feast, my scale-model lobsters, latest entries on a long roster of pets-for-a-day, scratched and swam in a bucket we'd found.

I awoke to a full moon and a clanking over by the bucket. Pat passed my elbow-jab down the line and we all sat up, too late to rescue our pets from a masked gourmet in a fur coat. But when that keen raccoon nose aimed at our larder, we drew the line. "Shoo! Scat! Git!" Off the big fellow scampered. The food slept in with us that night.

Growling clouds flung down slanting needles of rain and machine-gun bursts of hail all the next day. We split wet logs for the dry kindling inside and nursed a fire under a plastic-tarp front porch. A turtle, a salamander, and a toad checked into the bucket for brief stays, but all were eclipsed by what arrived next.

"Can I keep it?" Scott asked after a sortie to the river for a drink. To his proudly displayed ankle clung a two-inch black bloodsucker. "Awhile?" he wisely added.

"Keep *that?*" asked the world's gamest mother.

"It looks real neat," he explained. And that seemed to settle the matter. Assigned to a guest room in a plastic bag, the leech held Scott spellbound all afternoon.

A fiery dawn scattered sparks on the liquid ribbon at our doorstep. Four mergansers paddled upstream, bobbing and snatching at who knows what for breakfast. A fidgety warbler set a sapling aquiver, and around camp gnarled bushes tempted us out of bed with their fat blueberries.

Humans seem trivial intruders in such a superbly balanced realm, where eggs hatch and leaves rot and snow melts on a timetable that needs no tinkering. Mosquitoes had found the balance tipped in their favor with us around. But the forest took little note when we packed up and migrated back to asphalt and electricity, supremely thankful that there's still a place where men don't matter.

Vacations die hard in this family. We couldn't go home without one more hike in the woods, one more view from a mountaintop. But an angry thunderstorm dragged a curtain of rain over Whiteface Mountain just as we arrived at the summit. There went our view. Into the little stone observatory we scurried, to swap hellos and small talk with tourists who had gained the top by car and elevator.

"Are you Forty-Sixers?" asked one middle-aged couple. We looked blank, so they told us how an early survey had found 46 Adirondack peaks rising over 4,000 feet. Whiteface was one. Anyone who scales them all is a Forty-Sixer. Some offer easy trails, others no trails at all; the climber must bull his way through the brambles, compass in hand, and find his own way to the log book at the top. There his signature proves his feat.

"Climbed one yesterday," said the husband, just a little too casually, I thought. But Pat took the cue: "How many does that make for you?"

"Forty-six," they beamed. It had taken them 10 vacations to climb this piecemeal Everest. What would they do now? "Climb 'em all again!"

And what would we do, I wondered as we enjoyed our freshly washed view at last. Would we make it back here sometime for another dose of these healing woods?

Again Pat took the cue. "Forty-five to go," she said.

DAY'S DYING GLORY PAINTS ROSY MEMORIES *of a vacation in the wilds. Nature pours out her paintpots for the family hiking between sunstruck guardrails to the pinnacle of Whiteface Mountain, named for its avalanche scars. A highway to the 4,867-foot height beribbons a ridge behind them; at its end waits an elevator to lift "motor climbers" the last 270 feet.*

When winter cloaks Whiteface, skiers speed down frozen slopes, then drink in panoramas that stretch away to New Hampshire and Canada as a two-mile-long chair lift whisks them back up. Below spreads Adirondack Forest Preserve, our largest state park, more than half of it privately owned, where 37 campgrounds, scores of tent sites, dozens of shelters, hundreds of miles of trails offer all outdoors—fine fare for campfire conversation while the embers toast a marshmallow treat.

MARTIN ROGERS

By Jay Johnston

AMATEUR AQUANAUTS PLUNGE INTO A WATERY WONDERLAND TO FATHOM THE

Splendors of a Dive-in Park

I spied him about the time he spotted me. No mistaking the undershot jaw and razor teeth that give the barracuda such a ferocious look—and bite. As the gray five-foot predator circled us, my wife Ginger saw him and pointed, then our teen-agers John and Ellen caught sight of him. We had been prepared for this moment by expert advice: "If you don't bother barracudas, they won't bother you. Don't panic if they join your underwater party." But the experts were up there and we were down here, within a lightning lunge of those evil-looking teeth.

We glanced at each other—and swam about our business. The words of wisdom prevailed, perhaps because we were surrounded by too much beauty. We weren't about to let one ugly intruder spoil our delight in John Pennekamp Coral Reef State Park, a 122-square-mile salt-water oasis off Key Largo, Florida. Making our debut dive in scuba gear, swimming in pale emerald waters 82 degrees warm and so

Aqualungers browse amid bristling antlers of elkhorn coral in Florida's Pennekamp preserve; Jerry Greenberg

crystal clear we could plainly see objects on the sea floor 20 feet below, we continued to explore the fantastic realm of a living coral reef, spawning ground for legions of brilliantly hued tropical beauties—as well as the curious barracuda. He kept us company in our "sightseaing," and in time we even grew accustomed to his fierce face.

Months before, when my own curiosity about Florida's undersea sanctuary and armchair musings on the challenge of skindiving had percolated to the point of active planning, Ginger had hesitated: "There are sharks and barracudas in that water, aren't there." It was a statement, not a question. Probably so, I had to admit, since the reef extends some six miles out into the Atlantic.

"Well," she declared, "I might—might, that is—go out in a glass-bottomed boat."

We did just that on our first day at Pennekamp, cruising out on the 49-passenger *Infante* to Molasses Reef Light at the park's southern edge. Through four huge windows in the *Infante's* bottom we gazed down into a strange and wonderful world. On the surface a dozen boats flying red-and-white diver's warning flags reminded us where the action was. Our appetites whetted, we could scarcely wait to plunge in. Even Ginger yielded—tank, mask, and flippers—to the lure of the reef.

We had never before fastened on a faceplate, so Tyll Sass, our Berlin-born, Cincinnati-bred instructor, began with fundamentals—free-diving drills beside the park marina. "With just a mask, snorkel, and flippers you can enjoy 90 percent of the underwater scenes here," he said. "Everyone can do it, young and old, and at his own pace."

After we mastered—well, got acquainted with—the snorkel tube, Tyll moved us on to scuba. Strapping the air tanks on our backs, he taught us how to breathe through

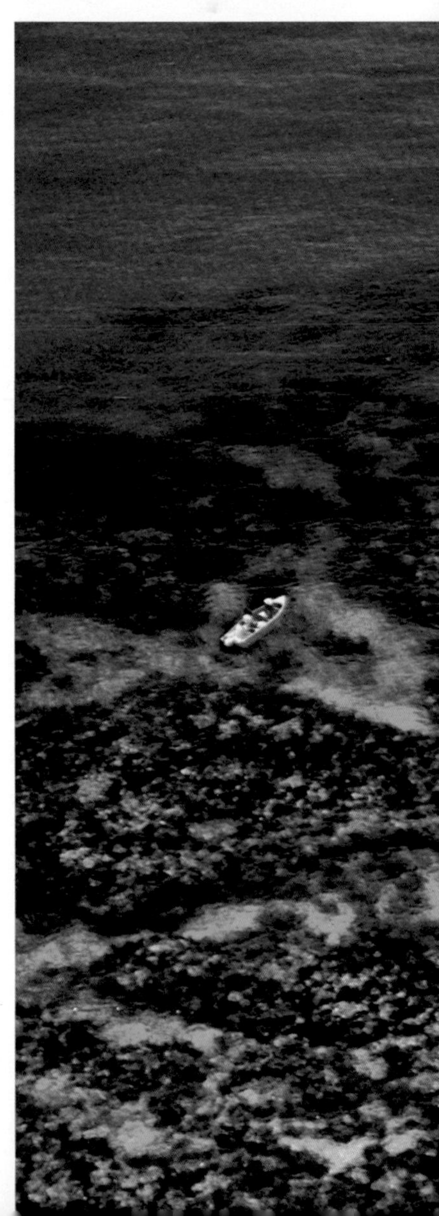

EAGER TO ROAM
THE CORAL REALM, *learners wade to scuba school in the Pennekamp shallows. The Johnston family begins with snorkels, later will heft self-contained underwater breathing apparatus (scuba) for deeper dives. After school they head for luminous playgrounds farther out where boats seem to float on air, and red-and-white flags warn, "Watch out for free divers." Below the surface awaits a shimmering world of color and life that dazzles a diver's eye.*

Novices seek expert advice (page 421) to avoid blunders that might leave them breathless.

the regulator, or hose; how to prevent fogging the faceplate (spit in it and rinse lightly: the salt-saliva coating does the trick); how to equalize pressure on the eardrums (press mask against the base of the nose and try to exhale).

He pounded home the rules of safety: If you jump in without knowing the depth, you may take bloody soundings on jagged coral. Swim upcurrent of your boat to assure an easier return. And of course, remember the recommended etiquette with sharks and barracudas.

On a bright July morning we sped seaward in a runabout littered with diving gear. Looking over it, I felt more like the skipper of an underwater demolition squad embarked on a mission than the head of a family bent on a carefree outing. We anchored at Grecian Rocks, midpoint in the

JERRY GREENBERG. OPPOSITE: OTIS IMBODEN, NATIONAL GEOGRAPHIC PHOTOGRAPHER

Graveyard of ships in sailing days, once mined by curio dealers and scoured by spearfishers, America's first underwater park today adorns a subtropical pleasuring ground that sweeps from the luxury towers of Miami to Key West and Everglades National Park. The 78,000-acre dive-in aquarium honors the memory of John Pennekamp, a Florida conservationist who strove tirelessly to protect the reef lest exploiters turn it into a watery desert. From park headquarters off Key Largo, mangrove-banked channels (above) lead some 300,000 visitors a year out where cormorants feed, porpoises play leapfrog, flying fishes skim the sea, and lighthouses keep a lookout at reef's edge. Here divers abandon shaded patio boats (opposite) to probe the sunken rampart's treasures at depths to 40 feet.

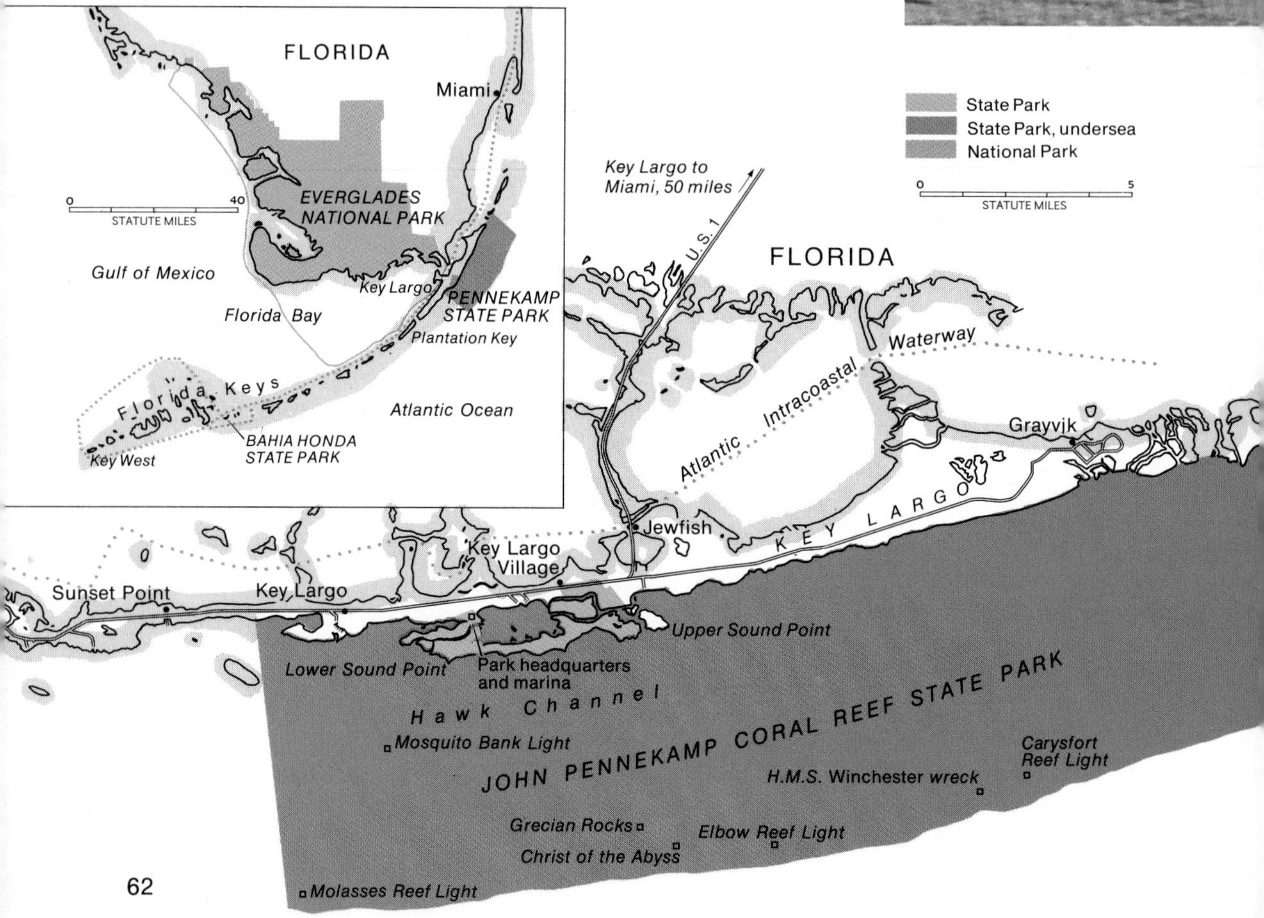

FLORIDA
Miami
0 40 STATUTE MILES
EVERGLADES NATIONAL PARK
Gulf of Mexico
Key Largo
PENNEKAMP STATE PARK
Florida Bay
Plantation Key
Florida Keys
Atlantic Ocean
BAHIA HONDA STATE PARK
Key West

State Park
State Park, undersea
National Park
0 5 STATUTE MILES
Key Largo to Miami, 50 miles
U.S. 1
FLORIDA
Atlantic Intracoastal Waterway
Grayvik
KEY LARGO
Jewfish
Key Largo Village
Sunset Point
Key Largo
Upper Sound Point
Lower Sound Point
Park headquarters and marina
Hawk Channel
JOHN PENNEKAMP CORAL REEF STATE PARK
Mosquito Bank Light
Carysfort Reef Light
H.M.S. Winchester wreck
Grecian Rocks
Elbow Reef Light
Christ of the Abyss
Molasses Reef Light

JERRY GREENBERG. OPPOSITE: OTIS IMBODEN, NATIONAL GEOGRAPHIC PHOTOGRAPHER. MAP BY BETTY CLONINGER, GEOGRAPHIC ART DIVISION

park, where at low tide protruding bits of reef remind you of pop-art ceramic creations. With shallow sandy sections and deeper spots of 10 to 40 feet, the area makes an ideal proving ground for novice snorkelers and scuba divers.

Snorkelers have an easy time getting started; they just jump in. Scuba entry is another matter. The 30-pound air tanks made us top-heavy when we stood up; in the rocking boat balancing became a precarious thing. Even if we'd managed to wobble to the side without tripping over our flippers or barking shins on the gunwale, any face-down dive might have damaged or dislocated the faceplate. So we followed the school solution: Sitting on the gunwale, back to the water, one hand on the mask and the other on the tank harness, we fell backward, heels over head.

Splash—splash—splash—splash. Seconds later we found ourselves hovering over the coral reef, one of the oldest animal communities on earth. Here soft-bodied coral polyps—tiny creatures with petal-like tentacles that build protective cups of lime—flourish in the warm sea. Billions of their limestone skeletons have formed the foundation of the reef. Now vast colonies of living coral animals grow on the dead and fashion a fantasyland of strange forms.

Gliding along twisting alleys carpeted with white sand, we passed clusters of golden staghorn coral, its pointed antlers standing as tall as a man; huge boulder-shaped brain corals with patterns of convoluted grooves that bear such a marked resemblance to the human brain; towering coral feathers and sea fans, graceful gorgonians swaying with the current.

Life filled every square foot of this coral metropolis. Around us swam schools of porkfish, yellow tails glinting like ornaments of gold. Parrotfish displayed their gorgeous green and blue dress; some even sported polka dots. Sergeant majors

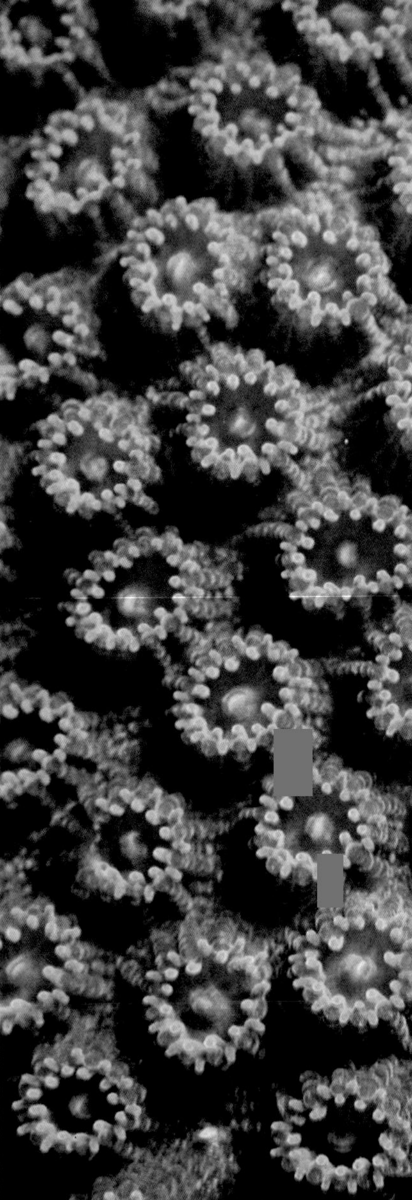

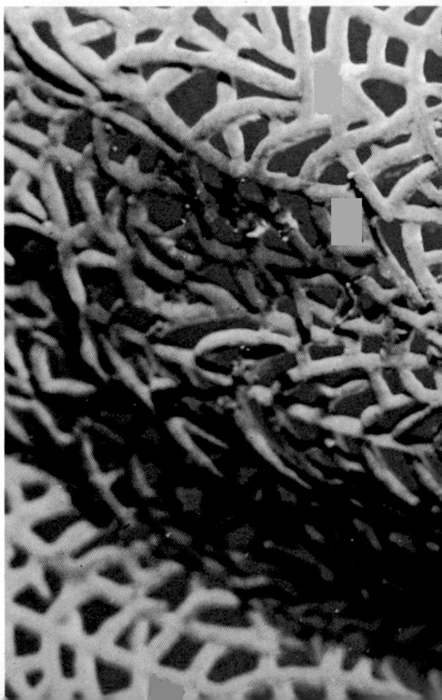

drilled smartly, flaunting black stripes on yellow uniforms. Spadefish swept by, silvery bodies bordered with ebony. All were amazingly nonchalant about our presence. Ginger, in a bright green suit, looked like an aquatic Pied Piper as schools of fish trailed her about. "No doubt following me to see where the big green one feeds," she concluded with a laugh after we had returned to the boat and recalled her magnetism.

"The fish seem to sense safety in the park," Tyll told us, adding that they appear in greater numbers here than in any other section of the 220-mile-long reef.

For safety's sake we swam in pairs. Once Ginger and I tried to practice descending the way Tyll had demonstrated —simply by exhaling and not breathing. Easier said than done, we discovered. Willpower collides with the powerful instinct to keep sucking that precious air. We had worked at it for several minutes before we noticed how far we had drifted from the boat. Now, on the long pull back, our aching muscles told us why Tyll had cautioned against slipping downcurrent of the boat.

We struggled aboard, finally, and sat gasping for breath. "Listen," Ginger panted, "next vacation, what do you think

IN THE LAIR OF AQUARIUS, NATURE'S PSYCHEDELIC SPLENDORS ENRAPTURE THE MIND. Sunlight filtering through Pennekamp's waters glitters against more than 40 kinds of coral, hundreds of species of tropical fish; swimmers stare, and the fish goggle back. Delicate asterisks of star coral owe their green beauty to algae that help them extract lime from the sea. Leopard-spotted snail (lower), called flamingo tongue, feeds on the soft coral filigree of a sea fan. Blue-dotted young damselfish will wave a yellow tail in maturity. Cloaked in hues befitting royalty, queen angelfish (lower right) grazes on plants with its brushlike teeth. Ferocious moray eel, guarding its coral cave (below), strikes with stunning swiftness, can kill a diver by holding him under. But most morays attack only in defense. Divers counter a more common hazard—painful pricks of spiny urchins and stinging coral—by wearing gloves (opposite).

JERRY GREENBERG

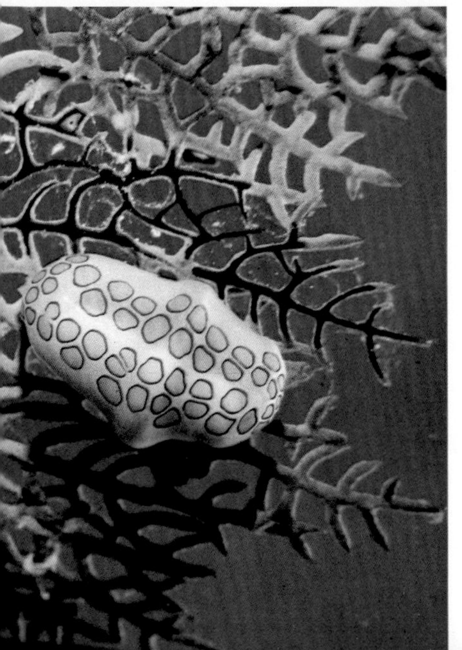

THE CHAIN OF KEYS OPPOSITE—MISSOURI (LOWER), OHIO, BAHIA HONDA, BIG PINE—ARCS TOWARD KEY WEST. EMORY KRISTOF, NATIONAL GEOGRAPHIC PHOTOGRAPHER

OVERSEAS HIGHWAY, WORLD'S LONGEST OCEAN-GOING ROAD, THREADS A 100-MILE RIBBON OF CONCRETE AND STEEL through the Florida Keys, tropic gems of wind-ruffled palms, snow-white shores, creamy surf. Pirate plunder lies buried in the sand, while tourist treasure abounds on every hand—emerald, turquoise, and sapphire sparkling in the ever-changing waters; pale gold rising from the sea each dawn, fiery gold afloat on the western horizon. Bahia Honda State Park (below and on rectangular key opposite) offers swimmers both Atlantic and Gulf of Mexico beaches. Houseboaters (above) linger at Key Largo, on the Intracoastal Waterway that follows the islets to the old Spanish port of Key West, where military jets whine and languorous breezes whisper mañana.

about a nice quiet cottage in the mountains with rocking chairs on the front porch?" The question came up again the time the shark joined us—actually the only one that came close in a dozen days of diving at Pennekamp.

John and Tyll were scuba diving and the rest of us snorkeling near the stern of the boat one morning when Tyll poked his head above water and yelled: "Shark! Everybody back in the boat!"

No group ever scrambled into a boat faster. Tyll told us the six-foot mako probably wouldn't have bothered us, but he believed it wiser for the snorkelers near the surface to get out of the water. "Some sharks feed on the surface," he pointed out, "and who knows when one might mistake a snorkeler for a thrashing fish?"

John had spotted the shark too. Had he been afraid? No. "Wasn't anything I could do about it," my 17-year-old shrugged. "Besides, Tyll was taking pictures of it."

Of course, the odds favored John. No one had been attacked by sharks or barracudas since Pennekamp opened in 1963. "We've never had a fatality of any sort on the reef," a park official told me, "though we've had some near ones—people who can hardly swim jumping into 35 feet of water with tanks and no instructions."

But over the centuries the reef has taken its toll in ships. Its edge comes up abruptly from the deep waters of the Gulf Stream and heavy seas break against that outer coral barrier, whose hidden fangs have holed the hulls of Spanish galleons, pirate vessels, and privateers. Here in 1695 the 60-gun British ship of the line H.M.S. *Winchester* broke her back on the reef and sank.

We saw some of her cannon, raised in 1939, standing guard near park headquarters on Largo Sound, surrounded by campgrounds and shops. Here a nature trail cuts through a mangrove swamp, and from the marina boats take divers out to the Christ of the Abyss, a nine-foot statue set in a hollow 30 feet below the surface.

Though the park shelters only campers, overnight lodging abounds on Key Largo and Plantation Key. In our Key Largo cottage facing Florida Bay we fell asleep each night to the music of coconut palms rustling in the trade winds, fronds clacking like castanets.

Then one day the music and the diving stopped. It was time to go. We looked out for the last time on the shining sea whose hidden marvels we had plumbed, and turned away. "Come back next year," Tyll Sass called, "and I'll teach you to catch lobsters 50 feet down in the coral caves."

John and Ellen traded glances. They would be taking summer jobs next year. Or would they?

SNUG IN THEIR PENNEKAMP SANCTUARY, *a school of striped porkfish and white grunts call a recess to swarm around a wandering fish watcher. He carries no spear; only hook-and-line anglers may pull in these food fish, along with the snappers, mackerel, groupers, bonefish, and other game species that forage in the coral gardens. Park rules sanction lobstering in season—by hand, slat trap, or net—so long as the ocean floor suffers no damage. Campers need venture no farther than the shallow coastal creeks to find grunt and mangrove snappers. A Key Largo sunset (opposite) silhouettes a sampling of the bounty that makes the angler's day compleat.*

JERRY GREENBERG. BELOW: OTIS IMBODEN, NATIONAL GEOGRAPHIC PHOTOGRAPHER

JOIN THE HAPPY THIRD
OF THE NATION THAT EACH YEAR
HANGS OUT THE SIGN . . .

GONE FISHING

Intent on his quarry of tadpoles and minnows, a boy works a bog in Massachusetts. A thousand miles south in the balmy Bahamas, a sportsman pits skill and sophisticated tackle against twice his weight in fighting tuna. Between these fishermen, so distant in their ways and their means, dwells the rest of an army of more than 60 million Americans —Izaak Walton's beloved "Brothers of the Angle."

Little wonder that angling's legions steadily swell, for they enjoy a continent filled with scrappy fish. In river and lake lurk tackle-smashing muskies and pike, while in a nearby brook dart dainty trout, so game that half-pounders bend your flyrod double. Other fresh-water fish abound: ubiquitous crappies, the peerless black basses—largemouth and small—sweet-fleshed perch, their cousin the walleye, and that iridescent prince of panfish, the bluegill.

Wet your line in southern California's creamy surf. Spunky corbinas, foraging in shallows, delight you with their fight, then again with their flavor. High tide rolls in, and with it ride spawning grunion, yours for the scooping. Beyond the breakers, fishermen seek yellowtails, voracious hunters that pursue their prey in wolfpacks. Up the coast, boatmen troll for the Northwest's salmon, as famed for gameness as for their great migrations.

Along the East Coast the vast continental shelf spreads a fishing ground for megalopolis. Crowding a pier, fishermen of all ages reel in fish of all descriptions, from flat

TADPOLE HUNTER STALKS HIS PREY IN MASSACHUSETTS; ROBERT W. MADDEN. RIGHT: DEEP-SEA FISHERMAN TACKLES A BLUEFIN TUNA OFF BIMINI; JAMES L. STANFIELD, NATIONAL GEOGRAPHIC PHOTOGRAPHER

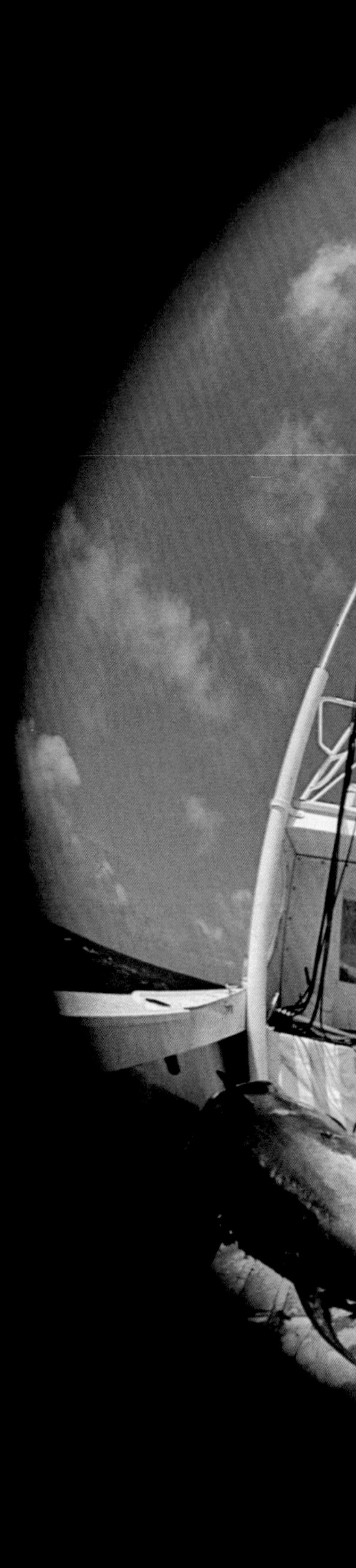

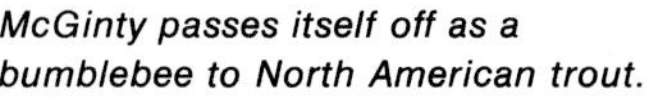

McGinty passes itself off as a bumblebee to North American trout.

Olive Dun, a classic example of the delicate dry fly, traces its English origins back five centuries in man's unquenchable quest for the trout.

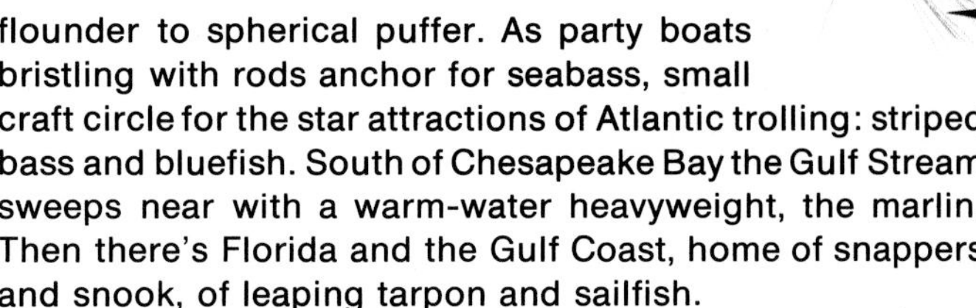

flounder to spherical puffer. As party boats bristling with rods anchor for seabass, small craft circle for the star attractions of Atlantic trolling: striped bass and bluefish. South of Chesapeake Bay the Gulf Stream sweeps near with a warm-water heavyweight, the marlin. Then there's Florida and the Gulf Coast, home of snappers and snook, of leaping tarpon and sailfish.

As an angler gets hooked on fishing (page 421), he succumbs to its glorious gadgetry—a new tackle box, lures to fill it, spinning reel to banish backlash, perhaps a collapsible, pocket-size rod in the event his business trip lands him by a bass pond. American fishermen spend nearly half a billion dollars each year on rods, reels, lines, and lures. But none delude themselves that money buys success. Huck Finns with cane pole and bobber still rule many a riverbank.

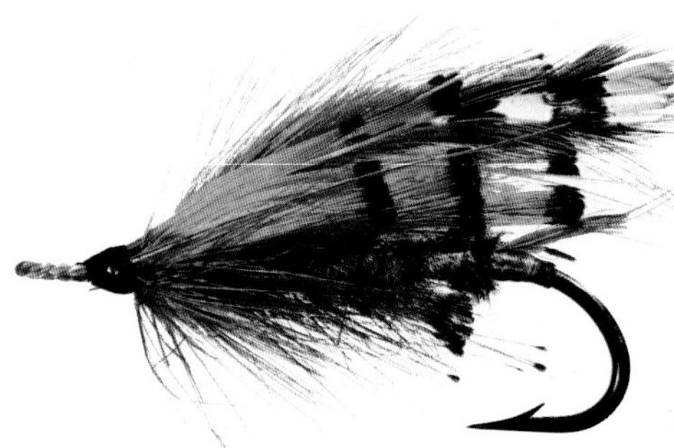

Durham Ranger, aglow with golden pheasant feathers, won fame by luring salmon from a distance both here and in its native British Isles.

Just as it fits each purse, fishing soothes each psyche. Need elbow room, a sylvan setting for musing? Try Colorado's Roaring Fork River (opposite). Gregarious? Join the gantlet that greets migrating chinooks on the Smith River in California (below).

Fishing, wrote George Orwell, is "the opposite of war." But fishermen constantly skirmish with their nemesis, Man the Polluter. No longer do leaping salmon fight their way up the tainted Connecticut River, nor do hordes of silvery, succulent shad choke the Schuylkill. And a canal that links the Great Lakes to the Atlantic has allowed the sea lamprey

Jock Scott, a British import that entices salmon and steelheads, wears the plumages of a dozen different birds from 5 continents.

Adams has fooled trout for five decades, ranks as an old reliable in a sport beset by uncertainty.

A LONER TRIES HIS LUCK FOR TROUT IN COLORADO; C. DAVID HISER. BELOW: BOATERS BUNCH AT A HOT SPOT FOR SALMON NEAR CRESCENT CITY IN NORTHERN CALIFORNIA; JAMES P. BLAIR, NATIONAL GEOGRAPHIC PHOTOGRAPHER

through to fix rasplike jaws on lake trout and whitefish and literally suck the life from booming fisheries.

Fortunately, Man the Conservationist makes amends, seeking to tidy up the waterways and restock them. In the 1960's he brought Pacific coho salmon to the depleted Great Lakes. There, gorging on alewives, they thrive with a zest that revives fishing. Striped bass, dogged fighters and delicious fare, star in another drama—one that fills fishermen with suspense. Because the oceanic fish enters fresh water to spawn, biologists wondered if it might forsake its wanderings and settle in man-made lakes. Now, with fingers crossed and rods ready, sportsmen see it slowly take hold in the fastnesses of fresh-water America.

Prone to noisy pre-dawn risings, guilty of long absences from home, the fishers call for special understanding. But they cannot be stopped. Let the lake freeze two feet thick (above); still they come—bundled anglers, heated cabin, cutting tools to chop a hole, and perhaps a scattering of lapel buttons demanding "Stamp Out Summer!"

And so they fish. On windswept Cape Hatteras, surfcasters perform a vesper ballet to the sea's rumbling rhythm (right). Their Western brethren drift in the enveloping solitude of Oregon's McKenzie River (opposite). All seek the thrill of a strike. Many get it. But should luck fail, none bemoan the time and effort. Herbert Hoover, a devotee of the trout, found an inscription somewhere that explains why: "The gods do not subtract from the allotted span of men's lives the hours spent in fishing."

FROM COAST TO COAST THE SEASON'S RIGHT WHENEVER THEY BITE: ANGLERS WADE NORTH CAROLINA'S GOLDEN SURF, HACK THE FROZEN ARMOR OF WISCONSIN'S STURGEON BAY, RIDE THE RIFFLES OF OREGON'S McKENZIE RIVER. ABOVE: DONALD EMMERICH. RIGHT: EMORY KRISTOF AND (OPPOSITE) BATES LITTLEHALES, BOTH NATIONAL GEOGRAPHIC PHOTOGRAPHERS

Hostelers' Holiday

By Chris Allen and David Kennedy

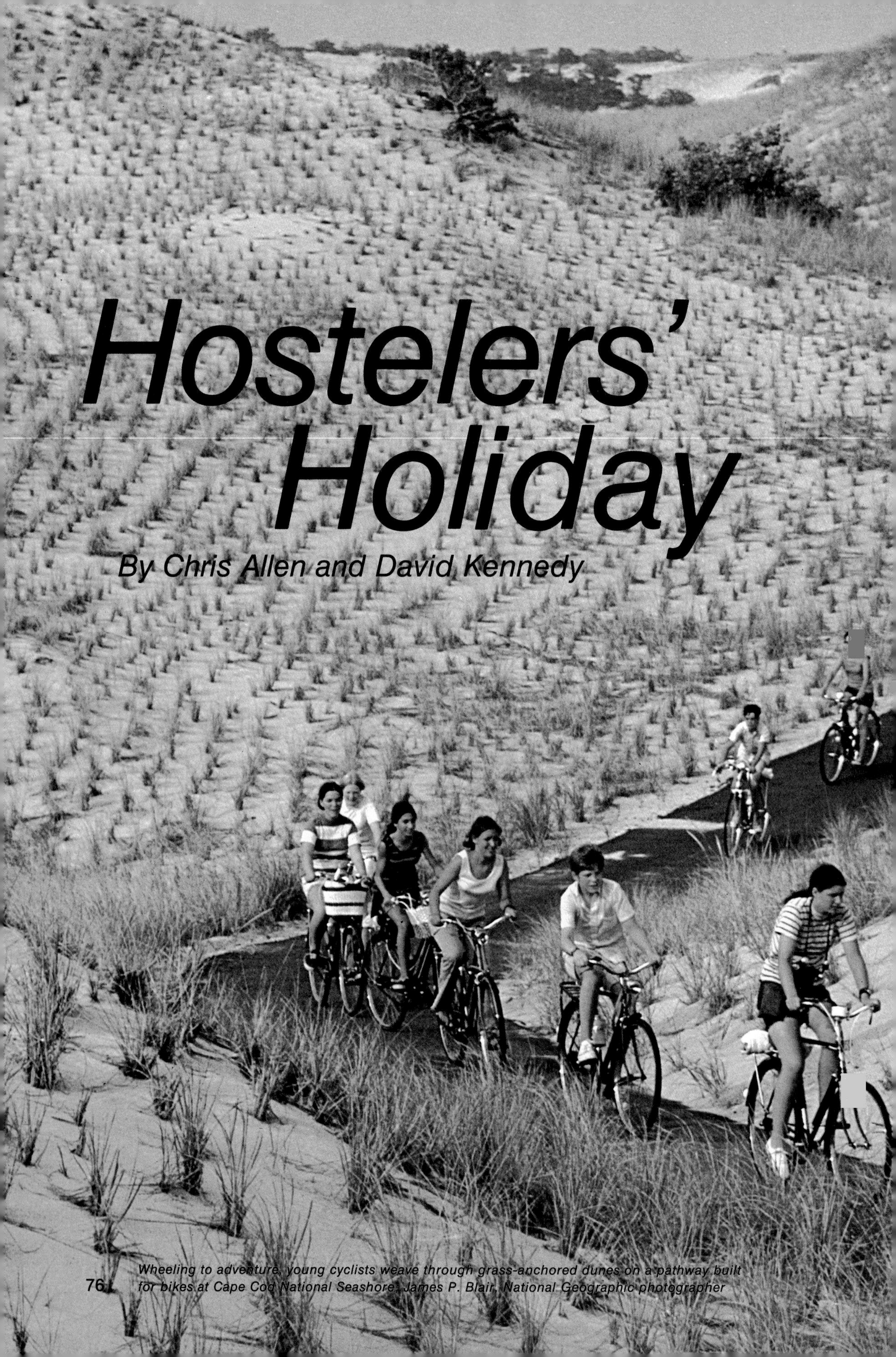

Wheeling to adventure, young cyclists weave through grass-anchored dunes on a pathway built for bikes at Cape Cod National Seashore. James P. Blair, National Geographic photographer

Yankee pedalers in Massachusetts, teen-agers Chris Allen (below) and Dave Kennedy (far right) found a welcome at the triangle sign of the American Youth Hostels. Near Orleans on Cape Cod they helped form a fireside foursome. On Nantucket Island they bunked at the Star of the Sea (left), an old Coast Guard post. Some 100 hostels in 22 states honor AYH membership cards (young and old may join, page 421); the AYH Bicycle Atlas shows safe routes, including bikeways marked by the new green symbol—even suggests an energizing snack called gorp: a tasty mix of peanuts, raisins, and chocolate bits.

We took a sharp right off the main road, coasted down a gentle hill, and began pedaling faster and faster. Around the bend waited the end of a long day. In minutes we saw it: a big white New England farmhouse and a shining jumble of handlebars and wheels. We sped up the driveway, dodged a basketball, and squeezed into a bike-filled garage. On legs that still seemed to be pedaling, we walked into that most welcome of places, a hostel.

After signing in and finding our bunks, we sank down in kitchen chairs to rest before cooking our supper of hot dogs and beans. From across the table came a hosteler's familiar question: "Where did you come from?"

We had quite an answer for him.

Dave and I had behind us more than 350 miles of hosteling in Massachusetts; our wanderings had taken us from the Berkshire Hills to Nantucket Island and the tip of Cape Cod. Now, back in the middle of the state, we had arrived at the Little Meadow Youth Hostel near Sunderland. Tomorrow we would pedal south to Connecticut. Our hostels there would be the homes of surprised aunts and uncles.

No need for relatives in Massachusetts, though. We found the triangular AYH symbol of American Youth Hostels on barns, private homes, backwoods bunkhouses—even in a church. As paid-up AYH youth members ($5 a year) all we had to do to check into a hostel was travel under our own steam: bike, hike, canoe, ski, or gallop up on a horse.

All hostels provide, for a small daily fee, a bunk, a kitchen, and a common room where hostelers can get together until lights out. But there's more to hosteling than having a place to spend the night. Hosteling is the people you meet, the America you can see only from a bike, the travel, the motion. . . .

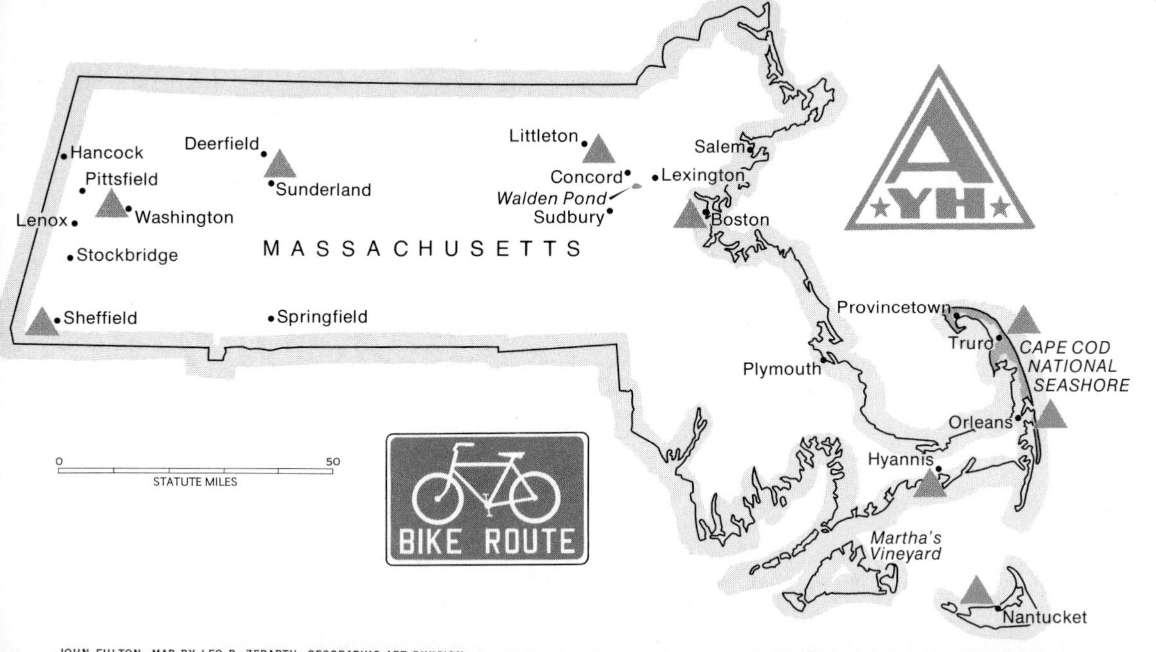

JOHN FULTON. MAP BY LEO B. ZEBARTH, GEOGRAPHIC ART DIVISION

"AND THIS IS GOOD OLD BOSTON, THE HOME OF THE BEAN and the cod, where the Lowells talk only to the Cabots, and the Cabots talk only to God." *So went the 1910 toast to the city that bred revolution in the 18th century, shone as America's Athens in the 19th, banned books in the 20th; the city that harbored slavers, then abolitionists whose "Battle Hymn of the Republic" rallied the North in war. A Lowell said, "Tradition is what keeps people from making fools of themselves." If so, Boston has made few fools.*

Old North Church (opposite) rose in 1723; the trumpeting angels appeared in 1746, loot of a pious privateer. Tories and Sons of Liberty traded glares at prayer in tense pre-Revolutionary days. Box pews, charcoal-burning foot warmers thawed winter worshipers. A tithingman's long pole, tipped by knob and feathers, woke Proper Bostonians snoozing at sermons. Men got poked, women tickled.

The Freedom Trail, guiding hikers through history, wends to the church. In its belfry hung the lanterns—"two, if by sea"—that sparked "the midnight ride of Paul Revere." The trail's sidewalk footprints swing past the Ebenezer Hancock house (right), decked with signs of the firm whose wares the Boston Tea Party dunked. Footprints lead to the Old South Meeting House, where colonials defied a king. A cobblestone circle marks the Boston Massacre; one who fell was Crispus Attucks, first Negro to die for American freedom. At the Old State House patriots cheered the Declaration of Independence, signed by five Bostonians.

Calvin Coolidge lauded Yankee virtues that built New England: eat it up, wear it out, make it do, do without. He found them useful in State House and White House; so do hostelers as they pedal their penny-wise, pound-wise way.

And the history. This is the way to learn it! Not far from our Boston hostel—the basement of Christ Church—loomed Dorchester Heights, a national historic site. There General Washington watched the evacuation of British troops from Boston on March 17, 1776.

The lights at Christ Church went out minutes after some late arrivals checked in. We were already in our bunks when we heard, "Only an Englishman would try to fold his trousers in the dark." The British had returned—a few, anyhow, on a hosteling tour of America. Later we had fun trading versions of each other's accents. And, sure enough, their pants *did* have sharp creases.

In the early morning light Boston Common looked bright and clean. We shared the broad, bench-lined paths with the pigeons. Cycling around and around a small fountain beneath huge office buildings, we watched the streets fill with people . . . and cars. No more bicycling today.

We locked our bikes and started off on the Freedom Trail, following the sidewalk's red line and red footprints to historic places. Alongside the Park Street Church, where abolitionists preached against slavery, two pretty girls

JOHN FULTON. OPPOSITE: THOMAS A. DEFEO

JOHN FULTON (ALSO OPPOSITE). PORTRAIT OF HAWTHORNE IN THE HOUSE OF SEVEN GABLES, SALEM

knelt at a grave in the Old Granary Burying Ground. They were rubbing a thick blue crayon on a sheet of paper taped to a headstone. As we watched, a name appeared out of the past—a widow who lived through the Revolutionary War. Near her lies Paul Revere, whom we were following on the Freedom Trail from his house to Old North Church. There we looked up at the belfry from which, "on the eighteenth of April, in Seventy-five," two lanterns signaled the advance of Redcoats on Lexington and Concord.

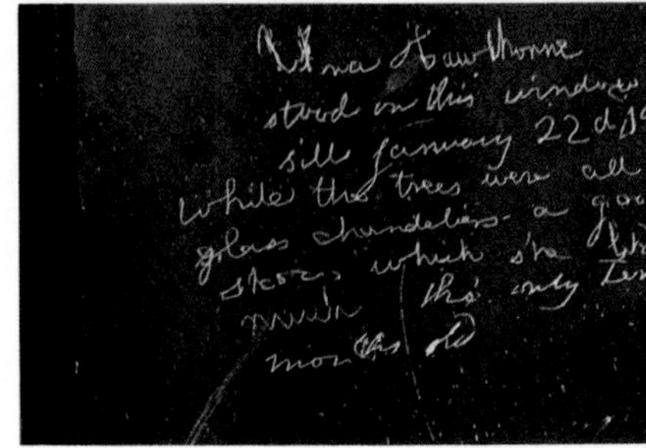

Stepping out of the cool shadows of the church, we turned onto one of the narrow streets that wind through the fruit stands, the awning-shaded groceries, and the bustle of the Italian market. This was Boston to us: aged churches overshadowed by skyscrapers, Revolutionary houses nestled between modern apartment houses, and old neighborhoods straddled by elevated expressways.

Cyclists pedal through a nation built for cars. Many of the best and safest routes for bikes don't even appear on automobile maps. So most hostelers quickly develop a faith in their own sense of direction.

People want to help, but often they themselves don't know. On the way to Concord, Dave asked directions from a man in a grocery store. That gave us 30 minutes of wrong-way pedaling. Then we tried a gas station attendant, who took the time to draw us a map. We felt we knew the way now, but we checked the route with a policeman. And we were finally on our way to the Friendly Crossways Youth

Hostel, just outside Littleton and within easy distance of Concord. When we registered—name, occupation (students), age ("under 18" column)—we noticed the name of a fellow hosteler whose occupation was "investment counselor." He had checked the "over 21" column.

Hallelujas—in Spanish!—woke us up next morning. We crawled out of our bunks to find ourselves in the middle of a Sunday service conducted by a church group of Spanish-speaking kids from New York City. They were early risers and, we found out later, great ping-pong players.

American literature came alive for us in Concord. We could imagine Ralph Waldo Emerson strolling from his white frame house, where his hat and walking stick still hang near the door. Outside in the garden would be his friend Henry David Thoreau, mending a fence. Maybe they would go up a shady street—as we did—to pay a call on Nathaniel Hawthorne, who lived in the Old Manse, built

"FROM AN EPOCH NOW GRAY IN THE DISTANCE, down into our own broad daylight," the words of Nathaniel Hawthorne have lured his readers—even those on bikes—to his Old Manse in Concord (opposite), where a guide gowned as in his era reads the tales he wrote there, Mosses from an Old Manse. *Visitors read words he etched with his wife's diamond on the windowpanes of his study. One (lower) captures a moment when his infant daughter Una "stood on this window sill" and looked out on an ice-coated day "while the trees were all glass chandeliers." Displeased with his tales and needing money, he took a job in Salem in 1845, resolving "to achieve a novel." He achieved a classic,* The Scarlet Letter.

by Emerson's grandfather. Until we walked where they had walked, we didn't really think of them as all living at the same time. Our English books had dates next to their names, but it had never gotten across to us. And how human they seemed as we looked at the Old Manse's everyday things: a large tin bathtub, a multicolored quilt, a fireside cradle. Interrupting her talk, our guide invited a young Japanese couple to put their baby son in the cradle, which rocked to life again.

We walked our bikes down the well-worn path from the Old Manse to Old North Bridge—"the rude bridge that arched the flood." Peering over a pack of Cub Scouts, we read Emerson's words on the pedestal of the Minuteman statue: "Here once the embattled farmers stood, and fired the shot heard round the world."

Past a firehouse, across a highway, past a trailer park, past a string of roadside signs, honked at by cars, we pedaled into a small parking lot. The cars would have to stop here. You have to walk to see Walden Pond. Along the steep banks, the sunlight shimmered through the tall oaks and groves of birches and fell in patches on the ground. We could see why Thoreau wrote: "I went to the woods because I wished to live deliberately. . . . I did not wish to live what was not life. . . ."

Breakfast is frantic in a hostel. Unless it's raining, the houseparents clear you out

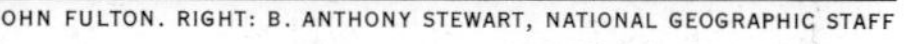

JOHN FULTON. RIGHT: B. ANTHONY STEWART, NATIONAL GEOGRAPHIC STAFF

"YOUTHFUL, EARLY-OPENED, HOPEFUL EYES" *scan the Concord of history and of Henry David Thoreau. "The question," he wrote, "is not what you look at, but what you see." Bikers on Old North Bridge see Redcoats marching on Minutemen, hark to words of Ralph Waldo Emerson: "Here once the embattled farmers stood, and fired the shot heard round the world." Nearby, Thoreau's Walden shimmers at sunset "like molten glass." He lived alone by the pond for two years, feeding frogs from his hand, quaffing the "tonic of wildness." In a cranberry, he said, you could taste "the flavor of your life." He felt no need to make peace with God: "I did not know we had ever quarreled."*

"A CONNECTION WITH THE LONG PAST," FORGED BY HAWTHORNE, awaits literary pilgrims searching his native Salem for "a rusty wooden house, with seven acutely peaked gables." One they find boasts a secret staircase (opposite). The "Old Witch House" of Salem conjures a photographer's figment (below). Here a Hawthorne forebear judged the first of the townsfolk doomed as witches. The hysteria in 1692 sent 19 to the gallows.

Henry Wadsworth Longfellow's poem, Tales of a Wayside Inn, *immortalized a tavern that still welcomes wayfarers on an old Boston post road. Its grist mill (opposite) forms a backdrop for a modern wedding portrait.*

after you do the breakfast dishes. Everybody hustles to cook and eat and wash and dry. Then there's a mad rush for bikes—and we're off for the day.

Today's trip would be a 17-mile ramble from Littleton to Sudbury and Henry Wadsworth Longfellow's Wayside Inn, which has offered "Food, Drink, and Lodging for man or beast" for 250 years. Dave and I were enjoying the past when we were yanked into the present. In the Red Horse Room, old even in Longfellow's day, we saw a TV on an antique table. We sat down to witness modern history—splashdown of Apollo lunar astronauts.

Life in the Space Age, though, means problems for bikers. We could find no safe bike route through the highway maze to Salem. A bus trip would mean dismantling our bikes; it's an art all cycling tourists should learn. But often it's hard to arrange for such bulky baggage on a bus or

JOHN FULTON

"'TIS THE GIFT TO BE SIMPLE,
'TIS THE GIFT TO BE FREE"

JOHN FULTON

A Shaker hymn to simplicity echoes over the sect's restored village at Hancock, where in the 1830's some 300 men and women worked, worshiped, sang, and danced—living in celibacy. Round barn reflects Shaker ingenuity: From a balcony wagons dumped hay into a central manger; one man fed 52 cows.

train. We hitched a ride with photographer John Fulton.

We found Hawthorne again in Salem, his home town and the seaport setting of his two most famous novels. In the introduction to *The Scarlet Letter* he tells about snoozers on the porch of the Custom House, where he worked as surveyor of the port. Dave slept soundly on the Custom House lawn while I hurried to finish *The House of the Seven Gables* before we visited it.

We stepped through the doorway that served in the novel as the entrance to Hepzibah's cent-shop. Our guide, a girl not much older than ourselves, showed us a false panel beside the fireplace in the dining room. The panel opened, disclosing a secret staircase.

Our tour group, Dave and I in the lead, climbed the winding stairs to a small, gabled chamber and crossed creaking floors to another room, this one dusty, roofed by massive beams, and full of old trunks and sea chests. A ladder led to a windswept lookout where wives searched the horizon for homecoming sailors.

For our western swing through the Berkshire Hills, we planned to use Camp Karu, a mountaintop hostel 10 miles east of Pittsfield, as our base for day-long trips to a Shaker village and a music festival at Tanglewood. We found the Berkshires a pleasure to our eyes but a burden to our legs. When we approached a hill we would groan—and shift. In low gear a cyclist loses speed but gains the power needed

to climb a hill. On the downside he shifts to high and gathers enough momentum to carry him over the next hill. But not always. Our rear luggage racks were hung with 20-pound saddlebags and sleeping bags. This load sometimes made the difference on steep hills, the difference being we walked our bikes up.

Now, one more hill—then the Mount Everett Youth Hostel, a little white cottage on a farm in Sheffield. Like all hostels, it was chartered by the AYH and watched over by someone who lived there. Our houseparent turned out to be Miss Mildred Roys, a lively lady in her eighties. We met her as she came out of the woods with two jugs of water. "There's a spring about half a mile down the path," she said. "There's a cistern in the barn, but that water's for washing." Later, we found the spring trickling into a rain gutter propped on a stick—Miss Roys's handiwork.

We were cooking supper, hoping to change dehydrated turkey and noodles into a casserole, when the door opened and a tired traveler stumbled in. "Just in time!" said Ken, who came equipped with a homemade bamboo flute, a fork, and an appetite.

Next morning, the three of us set off for Stockbridge and another cultural landmark—Alice's Restaurant. We followed the lyrics of Arlo Guthrie's talk-song: "Walk right in. It's around the back just a half mile from the railroad track." In Alice's we met the song's famed Officer Obie, off duty, eating lunch.

On to Camp Karu, Shaker Village, and the past. "Put your hands to work and your hearts to God," said Mother Ann Lee, founder of the Shakers. They first settled in Hancock in the 1780's. We couldn't imagine ourselves Shakers: "shaking, shouting, pacing, and singing" at services, not even speaking to girls, and our parents living in separate dormitory rooms. But in this museum village we could admire the

KEEPING ROOM OF WELLS-THORN HOUSE, DEERFIELD; ROBERT W. MADDEN (ALSO RIGHT). OPPOSITE: JOHN FULTON

"PHANTOMS. . . . WE MEET THEM AT THE DOOR-WAY, on the stair . . . silent as the pictures on the wall." Explorers of Massachusetts' past find in Deerfield evocations of Longfellow's "Haunted Houses"—a tomahawked door in the village museum, a time-burnished room "thronged with quiet, inoffensive ghosts." After the Deerfield Massacre of 1704, survivors counted 49 dead, 109 others carried off by Indian and French-Canadian raiders. Today's villagers boast of ghosts, maintain homes centuries old. Keepers of history, they reroute highway traffic, bury power lines, guard from blight a mile-long lane of elms and maples.

In nearby Amherst, Emily Dickinson lived, a recluse behind "the door I dared not open." But for those who toil up hilly roads in the springtime of their lives, she penned an image of joyous freedom: "And for an everlasting roof the gables of the sky."

"A MAN MAY STAND THERE AND PUT ALL AMERICA BEHIND HIM," as Thoreau did. Or youth may stand at sunrise on Cape Cod and look ahead to another day of quest. First landfall of Pilgrims' eyes, first New World soil they trod, the dune-barrowed arm still beckons: hostelers to bikeways, swimmers to a national seashore, beachcombers to hunt for salt-silvered driftwood in the wrack of the tides.

Shakers' ingenuity. Whatever they did, they did well. They were the first to sell packaged seeds in America. And they claim the invention of the clothespin.

Before the Berkshire Music Festival in Lenox, we found on the beautiful grounds at Tanglewood the replica of "The Little Red House," where Hawthorne lived for a short while. "I cannot write in the presence of that view," he once said. But here he wrote *The House of the Seven Gables*. The sun had nearly set in the hills behind the Red House when we sat on the grass outside the huge Music Shed. A bamboo flute . . . "Alice's Restaurant" . . . and now Mozart. Somehow, they all fit.

We leaned on the aft rail, watching the gulls swoop down to snatch bits of bread tossed into the churning wake of the ferry. A bell buoy clanged, and then out of the mist appeared Nantucket Island. We walked our bikes up a cobblestone street and started riding. For once, bikes outnumbered cars; Nantucket is a biker's paradise.

Our hostel, a gray, steep-roofed old Coast Guard lifeboat station, was surrounded by swaying seagrass. Bicycles of every color filled its corral. We found bunks in what had been the boathouse. Next door, in the station itself, were the kitchen, common room, and, upstairs, a girls' bunkroom. Every one of the 40 hostelers had a chore. Ours for that night was cleaning ovens. We worked fast. We could hear guitars and laughter in the common room.

The days went swiftly—swimming, sailing, cookouts on the beach. Too soon, we were on the ferry again, waving goodbye to Ana, Missy, Michele, Anne, and Nantucket.

Not goodbye to sea and sand, though, for we headed for Cape Cod and its string of hostels. We had miles of bikeways in the dunes, miles of national seashore, miles of surf. And for every "Goodbye" there were a dozen new "Hi's." Every hostel seemed jammed, but you could always find room and, in most hostels, a guitar.

At night, we sang a kind of theme song—"America," Simon & Garfunkel's version, lots of funny lyrics and then:

They've all come to look for America,
All come to look for America.

That's what we did. And after you've pedaled a mile of America, you feel as if you own it.

JOHN FULTON

Going Places East

"America is neither a land nor a people," Archibald MacLeish wrote in his poem *American Letter;* "A word's shape it is. . . ." See it now in the shape of Vacationland—"A shining thing in the mind." The East's beaches spread a golden carpet for the rising sun. Blue waters lap the shore, gleam through a lacework of waterways studded with lakes, bejeweled with ponds. Parks and forests entwine thrusting mountains. Cities glitter and beckon, from Boston's shrines and New York's skyline to Washington's monuments and Miami's glamor. Each city whirls like a carousel—but we can step off and relax among folk who never stepped on. We can walk into the past of colonial streets, windjammer ports, or Old World farms. Magic-carpet superhighways make distant delights seem next door. We can even enter the future, treading the rocket-lined paths of America's spaceport. Here man flung himself starward, looked back, and saw a vision given word-shape by the pen of MacLeish: ". . . the earth as it truly is, small and blue and beautiful."

"Vacationland" design by Tasi Gelberg Pesanelli, Inc. Sculpture by Don Turano, photographed by National Geographic's Robert S. Oakes

Signs of good times spring up across America's varied East.

Here you're never far from a campground  or a spot where the big fish bite . Come on in, the water's fine for sport  at seashore, lake, and stream. Mountain country means high times in summer , snow sports in winter . Hiking trails  and cycling paths  keep even city folk fit. Meet Indians at reservations ; shoot wildlife with a camera at sanctuaries . Sample the old frontier  at the West's doorstep. (See the West's sculptured panorama on page 271.)

"First are the capes,

then are the shorelands, now

The blue Appalachians faint at the day rise. . . .

The Lakes scatter the low sun. . . ."

Archibald MacLeish

MAINE: 1 Seafoods Festival, Rockland, Aug.; hail King Neptune and his ocean bounty.
2 Sloop Days, Friendship, July.
3 Windjammer Days, Boothbay Harbor, July; boat parade, lobster feast, dance.
4 Antique Show, Camden, July; displays of china, silver, furniture.
NEW HAMPSHIRE: 5 Craftsman's Fair, Newbury, Aug.; Yankee wares crafted and sold.
6 Fall Foliage Festival, Warner, Oct.
7 Dartmouth Winter Carnival, Hanover, Feb.; snow sculpture, ski meet, ice hockey.
8 World Sled Dog races, Laconia, Feb.
VERMONT: 9 Winter Carnival, Middlebury, Feb.; ice show, snowshoe race, ski jumping.
10 Franklin County Maple Festival, St. Albans, April; sugaring, pancake breakfasts.
11 Marlboro Music Festival, July-Aug.
MASSACHUSETTS: 12 Race Week, Marblehead, July; sailing regatta of 1,000 boats.
13 St. Peter's Day Fiesta, Gloucester, June; dory race, fireworks, blessing of the fleet.
14 Jacob's Pillow Dance Festival, Lee, and Berkshire Music Festival, Tanglewood (Lenox), both July-Aug.
15 Antique Collectors Weekend, Old Sturbridge Village, Oct.
16 Eastern States Exposition, West Springfield, Sept.; livestock, horse shows.
RHODE ISLAND: 17 Arts Festival, Providence, May-June; painting, sculpture.
18 Jazz Festival, Newport, July.
CONNECTICUT: 19 Barnum Festival, Bridgeport, July; circus parade, antique autos.
20 Shakespeare Theatre, Stratford, June-Sept.
21 Yale-Harvard Regatta, New London, June.
NEW YORK: 22 Winter Carnival, Saranac Lake, Feb.; snowmobile races, ice hockey.
23 Old Whalers Festival, Sag Harbor, June; whaleboat races, harpooning contest.
24 Flower Show, New York City, March.
PENNSYLVANIA: 25 Woodmen's Carnival, Galeton, Aug.; tree felling, logrolling.
26 Pennsylvania Dutch Folk Festival, Kutztown, July; shoofly pie, hex sign art.
27 Bach Music Festival, Bethlehem, May.
28 Mummer's Parade, Philadelphia, Jan.; costumes, string bands, clowns.
NEW JERSEY: 29 Arts-Crafts Festival & Antique Fair, Cape May, Aug.
30 Miss America Pageant, Atlantic City, Sept.
DELAWARE: 31 Old Dover Days, May; musket drill, colonial dances, playlet.
32 32 Winterthur, April-June, Sept.-Oct.; gardens in bloom at an Americana museum.
MARYLAND: 33 Clam Festival, Annapolis, Aug.
34 Hard Crab Derby, Crisfield, Sept.
35 Calvert County Jousting Tournament, Port Republic, Aug.; ring spearing, courtly ritual.
DISTRICT OF COLUMBIA: 36 Cherry Blossom Festival, April; spring adorns Washington.
37 Smithsonian Folklife Festival, July; crafts fair, music, dancing on the Mall.
38 Christmas Pageant of Peace; yuletide garlands the Nation's Capital.
VIRGINIA: 39 "The Common Glory," Williamsburg, June-Aug.; Spirit of '76 drama.
40 "Trail of the Lonesome Pine," Big Stone Gap, June-Sept.; hill folk musical.
41 Apple Blossom Festival, Winchester, May.
42 Wild Pony Roundup, Chincoteague, July.
43 Azalea Festival, Norfolk, April.
WEST VIRGINIA: 44 Mountain State Art & Craft Fair, Ripley, July.
45 Folk Festival, Glenville, June; music, drama, auction, do-si-dos.
46 Forest Festival, Elkins, Oct.; lumber-train rides, jousting, tree felling.
NORTH CAROLINA: 47 Craftsman's Fair, Asheville, July; skills of potters and weavers.
48 "Unto These Hills," Cherokee, June-Aug.; drama of Indian exile to Oklahoma.
49 "The Lost Colony," Roanoke Island, June-Aug.; story of ill-fated settlers.
50 Highland Games & Scottish Clans Gathering, Grandfather Mountain, July; bagpipes, kilts.
SOUTH CAROLINA: 51 "The Liberty Tree," Columbia, June-Aug.; state heritage drama.
52 Charleston homes tour, March-April.
53 Camellia Show, Georgetown, Feb.
FLORIDA: 54 "Cross and Sword," birth of St. Augustine, oldest city in U. S., June-Aug.
55 Fiesta of Five Flags, Pensacola, June; treasure hunt, aerobatics, regattas.
56 Shell Fair, Sanibel Island, March; outdoor art show, aquarium, exotic shells.
GEORGIA: 57 Arts Festival, Atlanta, May.
58 Arts Festival, Savannah, April; ballet, concerts, plays, paintings.
ALABAMA: 59 Tennessee Valley Fiddlers' Convention, Athens, Oct.
60 Azalea Trail, Mobile, Feb.-March; 35 miles of flowers wind through the city.
MISSISSIPPI: 61 Natchez Pilgrimage, March; tour of mansions built by King Cotton.
62 62 "Gold in the Hills," Vicksburg, March-May, June-Aug.; drama of Little Nell.
LOUISIANA: 63 Mardi Gras, New Orleans, Feb.
64 Championship Pirogue Races, Lafitte, May; marsh canoes paddled for prizes.
65 Jambalaya Festival, Gonzales, June; Creole cooking contests.
TENNESSEE: 66 Fish Fry, Paris, April; catfish, hush puppies, hootenanny, parades.
67 Iroquois Steeplechase, Nashville, May.
KENTUCKY: 68 "Legend of Daniel Boone," Harrodsburg, June-Aug.; hilltop drama.
69 Kentucky Derby, Louisville, May.
70 "The Stephen Foster Story," Bardstown, June-Aug.; medley of Old South favorites.
71 Big Singing Day, Benton, May; choral festival of ancient Welsh hymns.
OHIO: 72 State Fair, Columbus, Aug.
73 Swiss Festival, Sugarcreek, Oct.; yodeling, costume parade, games, cheese.
74 Pumpkin Show, Circleville, Oct.; parades, pie-eating contests, pie auction.
MICHIGAN: 75 Tulip Festival, Holland, May.
76 76 Country Fair, May, and Old Car Festival, Sept., Greenfield Village, Dearborn.
77 Lilac Festival, Mackinac Island, June.
INDIANA: 78 Covered Bridge Festival, Rockville, Oct.; visit 37 of them.
79 Indianapolis 500-Mile Race, May.
ILLINOIS: 80 Lakefront Festival, Chicago, Aug.; boat parade, bands, swimming meet.
81 "Abe Lincoln in Illinois," New Salem State Park, Aug.; outdoor drama.
WISCONSIN: 82 Snowmobile Derby, Eagle River, Jan.; drivers throttle up for world crown.
83 "Wilhelm Tell," New Glarus, Sept.; story of the Swiss freedom fighter.
84 Old Milwaukee Days; Fourth of July celebration, historic circus-wagon parade.
85 Lumberjack World Championship, Hayward, July; logrolling, tree topping, sawing.
86 Scandinavian Festival, Washington Island, Aug.; smorgasbord, folk dancing.
MINNESOTA: 87 Winter Carnival, St. Paul, Jan.; toboggan run, ice fishing.
88 "Song of Hiawatha," Pipestone, July-Aug.; Longfellow's poem enacted outdoors.
89 Minneapolis Aquatennial, July; canoe and hydroplane races, turtle derby, fish fry.
IOWA: 90 State Fair, Des Moines, Aug.
91 Oktoberfest, Amana Colonies, Oct.; beer, bratwurst, and oom-pah-pah.
MISSOURI: 92 National Festival of Craftsmen, Silver Dollar City, Oct.
93 Tom Sawyer Days, Hannibal, July.
ARKANSAS: 94 White River Water Carnival, Batesville, Aug.; boat and water shows.
95 Ozark Folk Festival, Eureka Springs, Oct.; square dances, barefoot ball, gospel songs.

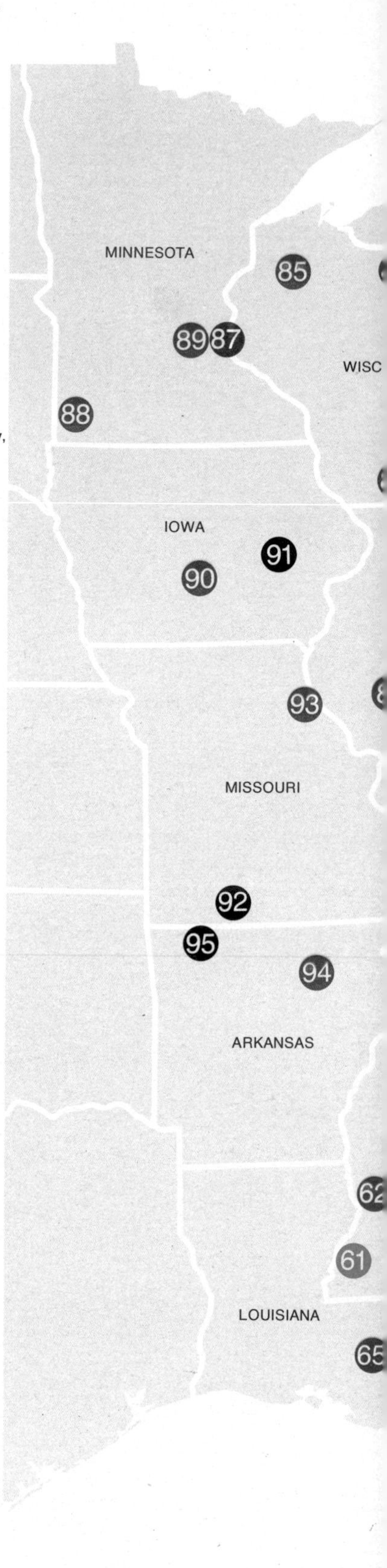

MAPS BY BETTY CLONINGER AND MONICA WOODBRIDGE, GEOGRAPHIC ART DIVISION

HAPPENINGS EAST

Do-si-do or Best of Show! Flaming leaves and harvest sheaves, Mardi Gras and oom-pah-pah, Yankee fairs and Ozark wares, Pennsylvania Dutch and Ohio Swiss, Louisiana Cajun and Carolina bagpiper. Sloop regatta, pirogue race, turtle derby, hard crab derby, Kentucky Derby! All year round, all over the East, in metropolis and heartland hamlet, in seaside resort and hilltop town, proud people remember their heritage, practice their arts and crafts, offer the fruits of land and sea. Color-coded map matches numbered list. Try a lobster feast in Maine in summer. See a snowshoe race in Vermont in winter. Square dance in Arkansas in fall. Join the spring sing in Kentucky. State agencies listed on page 422 can provide details and dates.

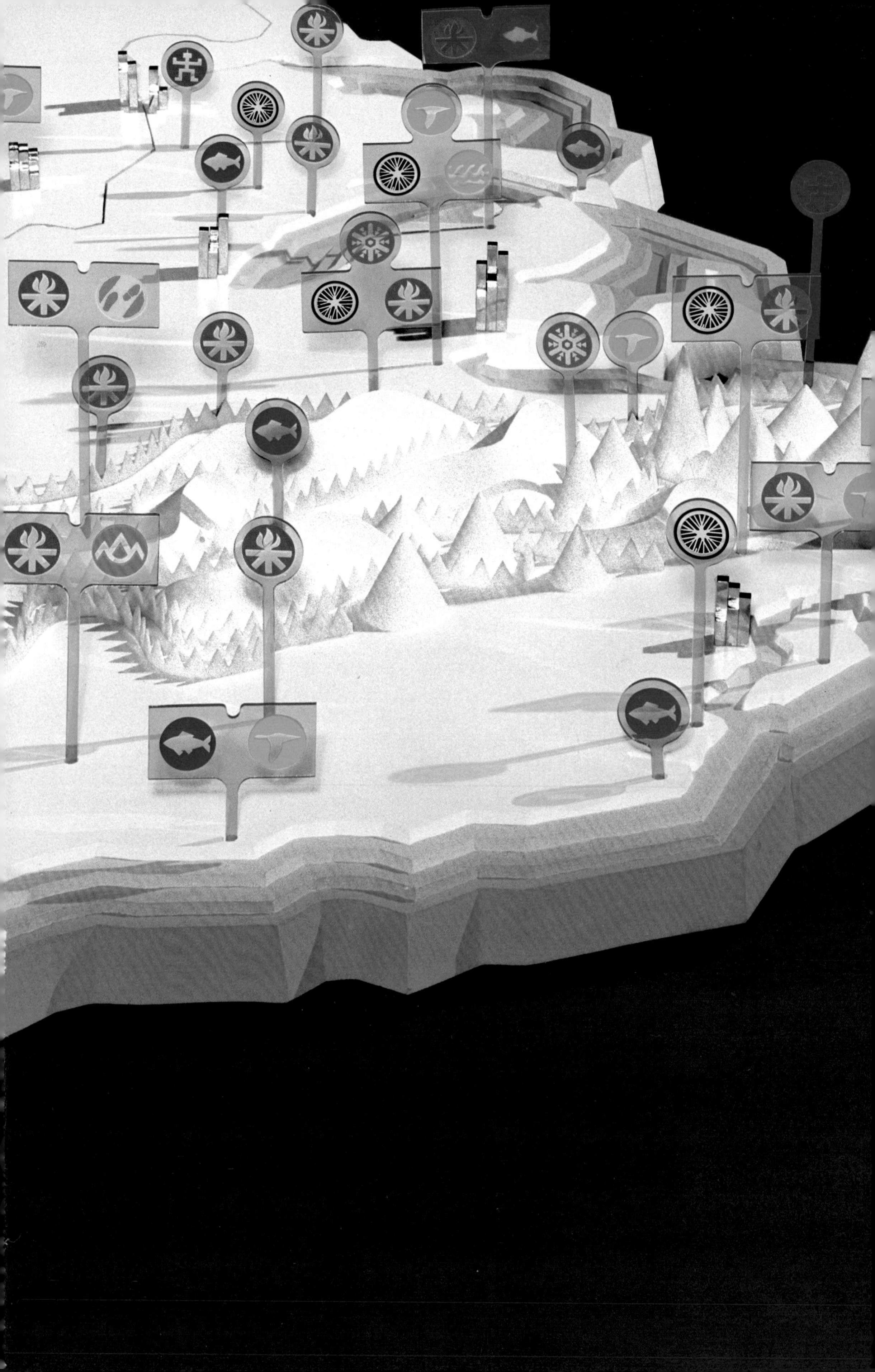

PARKLANDS

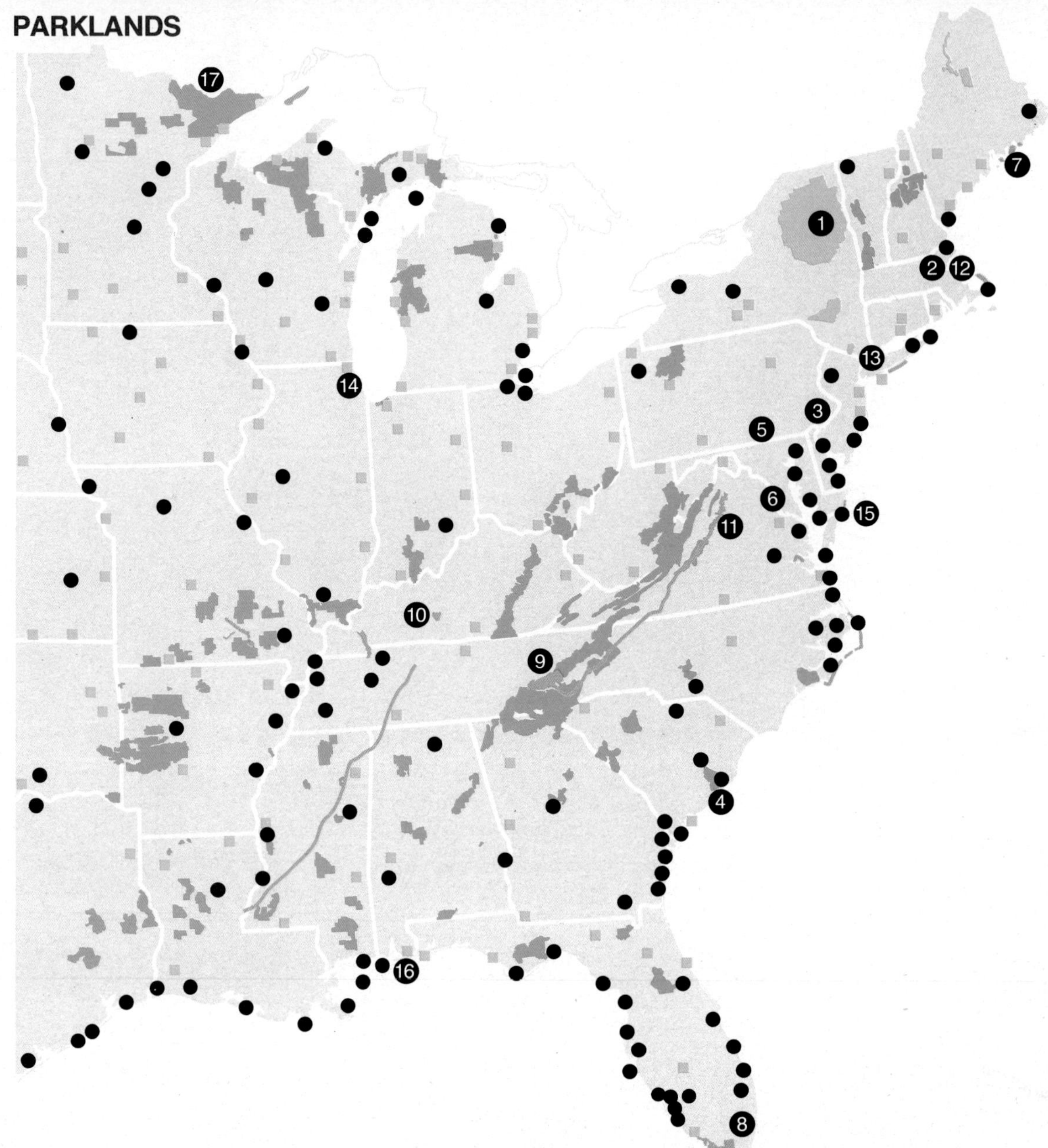

We have built so many cities on the East Coast that we call it Megalopolis, the "Great City." But amid this sprawl, oases and shrines of history endure. Beyond, just hours from teeming streets, beckon sylvan sanctuaries like New York's Adirondack Forest Preserve 1, largest state park in the U. S. On hallowed land we relive our past: from Concord and Lexington 2 to Independence Hall 3 in Philadelphia; from Fort Sumter 4 in the South to Gettysburg 5 in the North—and the House Where Lincoln Died in the heart of Washington, D. C. 6, city of 710 parks. The East's national parks offer a spectrum of splendor —from Maine's Acadia 7, greeting dawn from the top of our Eastern Seaboard, to Florida's Everglades 8, our largest subtropical wilderness. A fourth of the people in the U. S. live within a day's drive of the Great Smokies 9 and matchless greenery: 1,300 kinds of trees, shrubs, and herbs. Underground grandeur glitters in Mammoth Cave 10; Skyline Drive winds 105 miles through greens and golds of Shenandoah National Park 11. State and city parks spread like big backyards: Boston Common 12, the Nation's first; New York's Central Park 13; Des Plaines River Preserves 14, in the suburbs of Chicago. Wildlife refuges ● shelter creatures for the seeing: wild ponies and 275 species of birds on the Chincoteague dunes 15; sea turtles and pelicans in the bayous of Petit Bois 16. National forests shelter campers, waterfall-watchers. In Superior 17, Boundary Waters Canoe Area paddlers dip into two nations.

National Park System
National Forests
State Parks, Forest Preserves

VATERWAYS

Eastern bathers, beachcombers, ›oaters, and baskers, hemmed by , cottage-crowded coast, frolic ree on national seashores: historic Cape Cod 1; Fire Island 2, New 'ork's last wild strand; Assateague sland 3, 35-mile barrier reef; Cape Hatteras 4 and Cape Lookout 5 on North Carolina's Outer Banks. 'ans of the Chesapeake & Ohio Canal 6 ride mule-drawn arges, paddle canoes, ice-skate n winter. Indiana Dunes 7 and Pictured Rocks 8, national akeshores, preserve splendors, as o the Boundary Waters Canoe Area 9, which restricts motors, nd the Allagash Wilderness Vaterway 10. Hushed woodlands eckon boats to the Ozark Scenic Riverways 11, Table Rock Lake 12, nd the Eleven Point 13, part of the Vild and Scenic Rivers System; his includes the St. Croix 14 and he Wolf 15. Boaters also follow he Intracoastal Waterways 16 long the Atlantic and Gulf Coasts. he East's largest water layground, TVA's man-made Great Lakes of the South" 17, parkles in seven states.

Water recreation areas

'RAILS

Most of the East's Indian aths vanished under wagon vheels and highway pavement. But a woodland web still invites he footloose to our most opular outdoor sport: hiking. Not far from city sidewalks 2,000-mile green walk—the Appalachian Trail 1—winds hrough 14 states. The Long 'rail 2 hitches to the A.T.; he Finger Lakes Trail 3 aims o span New York. More than ,000 miles of footpaths lace the Adirondacks 4. Riders amble he Horse-Shoe Trail 5 from 'alley Forge on the pioneers' Conestoga Road. Part of the Buckeye 6 is the old towpath f the Ohio-Erie Canal. The New England Trail 7 circles the 'ankee states. Other highways rack our history: the Natchez race 8, Lincoln Heritage 9, Mississippi River Parkway 10, Ozark Frontier 11, Hiawatha Pioneer 12, Dixieland 13. Bikeways span Wisconsin 14, lodge dunes at Cape Cod 15, hread parks in Philadelphia 16, New York 17, and Chicago 18.

Wilderness Trails

Heritage Roads

Bikeways

Pennsylvania Plain and Fancy

Follow the dirt road that slices into the rich, rolling Pennsylvania farmland outside Lancaster. The road bends and twists, sweeps around a patch of brambly woodland, then dips sharply. At the bottom of a long hill, over a meandering creek, a covered wooden bridge reaches out like a sturdy right arm that grips the far opposite bank.

That faded spot on the span once bore a sign: "Walk your horse." Now a rattle of iron-bound wheels and a hollow *clip-clop* of iron-shod hoofs make xylophone music on the bridge's timber floor. The music swells and dies; horse and carriage, a dark silhouette in the tunnel mouth, are re-created by the sun.

The black-bearded driver, wearing a broad-brimmed hat square on his head, sits straight and stern. The woman next to him, shadowed in a coal-scuttle bonnet, looks up from the baby cradled in her arms. Young, strong, plain, hers is a mother's face from another time.

For the bridge spans more than a stream. It beckons visitors to cross from today's complex world to a realm where a simpler life somehow endures—the realm of the Pennsylvania Dutch.

Beyond the bridge, framed at its far end, is their land: a green field of corn, a red streak of silo, a white splash of farmhouse. Upstream are two of their sons: barefoot boys squatting on rocks, fishing. Straw hats lie on the bank. White suspenders criss-cross a blue shirt and a green one, holding up ample black "barn-door britches."

The boys live in long-past yesterdays, true to a faith that shuns change. Their heritage goes back to William Penn, who lured their forefathers to America in 1681 with the promise that "land was plentiful, peace abode, and every man could worship God according to his own conscience." Swiss and Germans, fleeing religious persecution, came in waves. They settled in the verdant valleys of the Susquehanna and Schuylkill, joining with English Quaker pioneers. The newcomers came to be called Pennsylvania Dutch—actually *Deutsch* slurred by English tongues.

Two ways of life grew side by side. The "Gay," or "Fancy," Dutch (Reformed, Lutheran, United Brethren, and others) adopted many of the customs of the world around them. They gathered about Kutztown, where their annual festival, with a smile under every sunbonnet (opposite), keeps alive a legacy of gaiety.

JOHNNY CLAYPOOLE'S HEX SIGN OF HEARTS AND FLOWERS AND DISTELFINKS, AND AN OLD-FASHIONED GIRL ENCHANT KUTZTOWN'S FOLK FESTIVAL; MARTIN ROGERS

The "Plain" Dutch (the Amish, River Brethren, Dunkers, Mennonites) settled around Lancaster. Their strict doctrines impelled them to remain apart; many stay apart, outnumbered nine to one by the Gay Dutch.

Mennonite sects range from the "Black Bumpers," who drive cars but blacken the chromium to prevent pridefulness, to the General Conference Group, who dress "like the world" and enjoy TV and telephones. River Brethren and Dunkers baptize outdoors by immersion—even if the ice must be cracked. But it is the Amish, "plainest of the plain," who have long fascinated visitors to Lancaster County. Named for its founder Jacob Amman, the Amish sect split from the Mennonites in the late 1600's and has remained aloof ever since.

"To be separate from the world means to the Amish to be different from the world," writes one authority on the Amish who lived with a Plain family. To make the separateness more vivid, the Amish cling to the old and the plain—in clothes, house furnishings, religious customs, and the German-sprinkled Pennsylvania Dutch dialect. "We know how the *alt* [old] works," they say. "How can we be sure of the *nigh* [new]?"

Green pastures and golden corn shocks surround homes near Lancaster, hub of Plain Dutch farmlands and whimsically named hamlets—Bird in Hand, Blue Ball, Intercourse. The Fancy Dutch cluster around Kutztown. An Amish farmer (below) cultivates tobacco by mule power, a Plain person amid plenty. Men smoke cigars or pipes, rarely cigarettes, and begin to grow beards on their wedding day. Pacifists, they shave upper lips, fasten garments with hooks and eyes, for moustaches and buttons once marked the military man.

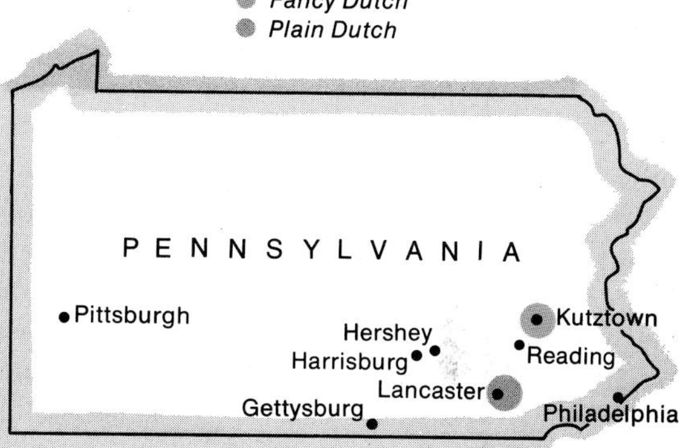

WILLIAM ALBERT ALLARD. MAP BY GEOGRAPHIC ART DIVISION

Visitors know when they have arrived in the land of the Plain People: power lines, telephone poles, and TV antennas disappear. The countryside becomes a quilt of meticulously tended fields seamed by road and stream, with sturdy farmhouses and barns (above). In neat farmyards cuffless black trousers, bright workshirts, and long dresses of purple or green or blue billow on washlines. No clackety gasoline tractors fog the air with sound and fume. Farmers consider such worldly conveniences sinful. Wasteful, too: "If you put gasoline in a tractor, all you get out is smoke."

Horses draw Amish plows and carriages

THEIR FAITH ROOTED IN THE PAST, AMISH WOMENFOLK TROOP TO TOIL WHILE AMISH KINDER FILL THE ONE-ROOM STUMPTOWN SCHOOL; WILLIAM ALBERT ALLARD

and help fertilize the land. Chill streams and smokehouses preserve their food. Wood-burning stoves heat their homes. They pump water by hand. If an Amishman should hitch a windmill to his pump, a neighbor will rebuke him for "making God do his work." Insurance and lightning rods are frowned upon as attempts to thwart God's will.

But when lightning strikes a barn and burns it down, neighbors come from miles around. Men and boys arrive with hammers and brawny arms. Women and girls (opposite) bring milk cans brimming with peppermint water and baskets of food, perhaps cracker pudding and *schnitz un gnepp,* a treat of dried apple slices and dumplings.

To the "outlander" (anyone not Amish), a tour of the countryside may inspire musings about the price of being plain: The barefoot, prayer-capped women walking a narrow road look somber; the schoolhouse with rooftop bell and waiting hand pump seems bleak.

Most of the one-room, eight-grade schools, built long ago by the Amish to keep their plain *kinder* apart from the fancies of modern life, are extinct. In a compromise with state law requiring education until the age of 17, most Amish children go to public school until they are 14. After that they begin a life of farming, continuing their schooling three hours a week.

The Amish have their times of fun and laughter, of song and even dance. These moments the visitor rarely sees. For they take place within the inner world of the Amish—the family farmstead, which also serves as a birthplace and a place for weddings and funerals.

AMISHMEN AND OUTLANDERS SIZE UP A MULE ON THE AUCTION BLOCK IN THIS SERENE COUNTRYSIDE WHERE HORSE-AND-BUGGY DAYS LINGER; WILLIAM ALBERT ALLARD

A Sunday sightseer may pass a farmyard filled with buggies. The house, on this Sabbath, is a church, where a congregation gathers for services lasting most of the day. At night, though, the youngsters will enjoy a "singing" in the barn. They'll sing hymns. But they'll square dance too. And laugh at jokes and riddles: "A man was running across the bridge. Yet he walked." Give up? *Yet* was his dog.

The Amish love the land and have harvested a bounteous reward. Yield per acre on their farms ranks among the highest in the Nation. They spurn worldly things; yet they do not consider making money sinful. Shrewd traders, they love a bargain—a good horse, a second-hand plow. The men mingle with outlanders at auctions, making bids with a slight

lift of the chin, a raised finger, a wink.

These Amish folk have come to accept inquisitive tourists with indifference—until a camera appears. Then their indifference vanishes—and so do they. They believe that to pose for a picture—a "graven image"—violates God's will. Even the rag dolls of little Amish girls are faceless. (With gentle persuasion, William Allard won permission to make the unposed photographs on these pages for the National Geographic Society.)

Unless you are the school teacher, feed dealer, family doctor, or a lifelong neighbor, you will usually not be welcomed inside an Amish farm. But should an Amishman say, "Will you stay with us, once?" you would enter a house simple and sufficient. White muslin curtains the windows. Plants in jars and tin cans line the sills. (The Amish waste nothing.) Straight-backed chairs surround the table in the big kitchen, where the family spends most of its time. A padded rocker stands near the cast-iron stove in the "fire corner." A pressure lamp hangs from the ceiling. Flowers and ivy twine around a wind-up wall clock "just for pretty."

The typical home swarms with children; the Amish cherish "the Lord's families." Although they dress their children in adult style, they expect youngsters to be *nixnootzich* (mischievous). And they expect their sons to sow a few wild oats before settling down. Young men setting out for Saturday-night sprees in Lancaster draw lots. The loser must stay sober enough to drive the horse and buggy safely home.

Young women have no such freedom; they spend their teen years preparing for marriage. When a girl is being courted, however, her swain may lure her out for a buggy ride. Both families pretend not to know about the trysting.

Young love usually ripens, like the harvest, in autumn, for weddings always take place after the crops are in. After a honeymoon of several weeks—visiting relatives on both sides, getting practical gifts—bride and groom return to his family. He may start his own farm or take over the old farmstead. His parents

KUTZTOWN FESTIVAL BUBBLES WITH YOUTHFUL ZEST AND APPLE BUTTER IN AN IRON KETTLE; MARTIN ROGERS (ALSO PAGES 112–113)

then will move into a wing called the *groose-dawdi haus* (grandfather's house).

Outlanders are rarely invited to Amish weddings. But you can attend a portrayal of one at the Pennsylvania Dutch Folk Festival in Kutztown. Each year during Fourth of July week the Gay Dutch gather there to exuberantly celebrate their heritage—and to give visitors "a happy heart and a full stomach."

The Plain Dutch take no part in so worldly an event. But the Gay Dutch, with common ancestors, customs, and crafts, find it easy to impersonate their sober brethren. In the enactment of an Amish wedding, you can almost feel like one of the guests at the bride's house, sitting on a wooden bench....

Surrounded by giggling friends, she wears a solid-color, shiftlike frock, white apron and *halsduch* (neckerchief), and a white cap tied at the throat by two narrow ribbons. High-top shoes peep from below her long skirt. Neither she nor the other women wear jewelry or carry flowers. The groom stands stiffly in black trousers, vest, and coat.

The real wedding's sermons and hymns (many echoing Gregorian chants) last for hours. Kutztown's dramatized wedding isn't *that* real. But authenticity and the understanding of the Gay Dutch are reflected in the staging of the wedding and in "Men of One Master," a pageant that vividly recalls the Amish struggle to survive in the modern world.

the boards drum with a dancing free-for-all until the fiddlers beg for mercy.

The Kutztown festival, begun by college professors and run by the Pennsylvania Folklife Society, displays crafts that live today as they did centuries ago. No one had to resurrect Pennsylvania Dutch folk arts; they have never died. All over the 35-acre fairground men and women in colorful garb work at skills as their forefathers did. A printer turns out broadsides on a press Ben Franklin would recognize. A *maydel* (girl) inscribes a birth certificate in *fraktur,* thick black handlettering. A father and son carve wooden eagles.

Rug-makers and basket-weavers with nimble fingers fashion varied designs. Baskets start, as they always have, with hand-drawn strips of wood trimmed on the

The author and director of both productions was born into an Amish family. But in his childhood his relatives and he were *oust* (expelled) from the church because his grandfather installed a bathtub in their farmhouse.

Kutztown's Gay Dutch amateur actors switch easily from somber Amish rites to livelier pursuits—cavorting in costume on the Folk Festival Common (above)—or swinging to the foot-stomping rhythm of the Kutztown Reel (overleaf). Experts demonstrate Gay Dutch jigging and hoedowning and quick-stepping Western square dancing each afternoon on the canopied stage. Spectators are welcome to have a go. At night, champion sets compete for prizes and

schnitzelbank (shaving bench). And rugs still come forth from humble rags.

Women stitch quilts and bonnets, knit gloves, make grandmother dolls with dried-apple heads (far right), paint toleware, and show mini-skirted housewives how to dye yarn in kettles; the vegetable-dye recipes are heirlooms.

The candlemaker (lower) patiently dips his heavy twine into beef or mutton tallow, forming candles as the old-time chandlers did. Their thick-wicked products gave a brighter light than homemade candles poured in thin molds.

Crowds always gather around the painter of hex signs (below). These bright patterns have become the trademark of everything "Dutch." Can geometric designs of stars, flowers, hearts, teardrops, and *distelfinks* (thistle- or goldfinches) bring wealth and good health, make rain, and banish evil spirits? Outlanders seem to think so. Repeatedly they return to the festival to tell the hex artist how well his signs worked. "Everything went great last year," a New York woman reported. "My children got through school, my husband's business prospered—all because of your hex sign." Occasionally a buyer will indignantly complain about a sign that brought bad luck.

Folklore experts insist that hex signs are merely decorative—"chust for nice." The Gay Dutch put the hex on hope

FESTIVAL FOLK KEEP A HERITAGE ALIVE WITH HANDS, HEIRLOOMS, AND HEARTS AS GAY AS HEX ARTIST CLAYPOOLE'S PAINTS; MARTIN ROGERS

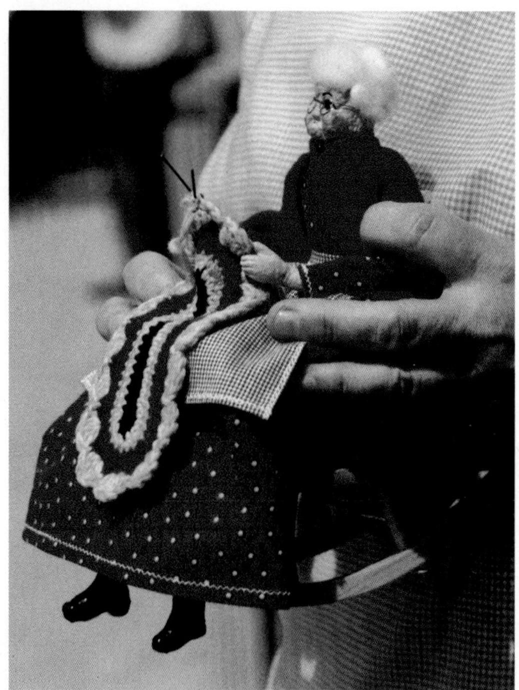

chests, quilts, dishes, even baptismal certificates. And, of course, on barns.

The Plain People never use the hex. But superstition thrives in both Plain and Gay cultures. European folklore is kept alive by practitioners wise in the ways of bees, snakes, and herbs. "Powwow" doctors, speaking "words directed by God," talk to cure the sick. "Dowsers" perform at the festival, showing how to find subterranean water by feeling the pull of a divining rod. And you may meet the Almanac Man. He'll tell you when to plant your crops, paint your fence, and—if you're an earthy Pennsylvania Dutchman with a sense of humor—when to romance your wife!

Being Pennsylvania Dutch is *wunderlich,* say its Gay people, and their preoccupation at the festival consists of sharing this wunderlich feeling with visitors. They particularly share

MARTIN ROGERS

Gay Dutch Country Kitchen fills family feasters (opposite) with favorites from a menu like this:

Fried Fresh Sausage
Potato Filling • Dried Corn
Lettuce and Egg Salad with Cooked Dressing
Apple Butter • Chow Chow • Cottage Cheese
Homemade Bread and Butter
Raisin Pie • Coffee

the wonderful habit of *fressing* (eating). All the Dutch, Plain and Fancy, love food. They agree: "Man and wife are one. But each has a stomach."

Chicken corn soup, sauerkraut and dumpling, *hinkle bott boi* (chicken pot pie), shoofly pie (sugar and molasses in a crumb-covered shell), the seven sweets and seven sours (including widely known favorites like candied watermelon rind and pickled onions)—all could come from the wood-burning stove of an Amish frau or the wood-burning stove of the festival's Country Kitchen.

This bustling outdoor cookery serves up hearty meals for craftsmen and festival workers. One day it may be *gashmelted die noodla* (buttered noodles with crumbs). Another day there's pig stomach stuffed with sausage and potatoes.

Hungry? Sample a giant pretzel, or funnel cakes sizzled right before your eyes (left). Better yet, answer the call *Koom essa!* at the food tents or at the pavilion, set up for family-style dining. Cooking is a family matter, too. Before the festival starts, wives in home and church kitchens jar gallons of chow chow (a sour: chopped vegetables, sugar, vinegar), pickled red beets, pepper hash, and other relishes. During the festival menfolk bake hams and fry chickens through the night while wives make batches of shoofly pie and milk tarts. Early each morning the old folks gather to peel and chop fresh vegetables. And the young people hustle about serving the steaming platters of food from noon "till everything is all."

Their reward comes as they watch the incredulous faces of outlanders confronted by plates mounded with chicken and ham, corn and beans, *schmierkase* (cottage cheese) and *lodwarrick* (apple butter).

Never mind the translations—or the waistline. As the Pennsylvania Dutch say, "A fat wife and full barn never did any man harm."

What So Proudly We Hail

Bursting rockets pinwheel across the heavens to splinter against the marble shaft and shower it with stars. On the green below, a hundred thousand faces beam at this Yankee-Doodle-Dandy display of Independence Day pride. The great white obelisk, thrusting 555 feet into spacious skies, has lured us like a beacon from sea to shining sea to our Nation's Capital.

Aptly, we begin at the Washington Monument, shrine to the Father of our Country. On July 4, 1848, its cornerstone was laid with the silver trowel Washington used in setting the Capitol's cornerstone 55 years before. In the throng stood a young Congressman from Illinois, Abraham Lincoln. The Monument's stump (the capstone was not set until 1884) would witness his days of agony and glory.

In daylight we ascend the shaft with a 70-second elevator ride, or test our legs against its 898 steps; then we gaze on Lilliputian Washington, an unrivaled view of the White House, the Lincoln Memorial, the gleaming arc of the Potomac.

Now into our waiting Tourmobile. Foot saver with picture windows (right), the bus circles the Mall, core of visitors' Washington, and links historic buildings with treasuries of the world's art and wonders. We'll explore them all, but first to the Capitol. "Here, sir," said Alexander Hamilton, "the people govern."

General Grant on horseback guards the western approach. How mighty the dome appears, a white cloud crowning the hill. Within, corridors seem yet to echo the fiery words of Henry Clay, John C. Calhoun—and Daniel Webster: "Liberty and Union, now and forever, one and inseparable."

Guided tours start in the Rotunda and go past statues of great Americans. Will Rogers in bronze stands "where I can keep my eye on Congress." Keep *your* eye on Congress by requesting a gallery pass from your Senator or Representative. (Free subways will take you to his office building.) Then take your seat as lawmakers forge our country's future.

After lunch in a Capitol cafeteria you can stroll over to the Supreme Court to see more history in the making. All rise as nine black-gowned justices enter. "Oyez! Oyez! Oyez!" calls the marshal, admonishing litigants "to draw near and give their attention."

Next door you can wander the Library of Congress; its 16 million volumes grew from Thomas Jefferson's collection. Prefer the Queen's English? Walk round the corner to the Folger Shakespeare Library,

FIREWORKS ETCH SUMMER SKIES OVER THE WASHINGTON MONUMENT AND THE CAPITOL; JAMES P. BLAIR, NATIONAL GEOGRAPHIC PHOTOGRAPHER. RIGHT: TOURMOBILE PLIES THE MALL; JOHN FULTON

with its replica of the Globe Theater. We leave Capitol Hill reminded of a character in *Henry VI,* "wishing his foot were equal with his eye."

But the Mall beckons with ice cream men and hurdy-gurdy carousel. During July's Festival of American Folklife the mile-long green sprouts tents; in their shade Kentucky woodcarvers, Appalachian toy makers, Navajo weavers, Texas chili makers show their skills.

Now pick a building—that turreted red castle, first home of Smithsonian exhibits. Established in 1846 with a bequest by British scientist James Smithson, the Institution became, said Mark Twain, "the Nation's attic." You could spend a lifetime roaming the corridors of its seven buildings on the Mall and still not see all its wonders. But let's try!

We stand at the Museum of History and Technology to watch *Infinity,* a ribbon of stainless steel by Jose de Rivera (below), slowly revolve. Inside swings a 73-foot Foucault Pendulum, proving before your eyes that the world turns. Beyond hangs the Star-Spangled Banner that Francis Scott Key saw "by the dawn's early light." First Ladies cluster in inaugural gowns (opposite). A parade of old cars—"That's a 1903 Winton"—draws the menfolk.

A triumph of taxidermy, an elephant 13 feet at the shoulder, guards the Museum of Natural History rotunda. (The 92-foot blue whale is fiberglass.) Dinosaur skeletons roam one room; in others Eskimos pursue seals, Aztecs offer a human sacrifice. Amid a glitter of gems, the Hope Diamond flaunts its 44.5 carats.

But more valuable than jewels is the lunar lump (opposite lower) that Apollo 11 astronauts brought back. Showcased in

SMITHSONIAN EXPLORERS STUDY GOWNS OF FIRST LADIES, A MOON ROCK, A REVOLVING "INFINITY": JAMES E. RUSSELL, NATIONAL GEOGRAPHIC STAFF; ROBERT W. MADDEN, JOHN FULTON

Many-faceted Smithsonian Institution dazzles with variety: Grinning Punch decorated a tobacco store; an Aztec calendar portrays the universe. Leonardo's Ginevra de'Benci graces the National Gallery; fire hose wagon in Museum of History and Technology was hauled by men; white tiger cub stars at the National Zoological Park. William Pitt orates beneath a National Portrait Gallery skylight. Lindbergh's transatlantic monoplane soars in the Arts and Industries Building. Robert W. Madden, Donna Grosvenor (lower left), and James E. Russell, National Geographic staff (opposite).

the Arts and Industries Building, the chunk of rock drew 600,000 viewers in eight weeks, eclipsing Smithsonian records. One earthling exclaimed, "Just like any other rock!" Most stand awed by this talisman of man's future in space. Sharing museum inner space are John Glenn's *Friendship 7* and Charles Lindbergh's *Spirit of St. Louis* (below).

The Muses reign in the neighboring Freer Gallery of Art, godown of oriental antiquities and Whistler paintings, and in the National Gallery of Art across the Mall. Housed in the world's largest marble structure, the National Gallery collections bedazzle the eye with early Italian masterpieces, works by Rembrandt, Rubens, El Greco, Van Gogh, Gauguin, Picasso, Constable, Homer—and the only Leonardo da Vinci in America (opposite, left center). Don headsets for lectures while you gaze. Some marvel silently; some rhapsodize—as did one mini-skirted lass: "Man, I mean Man, like Wow!"

At the National Portrait Gallery, a few blocks from the Mall, see the men and women who shaped our destiny—from British statesman William Pitt (opposite) and Pocahontas to Dwight Eisenhower and Albert Einstein. Originally the Patent Office, "temple of the useful arts," the building served also as a temple of mercy. Here Walt Whitman and Clara Barton ministered to Antietam's toll of maimed and dying. At war's end joy reigned: Four thousand guests dined and danced here at Lincoln's second Inaugural Ball.

Weeks later a shot rang out in Ford's Theatre, a block away. Restored after a century's neglect, the red-brick theater again lights its stage. In the basement museum you can see the derringer that killed the President. Across the street in the Peterson House, where Lincoln died, dimly lit rooms remain palled with sorrow.

The mystique of Lincoln pervades Washington: at the Capitol steps, where he pledged "to bind up the Nation's wounds"; in the White House, where he signed the Emancipation Proclamation; and at the Lincoln Memorial, where he belongs to the ages. Olympian in this city of shrines, the memorial is graced by 36 Doric columns, one for each of the reunited states at his death. Inside, pilgrims brought by the busload study the brooding figure by Daniel Chester French and read: "In this temple as in the hearts of the people for whom he saved the Union the memory of Abraham Lincoln is enshrined forever."

COLONNADED LINCOLN MEMORIAL WELCOMES ITS THRONGS; JOHN FULTON. BELOW: PISTOLS BLAZE AT FBI HEADQUARTERS; THOMAS NEBBIA

Before leaving the memorial (above) look east to see the Washington Monument glimmering in the Reflecting Pool. In winter the pool ices over: Bring skates!

At the Federal Bureau of Investigation in the Justice Department young visitors spend an hour as agents. They drop into the crime laboratory to see scientific sleuths. At the range they watch tracers riddle paper criminals (right), then take home the targets. In the fortresslike National Archives next door they view the documents that underpin our Nation: the Declaration of Independence, the Constitution, the Bill of Rights.

Bills of another sort—greenbacks—roll off presses at the rate of some 60 million dollars a day at the Bureau of Engraving and Printing, and it won't cost a penny to watch. Admission's free also to the floral splendors of the National Arboretum

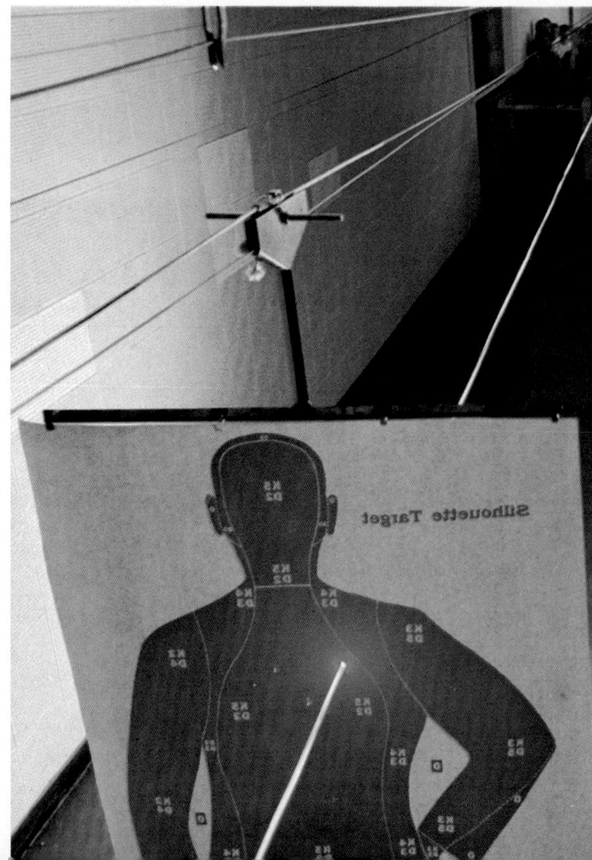

THE WORLD TURNS AT THE NATIONAL GEOGRAPHIC SOCIETY'S EXPLORERS HALL; EMORY KRISTOF, NATIONAL GEOGRAPHIC PHOTOGRAPHER

and to the National Zoological Park, where you can say hello to the white tigers.

Roam Georgetown with its historic homes and swinging bistros. Board a mule-drawn barge gliding the Chesapeake and Ohio Canal, woodland memento of America's westering. Survey progress on the National Cathedral, abuilding in Gothic style.

Flags bedeck Massachusetts Avenue's Embassy Row; its diplomats add dashes of cosmopolitan color. Indians in turbans and Africans in robes cheer a cricket match; a muezzin's evening chant wafts from a mosque; Parisian sidewalk cafes offer solace to the soles.

The world comes to you in Explorers Hall at National Geographic headquarters (above). Displays spur the imagination: You challenge Mount Everest, discover a stone god in a Mexican jungle, push to the North Pole with Peary's ice-battered sledge. In Lafayette Square, a short stroll down

16th Street, tulips lay siege to Andrew Jackson astride a bronze horse (below). Across Pennsylvania Avenue, route of Presidents, the White House awaits. As one of two hundred million landlords, take your place in line by the East Gate. Note the South Lawn's magnolia trees planted by Jackson; helicopters dodge them bringing visiting Chiefs of State.

Twice blackened by fire, and faithfully restored, the lovely white dowager lifts the spirit as you tread East, Green, Blue, and Red Rooms. There you'll find Stuart's portrait of Washington saved from the Redcoats by Dolley Madison, memorabilia of Monroe, Van Buren, two Roosevelts. Gold and crystal in the State Dining Room bespeak pomp and circumstance.

Beyond the Watergate where band concerts enliven the evenings, across the Potomac in Arlington National Cemetery, a sentry keeps vigil by the Tomb of the Unknowns. Among stately oaks and rows of tombstones, memories crowd. A young President exhorts, "Ask not what your country can do for you—ask what you can do for your country." A restless flame marks John F. Kennedy's grave. Nearby stands the mansion where Robert E. Lee dwelt before the hell of civil war. Down the river, our first President lies at his beloved plantation home, Mount Vernon, mecca to millions.

Washington chose the site for his namesake city. L'Enfant planned it "on such a scale as to leave room for that aggrandizement and embellishment which the . . . wealth of the Nation will permit it to pursue." And he planned well.

Each of us carries away his own vision of Washington. For many of us it is the pinkish haze of cherry blossoms ringing the Tidal Basin and Jefferson's memorial (opposite). Here he pledges "eternal hostility against every form of tyranny over the mind of man." And in the shimmering blossoms of spring we see the promise of our still-young land.

TULIPS MARCH ON ANDREW JACKSON'S STATUE AND THE WHITE HOUSE; CHERRY BLOSSOMS FRAME THE THOMAS JEFFERSON MEMORIAL.
B. ANTHONY STEWART AND (OPPOSITE) W. E. GARRETT, BOTH NATIONAL GEOGRAPHIC STAFF

A Christmas Card from Williamsburg

The Night Watch lifts his lantern high above his head. Militiamen sweep their pine-tar torches through the bonfire, form a flaming column, and march off at the head of a happy hurly-burly of paraders. "Light your candles!" The watchman's iron-lunged command rings through the cold December night, and dark houses and inns flicker to life. Windows in the Capitol open golden eyes, and from the cupola atop the Governor's Palace (above) a lantern shines over the city like the Christmas star. The Grand Illumination is underway, heralding Christmastide at historic Williamsburg.

Now begins a festive fortnight whose joy and radiance add an extra measure of richness for visitors seeking the spirit of the past in Virginia's restored colonial capital. This is Christmas as it used to be. Wreaths and swoops of greenery bedeck the town. Somewhere around the Inn lies the hidden Yule log. Anyone can join the search. The lucky finders haul it to the hearth and set it ablaze, pouring a glass of wine over it as a final toast. By time-honored custom visitors feed the flames with sprigs of holly in hopes that their sorrows will turn to ashes.

Music fills the air as carolers and balladeers render traditional tunes, and bewigged musicians play in stately concert at the candlelit Capitol. Fireworks and pageantry enliven the days; from Market Square comes the crack of musket and pistol as the "Christmas Guns" sound off. And around the groaning board merrymakers gather to feast and wassail.

Yet for all its furbelows and flourishes, Christmas in Colonial Williamsburg is a time of mellowness and harmony. The lights in the windows cast a warm, uniform glow, with none of the garishness of Christmas lights elsewhere. And, like the master clockmaker and engraver opposite, the people of the town seem to embody the graciousness and assurance of the 18th century. These gentle and generous folk tend Williamsburg's 90 acres of gardens and greens, exhibit its crafts, live in its original and reconstructed homes and shops, interpret its past, protect its heritage. For them, as for their counterparts in the 1700's, winter marks the least tumultuous time of the year. In bygone days the fall meetings of the General Assembly and General Court brought the wild, crowded "Publick Times," when travelers fell three a bed in the Raleigh Tavern, slept in the halls and stairwell

FROSTED CRAPE MYRTLE FRAMES THE GOVERNOR'S PALACE AND (OPPOSITE) AN ENGRAVER DESIGNS A MEDALLION AT THE GOLDEN BALL; JAMES L. AMOS, NATIONAL GEOGRAPHIC PHOTOGRAPHER

of Christiana Campbell's Tavern. When the lawyers, traders, and politicians departed, the clamor ebbed and Williamsburg resumed its serene winter ways.

Today the Publick Times peak in summer, when tourists flock to the "green country town" in an endless stream. The pace slows in the cold months; yet the appeal of Williamsburg's intimate, family-style Christmas celebration draws a devoted band of travelers who reserve lodgings—including 18 charming houses in the restored area—up to a year in advance.

As the blazing torches of the Grand Illumination parade light the way to yesteryear, visitors swing into step with townsmen in waistcoats and ladies in bonnets and farthingales. "Christmas is coming, the geese are getting fat," shrill the fifes. *Paradiddle double diddle flam!* beat the drums.

Ghosts of Christmas Past parade with them—ghosts of men who strode with regal air, and of men who dreamed and struggled and founded a new nation. Lord Botetourt, popular governor of this prospering and sometimes contentious colony, waves as his high-spirited team steps invisibly through the crowd. And isn't that lad with the red hair Tom Jefferson? He and John Page, students at the College of William and Mary, bound along in a holiday mood.

Behind the paraders as they march down mile-long Duke of Gloucester Street stands the H-shaped Capitol where Patrick Henry protested the Stamp Act with the fiery challenge, "If this be treason, make the most of it!"

Off to the right, at the head of its park, stands the lofty governor's residence, called the "Palace" ever since colonists complained about levies required by Governor Spotswood to complete it about 1720. Here one winter day in 1754 came a hard-riding young major named George Washington, to report on an incredibly dangerous mission into the

THE GRAND ILLUMINATION WELCOMES CHRISTMAS ALONG DUKE OF GLOUCESTER STREET; JAMES L. AMOS, NATIONAL GEOGRAPHIC PHOTOGRAPHER, AND NELSON H. BROWN

SPECIALTIES OF WILLIAMSBURG FEAST THE EYE IN THE RALEIGH TAVERN KITCHEN; JAMES L. AMOS, NATIONAL GEOGRAPHIC PHOTOGRAPHER (ALSO OPPOSITE)

western wilderness. His account of French hostility, of savage tribes hungry for settlers' scalps, presaged the bitter French and Indian War.

The taverns of Williamsburg would have offered that weary soldier warmth, merriment, and a hearty bill of fare. Today the taverns still set out such favorites of colonial trenchermen as fresh trout and succulent mutton chops, Welsh rabbit on toast, spoon bread and a ring of bread called Sally Lunn, rum-cream pie and cherry tarts. In Christiana Campbell's Tavern (below) balladeer Tayler Vrooman urges diners to "sing care away, with sport and play."

Though prepared for modern palates, the specialties reflect exhaustive research which has unearthed not only the recipes but also the news that Christiana Campbell was "a little old Woman, about four feet high & equally thick."

Final arbiter of what is to be seen, heard, and done in the city, the research staff has amassed a mountain of detail for a recent major expansion of the restored city. Today the familiar weaver, printer, silversmith, baker, bootmaker, and blacksmith still go about their daily business. But so do many others new to the Williamsburg scene—cooper, gunsmith, sand caster, and basket maker. And four important 18th-century survivals have been added to the tour of historic buildings—Wetherburn's Tavern, with its Great Room for balls and banquets; the elegant Peyton Randolph House, reflecting the wealth and taste of a

CAROLERS BRING CHEER TO THE MARY STITH SHOP; JAMES L. AMOS, NATIONAL GEOGRAPHIC PHOTOGRAPHER. OPPOSITE: FIGHTING FROST WITH FIREWOOD AT THE PUBLIC GAOL; PAUL CONKLIN

prominent patriot; the James Geddy House, home and shop of colonial smiths; and the college's Wren Building, oldest academic structure still in use in the United States. This campus centerpiece has stood in quiet dignity since 1698, its chapel and classrooms evoking memories of Jefferson, John Marshall, and James Monroe, who studied there.

And so the past lives, in the precisely accurate reconstructions, in the good cheer that warms the crisp nights of Christmastime, in the carols that echo through the town, in the heavy capes and three-cornered hats of the carolers, in reflected candlelight and hearths aglow with crackling logs.

Fires made winter tolerable, but feeding them proved a wearisome chore. In one plantation house, school, and kitchen, noted a colonial traveler, there were "twenty-eight steady Fires! & most of these . . . very large!" To keep them burning it was necessary that "a cart & three pairs of oxen . . . every Day bring in four loads of Wood, Sunday excepted."

But the flames that cheered could also cast a pall over the merriest of seasons. Holiday lights gleaming in the governor's mansion seem a reminder of the original Palace's sudden and fiery end. In December of 1781, a year after legislators had moved the capital 45 miles northwest to Richmond to escape British warships, the residence was filled with American soldiers wounded during the climactic battle of Yorktown. Three days before Christmas, an hour before midnight, sparks ignited the wooden interior; flames leapt from

the Christmas days of old, merry or mournful, tranquil or turbulent.

"Light your candles!" With each swing of his lantern the Night Watch summons shining tapers until a wake of twinkling windows spreads behind the paraders. *Paradiddle diddle flam!* The drums roll and the fifes squeal as the crowd churns through the heart of Williamsburg, past the Magazine and the Court House of 1770, past the glowing round windows of Bruton Parish Church, until it swirls to a standstill before the Wren Building. A hush spreads through the throng as it listens to the timeless words from St. Luke:

"And suddenly there was with the angel a multitude of the heavenly host praising God, and saying, Glory to God in the highest, and on earth peace, good will toward men."

the lower rooms, roared upward, and engulfed the building as the crippled and maimed struggled to escape. In three hours the mansion was a smoking ruin, its blackened walls glowering over charred paneling, smashed chandeliers, tumbled fireplaces, broken delft tiles.

One soldier was trapped, his spirit, perhaps, roaming the rubble for 150 years, until reconstruction of the Palace. None thought it would ever rise again. In the early 1900's a school building occupied the front yard. Then, in 1934, the country's loveliest phoenix sprang from the old ashes, rising on its original foundations, to the delight of countless republican multitudes, the sons of sons of revolutionaries ready to admire still the glamor and elegance of the aristocratic life. And eager to recall

Around the World in 60 Minutes

The charming Icelandic blonde fielded yet another question: "That tapestry, largest in the world, was made in Belgium with 90,000 miles of thread—enough to go around the world nearly four times." Delivering warm smiles and cool facts in Swahili, Urdu, Gaelic, and two dozen other tongues, guides from 30 nations lead 5,000 visitors a day through the United Nations, whose operations gird the globe in a bright tapestry of hope for mankind.

Crossing into international territory from the sidewalks of New York, juniors whose trick-or-treat collections for UNICEF help feed children in other lands join seniors who recall 1945, year of U. N. chartering in San Francisco

BEACON OF HOPE, THE SECRETARIAT BUILDING RISES FROM THE UNITED NATIONS ENCLAVE BESIDE NEW YORK'S EAST RIVER; DICK HANLEY, PHOTO RESEARCHERS, INC.
ABOVE: FIVE LANGUAGES WREATHE THE GLOBE ON A U.N. STAMP

under the shadow of atomic holocaust. Threading a mile-long route filled with peoples and art from 126 lands, they explore what Eleanor Roosevelt called "the only place in history where the whole world has hung its hat and gone to work on the common problems of mankind."

From a balcony (opposite) they survey the ceremonial staircase where heads of state have entered to address the General Assembly. In this "Parliament of Man" voices of the smallest country as well as the most powerful shall be heard. Earphones enable future statesmen, at the push of a button, to hear an instant translation of a speech in any of the five official languages: English, French, Russian, Spanish, or Chinese.

In the Security Council (upper right) delegates will gather at a moment's notice to thwart a threat to peace. Other council chambers echo with calls to revolution and war: peaceful economic and social revolution to better the lives of men everywhere; war on poverty, disease, and hunger.

Tours end in the lower lobby, where Manhattan subway riders and Ames, Iowa, students jostle for special-issue stamps, carvings from Cameroon, field studies from the Maldives. A visitor from Peru, Pakistan, Pennsylvania, or Paris pauses silently to pray for peace in the U.N.'s Meditation Room. Others hie to the Delegates' Dining Room above the river. Here, as in corridors, lounges, chambers throughout this forum of the family of man, voices rise that the guns may fall silent.

HOUR-LONG GUIDED TOURS OPEN EYES AND EARS TO THE WORLD OF THE U.N.; JAMES P. BLAIR, NATIONAL GEOGRAPHIC PHOTOGRAPHER

History Docks at Mystic

Shading his eyes from the sun's glare, the lookout scans the sea. Suddenly he stiffens. There . . . off the port bow! His voice rings clear: "Thar she blows! Blo-o-o-o-o-ows!"

The captain lets go the helm, jumps up and down, and shrieks, "Away the boats!"

The lookout sounds again, disdainful now. "You got it all wrong, Judy. First you say, 'Where away?' Then. . . ."

What matter that the lookout is a 13-year-old in mod-colored bell-bottoms? That the captain is only 10, and a girl? Or that the *Charles W. Morgan,* last of the great wooden whalers that "took the white bone in their teeth" and leaned before the wind in search of leviathan, has found her final berth in sand at the mouth of Connecticut's Mystic River? For the half million visitors who call at Mystic Seaport every year, the glorious Yankee age of sail comes to life. Mystic charms some with its venerable craft shops on cobbled Seaport Street that bespeak a simpler day. Others it hits with the impact of a frenzied sperm whale flipping his flukes in a geyser of spray.

They come by car, bus, or boat, and if they're lubbers on arrival in the morning, they've acquired a crust of salt by sunset. Adults, hoarding steps and nursing their feet, may prefer to set a leisurely course into New England's past. They pause at the one-room schoolhouse, peruse the apothecary shop, and get their bearings in the museums amid charts, old journals and logbooks, tea chests, ships in bottles, exquisite examples of scrimshaw (below). Village whittlers turned whalers etched such scenes on whale ivory during voyages that dragged on for three or four years.

But children react to the magnetism of the old ships with zest and run to meet them. There, beyond the *Morgan,* rides the school ship *Joseph Conrad,* built in 1882. Capt. Alan Villiers in the mid-1930's sailed this square-rigger on a 58,000-mile voyage around the world. Other hulls lift to the gentle swells of the snug harbor: the *L.A. Dunton,* a Grand Banks dory fisherman that hailed from Gloucester

"A DEAD WHALE OR A STOVE BOAT!" THE WHALEMAN'S MOTTO FITS THIS SCENE SCRIBED ON THE TOOTH OF A SPERM WHALE THAT DID NOT GET AWAY. OPPOSITE: LEARNING THE ROPES CHALLENGES YOUNG MARINERS ALOFT IN THE SQUARE-RIGGER "JOSEPH CONRAD"; WESTON KEMP

and the last of her kind to be built; the New England pinky schooner *Regina M;* the Noank fishing sloop *Emma C. Berry.* A flotilla of others rests ashore along with the giant anchor (opposite) that belonged to a British man-of-war lost off Long Island in the Revolution.

To the ships, then. First the *Morgan,* with false gunports painted on, once meant to frighten "Feegee" cannibals. Mount the gangway and step aboard the 105-foot whaler, scarcely twice the length of the monsters she hunted. Now close your eyes and forget the bed of sand that grips her keel. Hear the planking under your feet hiss with rushing seawater; feel the ship lurch to the broad Pacific swells.

Shouts. A boat tows a whale alongside.

Smoke stings your eyes as you survey this scene of a century ago: From a platform rigged outboard, men slice into the giant beast with skilled thrusts of razor-sharp cutting spades. Other hands strain at a capstan that peels off long strips of blubber, and chop them into pieces—"Bible leaves." Greasy smoke pours from the brick tryworks

THE AGE OF SAIL LIVES ON AT MYSTIC SEAPORT, WHERE AN IMMENSE ANCHOR (OPPOSITE) SERVES AS A MAGNET FOR CHILDREN; WESTON KEMP

where blubber is rendered in huge iron caldrons. A grizzled seaman, reeking of whale fat and sweat, dunks a chunk of old bread into the boiling oil and hands it to you with a grin: "Have a doughnut."

With the last drop of oil stored in casks in the hold and the carcass cast loose to the sharks, you follow the weary crew below to their quarters. On 37 voyages, from 1841 to 1921, about a thousand men—old salts and adventurous farmboys—could call no home their own but this crowded, smelly forecastle. Here they ate their meager mess of salt

beef and dried peas; strained to read or carve by the stingy light of a single smoky lamp; lay on their cramped bunks and dreamed of green fields and home.

Youths of Mystic's Mariner Training Program climb the *Conrad*'s rigging (left) and there view the town as a homecoming sailor, famished for the sight of land, might have seen it. Beyond the oyster shack, stilting out from Seaport Street, the village nestles under its spreading greenery: neat homes, shops, stores, the white-spired chapel, the tavern with two doors—one for men and one marked "office" for escorted ladies—both opening into the same taproom.

For generations men of Mystic built ships—schooners, whalers, clippers—and sailed them to far corners of the earth. Finally steam overtook the windships; one by one they died, and the port died with them. Then in 1941 the Marine Historical Association, which created Mystic Seaport as a last port of call

CHIPS OFF A NEW BLOCK FALL AMONG VENERABLE FIGUREHEADS IN THE SHIP CARVER'S SHOP ON VILLAGE STREET; WESTON KEMP

for America's sailing past, brought the derelict *Morgan* from South Dartmouth, Massachusetts. Restored, she became the proud flagship of a growing fleet. As a setting for its vessel-lined wharves, the association scoured the East Coast for old maritime buildings and moved them to Mystic, re-creating a lively seaport village of a century ago. Now the sound of caulking hammers and the clang of metal on anvils bring the weathered buildings to life.

In the Nantucket Cooperage, a retired ship joiner explains how barrels were made. In the Peters-Driggs Shipsmith Shop an aproned smith with brawny arms fashions ironware of a bygone era. Sometimes he lets boys and girls pump the hand bellows. At the Ship Carver's Shop (above) a craftsman chisels a spread-winged eagle like those that adorned the transom of many a tall ship, while in timeless vigil stand figureheads, wooden widows of ships long lost.

Moonport U.S.A.

Crisply the numbers come over the speaker, every few minutes without halt or hold: "45 . . . 46 . . . 47. . . ." At their Go signal, a group swings out of the NASA Visitors Information Center, boards bus Number 47, and blasts off in air-conditioned comfort to tour the world's premier spaceport.

These visitors to the John F. Kennedy Space Center in Florida have peered into Apollo command and lunar modules, snacked on microwave-cooked burgers, relived the drama of flights on film: lift-off rockets delivering 7.6 million pounds of thrust, components falling away into blackness, craters yawning out a mooncraft window, searing re-entry, joyous homecoming to God's green earth. A lecturer has shown the basic simplicity of rockets, explained why an astronaut can "walk" in space at 17,500 miles an hour, answered a child's query, "How do you go to the bathroom in a space suit?"

Now, crossing from Merritt Island, the bus hums along a finger of Florida that beckons birds on the Atlantic flyway. Indians hunted here and left burial mounds. Spaniards, thirsting for water and gold, named the cape Canaveral, "place of tall cane." Americans renamed it Cape Kennedy, honoring the young President who in 1961 set the Nation "to achieving the goal, before this decade is out, of landing a man on the moon and returning him safely to the earth."

Today artifacts of 20th-century explorers stud the sands: gantries, blockhouses, antennas. "Remember the picture in 1962 of John Glenn walking out of a hangar in his space suit, carrying his air-conditioning unit?" asks the bus driver. "He came out of Hangar S, over there—first American astronaut to orbit the earth." A short walk for Glenn, a necessary walk before Neil Armstrong could take his famous step down onto the face of the moon, July 20, 1969—5 months and 11 days before the decade was out.

Steppingstones to the moon await at the next two stops: the Mission Control Center, whose pulsing consoles guided NASA's early manned flights; and the Air Force Space Museum, spiked with the world's largest missile collection. The museum, an off-duty pad formerly called Complex 26, witnessed the fizzles and "firsts" of experimental rockets after World War II. Out back a 1944 German V-1 buzz bomb poises on a pedestal. Beyond, small fry crawl under a Redstone to gaze at jets of the first operational ballistic missile, granddaddy of boosters for the one-man Mercury, two-man Gemini, and three-man Apollo missions.

MANKIND'S RADIANT DREAM RODE TO REALITY ON THE MUSCLE OF THE SATURN V (OPPOSITE) AND THE COURAGE OF APOLLO 11'S CREW, WHO JOURNEYED HALF A MILLION MILES TO THE MOON AND BACK IN A CAPSULE LIKE THIS; OTIS IMBODEN AND (OPPOSITE) O. LOUIS MAZZATENTA, BOTH NATIONAL GEOGRAPHIC STAFF

Past launch sites of Early Bird, Telstar, and other weather and communication satellites, past Minuteman silos, past the century-old lighthouse, the bus turns north along ICBM Road. Here service structures for ever mightier rockets (Atlas, Titan, Saturn) loom higher and higher.

Parents consigned to back seats by the space-age gap stretch to see the biggest of all—Complex 39, the moonport. Its construction taxed the Nation's purse; its size taxes the imagination.

The Vertical Assembly Building, hub of the complex, could swallow Washington's Pentagon in addition to Chicago's Merchandise Mart. Four U.N. buildings would fit through its 456-foot doors. In the cathedral light suffusing this gray-girdered temple of technology, the awed visitor descries tiny hard-hatted figures aloft. Sheltered from hurricanes, they can assemble four Saturn V rockets at a time within the central bay, 525 feet high. Components from across the continent, converging on the Cape by barge and by plane, swing on mighty hoists and hook one atop the other into space vehicles 36 stories tall, yet tooled more exquisitely than a jeweled watch.

Assembled on its mobile launcher, the rocket that will burst free of earth's grip at more than 24,000 miles an hour trundles 3½ miles to the launch pad on a transporter half as big as a football field. It clanks a mile an hour, gulping a gallon of fuel every 18 feet.

In bygone centuries Japanese designed serene gardens from which aristocrats could view the distant moon. Today America camps out to watch the moon come closer.

Whenever a space flight draws near, vacationing families flock like migrating birds to Cape Kennedy. Along the "Astronaut Trail" through Brevard County, No Vacancy signs light up before motels; trailers cram the campgrounds. And on beaches flanking the Cape, campers and station wagons disgorge tents and sleeping bags, camp stoves and folding chairs.

Within sight stands the greatest snap-together contraption of them all: the launcher and its precious vehicle, now flanked by a mobile service structure and gleaming as floodlit preparations fill the feverish night (page 146).

CAMPERS WITNESS HISTORY IN THE MAKING; O. LOUIS MAZZATENTA AND (RIGHT) OTIS IMBODEN, BOTH NATIONAL GEOGRAPHIC STAFF. APOLLO 11 EMBLEM, NATIONAL AERONAUTICS AND SPACE ADMINISTRATION

ASTRONAUTS ARMSTRONG, ALDRIN, AND COLLINS BLAST OFF FOR APOLLO 11'S LUNAR LANDING; JOHN SLACK

Morning sees the astronauts clamber into their cramped capsule atop the 364-foot rocket; VIP's and newsmen crowd the bleachers; NASA brass directs final checkouts in the Launch Control Center.

Countdown brings pulses up; batteries of binoculars lift along the beaches. A Niagara of flame engulfs the launch pad. Slowly the great white bird ascends atop a pillar of fire, then roars heavenward, five engines burning five million pounds of fuel in 150 seconds.

Hearts rise with the men riding a fiery chariot to the moon—blazing a path to Mars, to Venus, to worlds beyond the sun.

By Tom Allen

TIME AND TIDE UNVEIL A TROVE OF MARVELS FOR A

Seashore Treasure Hunt

She yells "Sea shell" at the seashore, palming a cockle at Sanibel Island, Florida; Paul A. Zahl, National Geographic staff

A ponderous shadow emerges from the midnight sea and lumbers up the beach to the high-tide line on Sanibel Island. The shadow sinks down until it looks like another hummock of sand. Lights flash on and we see her: huge carapace knobbed by barnacles, rheumy eyes blinking, rear flippers rhythmically scooping out an urn-shaped hole beneath her. A creature as much out of time as out of the sea, the 200-pound Atlantic loggerhead turtle has returned to her birthplace.

Nothing can stay her from a ritual as old as these sands—neither distracting lights nor a circle of wide-eyed children and sleepy adults. The eggs drop now: two, three, four, then faster and faster. A whispered count keeps quickening cadence: "... *twenty-three ... fifty-five ... one hundred....*" Charles R. LeBuff, Jr., of the U. S. Fish and Wildlife Service turns to my son Roger. "Like to help?" Eager 12-year-old hands transfer the eggs—soft, warm, the size of ping-pong balls—to containers destined for a hatchery. There, fenced off from crab, raccoon, and man, they will hatch in about two months. For some 20,000 years two-inch turtles have crept down this beach into the warm waters of the Gulf of Mexico, males to spend their lives at sea, females to live and mate there, returning to land only for the rites of renewal.

The great turtle stirs, thrashing the sand to wipe out all trace of her nest. She slowly turns and begins her crawl back to the sea. Children walk alongside, touching her, even straddling her. My daughter Connie hangs back. "She's crying," Connie says. Perhaps the female intuition of a 14-year-old is right. I'll explain later about the tearlike fluid secreted to protect the turtle's eyes. At this moment, as the turtle

LIFEGUARD FOR TURTLES ENDS HIS NIGHT WATCH on Sanibel Island off Fort Myers, refuge for the dwindling Atlantic loggerhead (lower right) and paradise for the shell collector. From May to August sea turtles crawl up the gulf beach after dark to lay eggs by the hundreds in flipper-dug holes. Searching for nesters' tracks, Charles LeBuff (above) patrols all night. Eggs he digs up hatch on a "farm" where hand-fed young spend ten months growing seaworthy. Conservationists hope to restore a Sanibel rookery that once held 2,000 nests and also seek to protect living shells.

Shellers harvest dead ones (upper right). Fan-shaped pen shells secrete gossamer filaments that Mediterranean artisans wove into a wondrous golden fleece.

JAMES W. LATOURRETTE, WOMETCO MIAMI SEAQUARIUM. UPPER AND LEFT: MARTIN ROGERS

THE SHELL GAME: PICK A NUMBER, ANY NUMBER. Buckets full, bags bulging, backs bent in the "Sanibel stoop," hunters comb the 12-mile-long island. They sift nearby Captiva, legendary pirates' isle for female prisoners, and the shellscape (below) on Upper Captiva.

disappears into the dark sea, I can believe that she cries in joy, celebrating a rite as beautiful as any I have ever seen.

For years we too have been summoned by the shore. My wife Scottie and I, born near the sea, had carried our children to it. First they sat at tide's edge and slapped Long Island Sound. Then they waded, dog-paddled, finally swam. We had watched them crawl, then toddle, then run, always back to us, always clutching a treasure—a sand-smoothed stone, a long-dead dogfish, a glistening shell. "Lookit!" had become "What's this?" Heads had bobbed farther from shore. Sand pails had given way to snorkels.

Now, on this island of shells, windrowed with wonders cast up by tropical tides and storms, we renewed the ritual of our summers. Connie, Roger, and Chris (16, in this Sanibel summer) had their own long beaches to run now, but they had not outgrown the sea or its treasures.

We began with shells—buckets of shells, bags of shells, even shells full of shells, splendid as their names: jewel box, ponderous ark, checkerboard clam, nutmeg, tulip, auger, turkey wing. We joined Sanibel's legion of the happily downcast, hunched to scan the sand.

One night, while Scottie and I walked the beach, distant lightning bathed the sky with eerie light. In those flashes we found ourselves looking down—for shells.

Each of us secretly hoped for the ultimate Sanibel find:

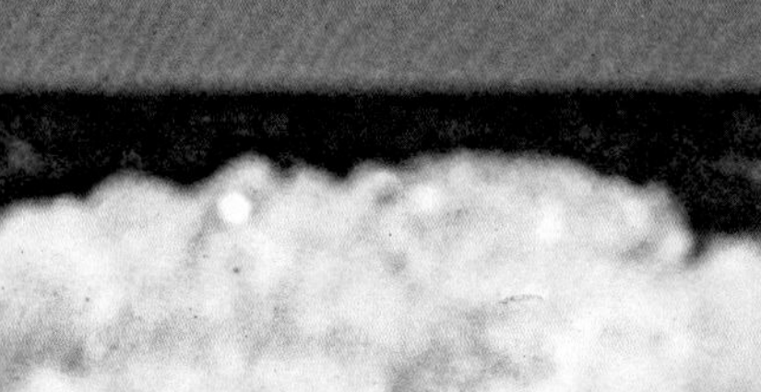

MARTIN ROGERS

OM ALLEN AND (ABOVE) OTIS IMBODEN AND (FAR RIGHT) PAUL A. ZAHL, ALL NATIONAL GEOGRAPHIC STAFF

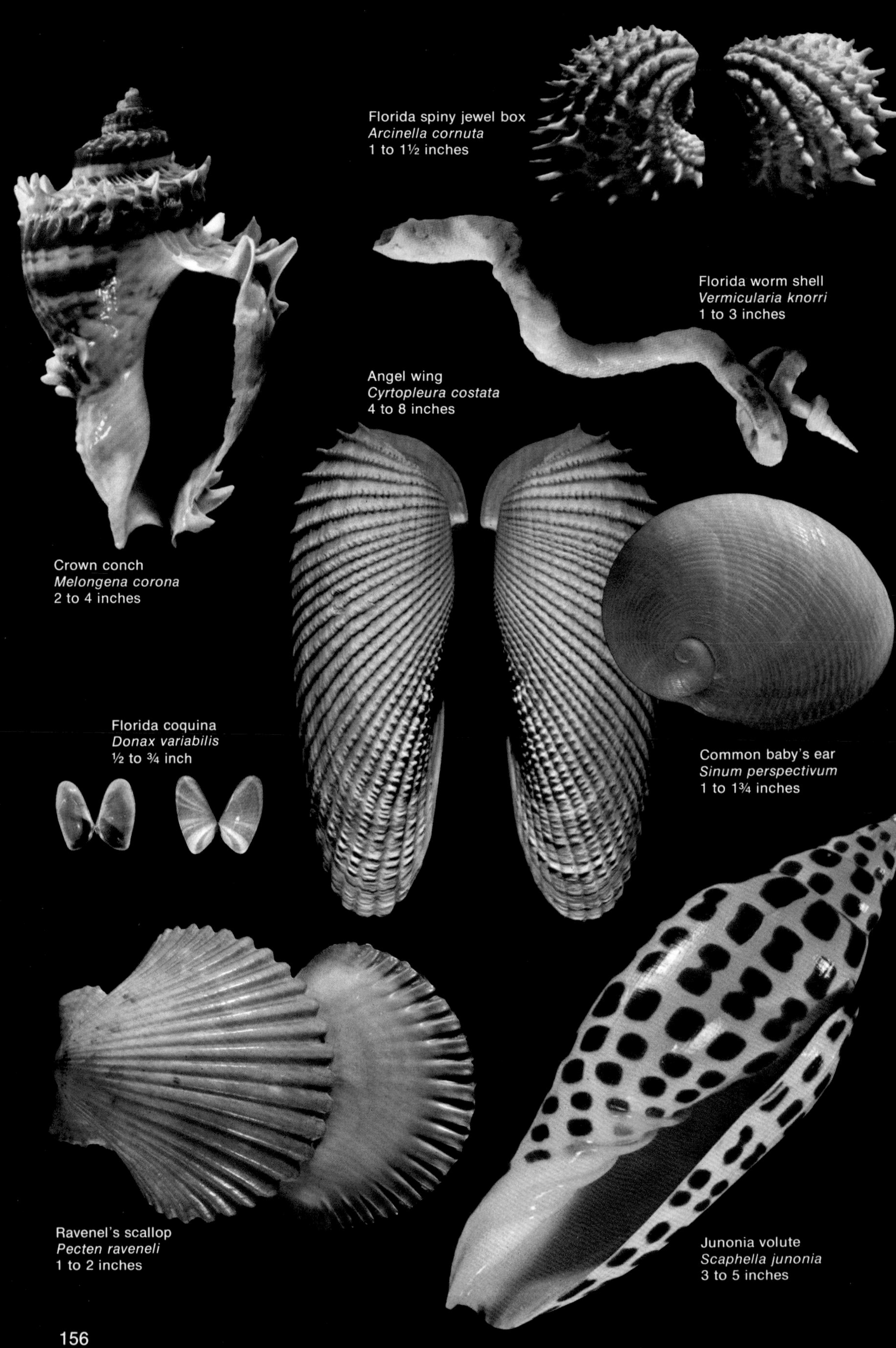
Florida spiny jewel box
Arcinella cornuta
1 to 1½ inches
Florida worm shell
Vermicularia knorri
1 to 3 inches
Angel wing
Cyrtopleura costata
4 to 8 inches
Crown conch
Melongena corona
2 to 4 inches
Florida coquina
Donax variabilis
½ to ¾ inch
Common baby's ear
Sinum perspectivum
1 to 1¾ inches
Ravenel's scallop
Pecten raveneli
1 to 2 inches
Junonia volute
Scaphella junonia
3 to 5 inches

BEAUTEOUS CASTAWAYS, ALLURING AS SIRENS, sea shells have enraptured man since he first walked a beach. Vessel of myth, wampum of Indians, the shell became a collector's item in the 1600's when exotics from the East Indies astonished Europeans. Mariners—even Captain Bligh of the Bounty*—shelled; their finds launched conchology, a science that now lists 50,000 species of marine mollusks.*

Sanibel's gems (opposite) draw collectors who seek most of all the junonia, namesake of Juno and rarest of the isle's 400 species. Florida beaches yield only about 100 a year. Within junonia dwells a body as lovely as the shell.

Ravenel's scallop, named for a pioneer American conchologist, recalls the symbol of Venus and emblem of medieval pilgrims. When scallops snap shells shut, squirting water jets them a yard.

The jewel box stays put, on rock or coral. The worm shell lurks in sponges; it begins life coiled, then unwinds. A mollusk builds its mansion with a mantle, a fold of flesh whose lime-secreting cells ooze a shell, layer by layer. Some cells bear pigments.

Angel wings "shoulder" their way a foot or more into mud, draw food through a siphon. Coquinas leap out of wet sand; waves whisk them to new spots where they thrust out feet to anchor.

Baby's ear, kin to moon snails, kills prey. Pinning a clam under a powerful foot, it holes the shell with a long, rasp-toothed tongue. Crown conchs, with such snouts, devour scallops, even gang up to eat a horseshoe crab alive.

Collectors, like the whelk cleaners at right, learn the where and how-to of their hobby from such books as R. Tucker Abbott's Seashells of North America. *Good shellers seeking undamaged live shells follow the rule: take only two of each kind.*

SHELLS FROM SMITHSONIAN INSTITUTION COLLECTION; VICTOR R. BOSWELL, NATIONAL GEOGRAPHIC STAFF. RIGHT: MARTIN ROGERS

the rare junonia. We had heard about it within hours after crossing the 3½-mile toll bridge and causeway to the island. An exquisite, creamy shell of spiraling dots, it normally dwells offshore. Storm—and luck—can toss one at your feet. "Found a junonia yet?" veterans gibe as they eye a beginner's haul, woeful second-raters to them.

No junonias. But we did find a fragile, translucent angel wing fallen in the sand, passed up by those who sought a pair. We did find stacks of silvery jingles that faintly echoed their name when we shook them in our hands. And we plucked spiny crown conchs in the shallows while batlike rays glided by, swimming as if on wings.

Soon we were finding more than shells. Chris shinnied up his first palm and proudly hauled down a coconut. Connie flushed hundreds of fiddler crabs that scuttled before her in a rustling tide of brandished claws. Scottie confronted a single crab, a pale, stalk-eyed phantom that frantically dueled with her feet. A hole-dweller on the upper beach, the ghost crab does not breathe air as a mammal does. It must bathe its gills in the sea. Scottie apparently had loomed as a barrier on one of its daily dashes for life.

Roger chanced upon a Wilson's plover on her nest in the sand. She limped off, dragging a wing—the "crippled-bird act." Seeing him as a predator, she was trying to lure him

after her and away from the nest. "You have to watch your step around here," Sterling Lanier, a Florida friend, warned us. "Some of these beaches are rookeries." That's all we needed to hear. With Sterling as our guide, Roger and I set off.

On a desolate northern beach Sterling motioned for quiet. "I don't see anything," Roger said softly. "Don't look," Sterling whispered. "Listen!" We heard the scolding *"Kreet! Kreet!"* moments before we saw the least terns diving at us. They fluttered over our heads, their cries crescendoing as we cautiously treaded our way. When their volume peaked, our search ended. There near our feet huddled twin puffs of down, newly hatched terns peering over bleached shards of sea shells.

Birdlife thrives on Sanibel, a sanctuary with 4,500 acres of swamp and shallows given over to a national wildlife refuge. An osprey broods her young atop a tall dead tree. Plummeting pelicans smash into the sea for prey. In the refuge we saw an anhinga, fresh from an underwater fishing foray, spread its great wings to dry. Yellow-crowned night herons waded for crabs. One waning afternoon we counted 21 species. Then more than a score of roseate spoonbills winged in and alighted on a mangrove island's tangled skyline. Their pink aura mocked the setting sun.

Because we saw so much life around us we sought it also in the shells. Beautiful as they may be on a cottage windowsill, they are empty. Lustrous, rainbow-dappled coquinas in collections look like pinned butterflies. But scoop up a handful of wave-

On the darkening beach of Sanibel they gather, still searching for shells—and something more:

washed sand and see these half-inch clams fluttering. Two barely visible siphons writhe from each tiny shell. One inhales water for its oxygen and morsels of food; the other pumps out water and waste. Put a coquina back on the sand and it daintily tips up, digs with a pointed foot, and disappears.

Wet sand became a stage. A fist-size cockle slowly opened, then suddenly thrust out a jumping jack of a foot and flopped over. Beneath our feet we watched humped wrinkles form. We followed the burrows to find gleaming, torpedo-shaped shells called olives. As soon as we put them down they tunneled away, making new wrinkles. In the intertidal underworld they joined others that we stalked: the wafer-thin sand dollar that can slip into the sand like a coin into a slot; the baby's ear, whose gelatinous body shrouds a delicate whorled shell.

The tide was going out and so was the day. Across a tidal pool prowled by scampering little crabs, across a sandbar patrolled by sunset shellers, we found the retreating edge of the sea. We were not alone. A moon snail rose from the watery sand. Her velvety body poured out and enfolded her smooth round shell. Each riffle that lapped her bore grains of sand that clung to an invisible film on her flesh. Slowly the grains became a wall—a sand collar to humans who find them brittle and dry on the beach. But it was indeed a wall—built to guard a treasure, the eggs of the moon snail. Kneeling in the twilight, we were witnessing another ritual of renewal.

communion with the sweep of shore, the whisper of wave lap, a sea gilded by the last light of day.

OTIS IMBODEN, NATIONAL GEOGRAPHIC PHOTOGRAPHER

Into the Wondrous Realm of Wildlife

Moss-hung cypresses loomed up from vast islands afloat on a still, dark mirror. Dense stands of black gum trees, sweet bay, and buttonbush rose like woven green walls along the narrow waterway. Our flat-bottomed boat, skimming the reflection of a primeval world, nudged a bank. It shuddered gently. And we sensed, as Indian hunters had, that this was a place like no other. They called it Okefenokee—land of trembling earth.

The ground itself seems alive in Okefenokee Swamp, actually an immense peat bog that filled a basin left by a retreating Atlantic Ocean. Peat rooted to the old seabed occasionally breaks off, forming islands. Step on one and you feel the thick mat quivering beneath your feet.

Swampers call the islands "houses" because they shelter so many of the creatures in this national wildlife refuge in southeastern Georgia. Turtles, some of them 100-pound "alligator snappers," sun on the banks. On branches above perch snake-necked anhingas, who look as if they had just winged out of the Age of Reptiles. White ibises sweep the sky. Black bears and white-tailed deer roam the forests.

Slow but steady, two rivers flow through the 630 square miles of Okefenokee—the Suwannee toward the Gulf of Mexico, the St. Marys emptying into the Atlantic. As our boat glided through water dyed strangely black by bog acid, I scooped up a handful and found it sweet.

Gator's-eye view of Okefenokee captures bearded cypresses and water lilies that will decay to peat and sustain the glassy bog; Robert F. Sisson, National Geographic photographer

By Robert M. McClung

TOM ALLEN, NATIONAL GEOGRAPHIC STAFF. BELOW AND OPPOSITE: ROBERT F. SISSON, NATIONAL GEOGRAPHIC PHOTOGRAPHER

We passed other boats filled with visitors enjoying the serenity and the dark beauty of the swamp. A pair of gorgeous wood ducks whistled by; flashing blue dragonflies played tag across the water; swallowtail butterflies dipped and fluttered in shifting patterns of color.

Near Billy's Island, onetime hideout of Seminole war chief Billy Bowlegs, we put-putted up to a "prairie"—a marsh carpeted by purple pickerelweed, white floating hearts, yellow water lilies. We paused to examine the snug nest of a round-tailed muskrat, then watched a cottonmouth sunning itself on a half-submerged log. I stared as another floating log slowly submerged and disappeared—an eight-foot alligator!

Once a lair of moonshiners and alligator poachers, Okefenokee has become a refuge for imperiled species and a paradise for wildlife watchers. Gators, nearly wiped out, now number about 5,000. Threatened birds like the osprey, bald eagle, and Florida sandhill crane dwell here in safety along with 200 other species.

Protected animals hold open house for animal watchers at hundreds of refuges like Okefenokee, from the Florida Keys to the Aleutians. In a career of studying and writing about wildlife, I have visited many preserves. I have seen hundreds of fleet pronghorns skimming across a dry lake bed in a Nevada refuge, and white pelicans soaring in perfect formation above Malheur Lake in Oregon. Once in Wyoming

DOMAIN OF THE ALLIGATOR, DEN OF BEAR AND BOBCAT, *Okefenokee Refuge opens a primal world to visitors who course watery trails in flat-bottomed boats (upper) or tread cypress-canopied boardwalks. Lazing gator (opposite) may snooze with jaws open so fish can swim into the big trap. For courting or combat, male American chameleon (above) glows with living color; body brightens, dewlap reddens. Near the refuge, guides at Okefenokee Swamp Park "talk" hidden gators into view, and Georgia's Stephen C. Foster Park offers camping and guided fishing.*

TOM MYERS. OPPOSITE: VAGN FLYGER. BELOW: ROBERT F. SISSON, NATIONAL GEOGRAPHIC PHOTOGRAPHER

"EVERY CREATURE IS BETTER ALIVE THAN DEAD . . . PRESERVE ITS LIFE," Thoreau pleaded a century ago as the blood of bird and beast stained the land. The wanton killing went on: bison, gunned down by the millions; elk, slain for meat and watch-fob teeth; passenger pigeons, decimated until flocks that once "darkened the sun" dwindled to a single bird in 1914, then none. But the ideal of preservation lived and grew into a system of wildlife refuges where men guard a living heritage (pages 100, 276). Some even cup it in their hands (left), caring for orphaned fox squirrels at Le Compte Refuge in Maryland.

Elk breed in Yellowstone and Grand Teton National Parks, bugling bulls tangling antlers for the possession of harems. In the fall the great herds migrate to the National Elk Refuge in Jackson Hole, Wyoming (below), a spectacular, cast-of-thousands show for closeup audiences. Visitors can help scatter feed from sleighs. To keep elk in balance with available habitat, refuge-controlled hunters trim herds.

Mountain lions and wolves once were the hunters. But predators—even the majestic golden eagle (opposite)—became man's prey, until he learned to rue the irreplaceable loss of a species. Today men struggle to succor the endangered ones.

BACK FROM THE BRINK, ALIVE AND WELL IN THE WIDE-OPEN WEST, *bison puff through rump-deep snows of Yellowstone, where another year-round resident—the red fox—makes the summer scene at right. Winter visitors, riding snowmobiles from Mammoth Hot Springs and West Yellowstone, may spot fox and bison, bighorn sheep, deer, and antelope.*

In all seasons wildlife transforms landscapes into lifescapes at national parks and refuges; some offer treasured views of species that need man's help to survive. Boaters flock to Texas shores to glimpse our pitifully few whooping cranes wintering in Aransas Refuge. Florida sanctuaries guard jeopardized cougars, manatees, Key deer. Grizzly bears, off the endangered list, hold their own in Western preserves.

At Oklahoma's Wichita Mountains Refuge whitetails (opposite)—our most abundant deer—share the woodlands with picnickers and campers. This showplace refuge also keeps alive a symbol of the Old West: a herd of the fabled Texas longhorn.

DAVID G. ALLEN. LEFT: WILLIAM ALBERT ALLARD. UPPER: FRANK AND JOHN CRAIGHEAD

I watched a herd of elk crashing through an aspen grove. And I have shared the silence of a mangrove thicket with an elusive little Key deer. Through the years I have seen more and more Americans share my delight at the sight of wild creatures roaming free, shielded from man's encroachments, living and dying by nature's laws.

Rounding a bend at the Wichita Mountains Refuge near Lawton, Oklahoma, one day, my family and I saw our first unpenned bison, a big old bull lying beside the road. When I stepped out to take his picture, he rose suddenly—1,500 pounds of flesh and bone and shaggy coat, with a head twice the size of a bushel basket. Without waiting for his next move, I scrambled back into the car.

Later, when we had driven farther into green prairies nestled amid the mountains, we navigated through a band of bison, mostly cows and frisky calves, progeny of eight pioneer bulls and seven cows that made an eighteen-hundred-mile trip from the New York Zoo in 1907. Today's herds will never replace the millions of bison that once darkened the plains, but they have reclaimed a nearly lost

LIKE PETALS SWEPT BY A SPRING BREEZE, EGRETS SAIL OVER SUN-TINTED SAW GRASS of Florida's Big Cypress Swamp. At its edge the National Audubon Society's Corkscrew Sanctuary protects a famed rookery amid our largest remaining stand of virgin bald cypress. In such enclaves the haunting call of the wild enjoins man to wield wisely his "dominion . . . over every living thing that moveth upon the earth."

national asset. Buffalo still roam at the National Bison Range in western Montana, at Fort Niobrara Refuge in Nebraska, and at Yellowstone and Grand Teton, which, like all our national parks, are wildlife sanctuaries.

Waterfowl refuges dot the wetlands on both coasts, along the Mississippi Valley, and in the Great Plains. At Brigantine Refuge on the New Jersey shore, bird-watchers may find most of the Atlantic brant population feeding in the marshes. At Virginia's Chincoteague, on a duned barrier island, migrants abound the year round—nesting, resting, or basking in winter haven. A herd of deer—descended from Japanese sikas released in 1923—wanders here, as do shaggy Chincoteague ponies whose origin is wrapped in legends of shipwreck and piracy.

Brigham, Utah, proclaims itself the "Gateway to the World's Greatest Waterfowl Refuge"—Bear River, covering a hundred square miles in the marshy delta where the river empties into Great Salt Lake. Here we saw sleek avocets feeding in their shoulder-to-shoulder march through the shallows. Black-necked stilts probed for insects in muddy tussocks. Flights of glossy ibis sailed majestically overhead.

In winter, Florida's many refuges and Everglades National Park bring birds and bird-watchers together. Roseate spoonbills preen atop mangrove thickets, giving the gift of their most brilliant plumage to the eyes of Christmastide visitors. The stately great white heron spreads seven-foot wings in its own refuge, a string of mangrove islands near Key West. At Pelican Island Refuge, not far from the Kennedy Space Center, I once counted 2,500 brown pelicans and 1,200 of their nests.

Pelican Island is where it all began: Theodore Roosevelt proclaimed the island our first national wildlife refuge in 1903. Since then national refuges have been established in 46 states, offering sanctuary to urban families as well as to wildlife (page 421). You need not travel far to find the special kind of peace that pervades a preserve.

I live in Amherst, Massachusetts, which, like many towns, has its own backyard sanctuaries. On our municipal conservation lands I can watch beavers and muskrats at work, glimpse a pileated woodpecker calling from a red maple grove, hear the screech of an owl. On one crisp fall day, I saw a bald eagle soar—and with him, for a moment, I soared.

LAURENCE R. LOWRY

By Charles W. Ebersole

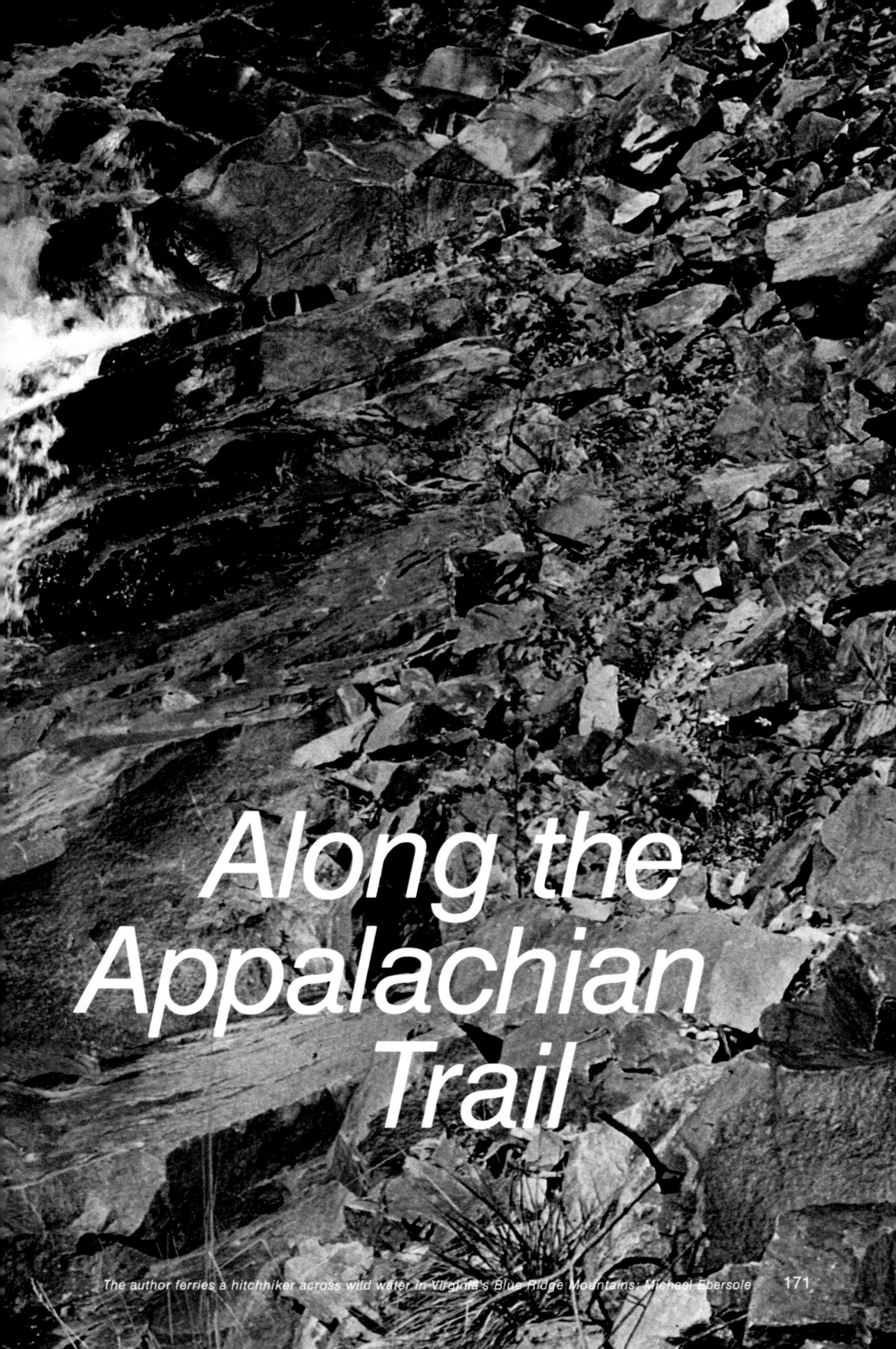

Along the Appalachian Trail

The author ferries a hitchhiker across wild water in Virginia's Blue Ridge Mountains; Michael Ebersole

Heavy boots clanking like ghost chains in the fog, we tramped the iron bridge over the steep-walled Nantahala River, bore left, and began our climb.

We skirted a pond, crossed a field. The Appalachian Trail guidebook made the route clear: Up ridge, down sag. Ascend slab ridge. Fill canteens at spring. Climb bald, dip into gap, mount steeply to crosstrail on crest. Turn right uphill. Ascend knife-edge of blue Nantahala slate.

By noon, seven grueling miles from the day's starting point, we stood on Cheoah Bald in North Carolina, my 17-year-old son Johnny, our beagle Snuffy, and I. We were all experienced hikers, but Snuffy was not the only one dog-tired. We had had it. Lunch and a brief stop rallied us, however. I began to feel new, invigorated. The rigors of the ascent were laurels earned. We were ready for more mountains. And we were mountain rich.

Peaks surrounded us, green-spired with spruce and fir, gray with the leafless tracery of hardwoods just before the surge of spring. Straight ahead, over the blue of Fontana Lake, rose the haze-curtained citadel of the southern Appalachians, the Great Smoky Mountains. Beyond, a rainbow of ranges rolled to Maine's granite monolith, Mount Katahdin. Behind us, 11 days of knobs, balds, ridges, and streams, lay the beginning of our journey, Springer Mountain, Georgia, southern terminus of the Appalachian Trail.

I had just retired as a chief metalsmith after 23 years in the Navy; Johnny had graduated from high school at midyear. And we had come east from Beeville, Texas, to take the measure of the 2,000-mile trail.

Linking peak to scenic peak, this cloud-piercing pathway stretches along the age-old, weather-molded Appalachian mountain mass. The trail seeks not an easy way but a remote, wilderness way. One of the longest continuous marked footpaths in the world, it offers the hiker a supreme test. For 10 years I had chased its arrow-shaped markers and white-paint blazes on tree and rock through my daydreams. Now footsteps followed fantasy.

When Johnny and I piled out of our sleeping bags that March 31 on Springer Mountain, it was 16° above zero. We almost piled back in. Frost bearded the ground; our canteens had frozen solid. But out beyond the laurel thicket that had broken the night wind off our one-man tents, miles of beauty and blisters beckoned. I grabbed my boots.

"Johnny, let's hit the trail."

We quickly broke camp and shouldered our gear—cook pans, ponchos, flashlights, fishing lines, extra clothes. Johnny zipped on Snuffy's pack, its denim pockets bulging with dog chow. Snuffy said "Let's go!" with his tail.

JOHN EBERSOLE. OPPOSITE: MARTIN ROGERS.
MAP BY VIRGINIA BAZA, GEOGRAPHIC ART DIVISION

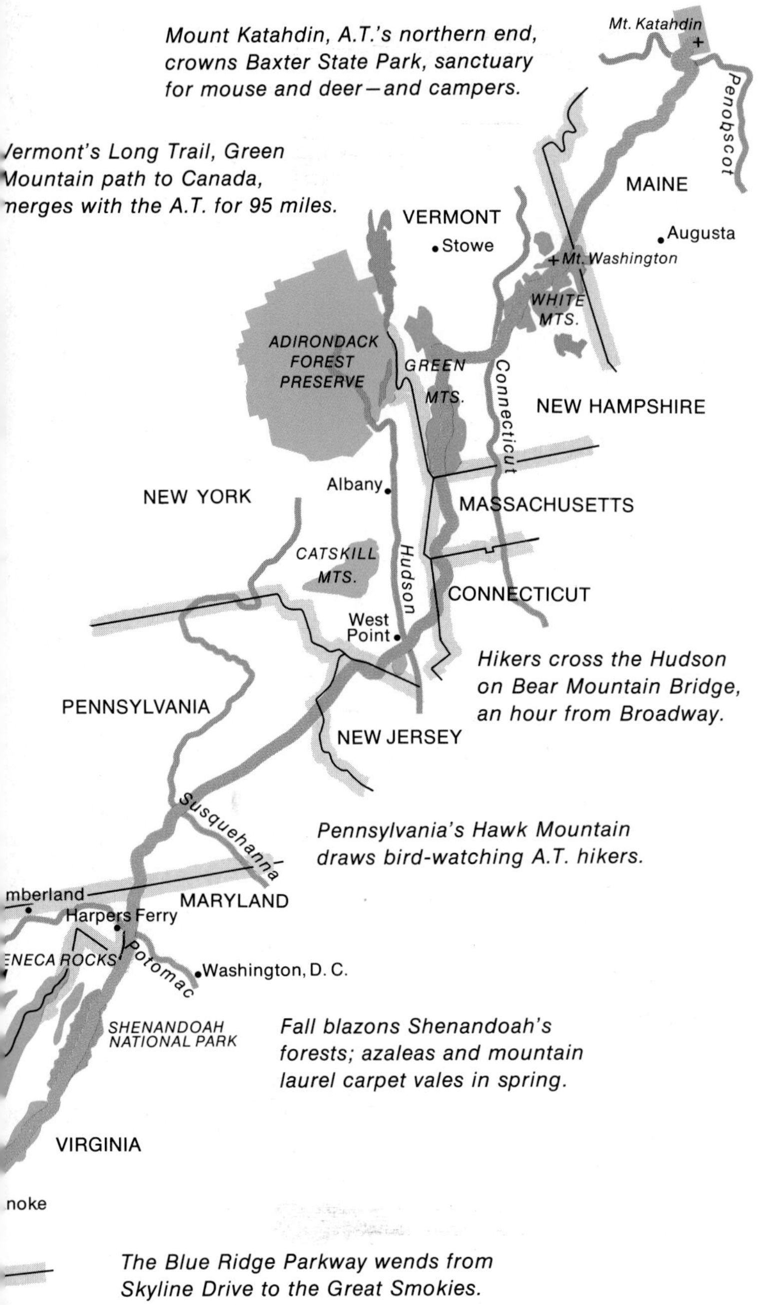

Mount Katahdin, A.T.'s northern end, crowns Baxter State Park, sanctuary for mouse and deer—and campers.

/ermont's Long Trail, Green Mountain path to Canada, merges with the A.T. for 95 miles.

Mt. Katahdin
Penobscot
MAINE
VERMONT
Stowe
Augusta
Mt. Washington
WHITE MTS.
ADIRONDACK FOREST PRESERVE
GREEN MTS.
Connecticut
NEW HAMPSHIRE
NEW YORK
Albany
MASSACHUSETTS
CATSKILL MTS.
Hudson
CONNECTICUT
West Point
PENNSYLVANIA
NEW JERSEY
Susquehanna
mberland
MARYLAND
Harpers Ferry
NECA ROCKS
Potomac
Washington, D. C.
SHENANDOAH NATIONAL PARK
VIRGINIA
noke

Hikers cross the Hudson on Bear Mountain Bridge, an hour from Broadway.

Pennsylvania's Hawk Mountain draws bird-watching A.T. hikers.

Fall blazons Shenandoah's forests; azaleas and mountain laurel carpet vales in spring.

The Blue Ridge Parkway wends from Skyline Drive to the Great Smokies.

Great Smoky Mountains National Park offers 600 miles of highland trails.

Chattahoochee National Forest guards A.T. terminus, 3,782-foot Springer Mountain.

Swath of solitude beside corridors of concrete, the Appalachian Trail sweeps close enough to major cities to offer 120 million people a long—or a short—hike. From Springer Mountain in the Blue Ridge crags of Georgia (below) to the top of Mount Katahdin in Maine, where the author signs the register (opposite), the trail threads 14 states. Four feet wide and 2,000 miles long, the A.T. cuts through eight national forests and two national parks, crosses 15 rivers, dips to sea level at the Hudson, climbs to 6,642 feet on Clingmans Dome in the Great Smokies. The trail courses the Appalachians, a chain with such massive links as the White Mountains, Alleghenies, Cumberlands. Volunteers publish guides (page 421) and mark the way with white-paint blazes, tacking on trees this symbol of the trail: A

Wrapped in soft blue haze, Georgia's Chattahoochee National Forest spreads before hikers in the

We moved out briskly as dawn blushed pink over a sea of peaks on our right. Down easy, graded paths, our first spurt of walking warmed us and soon put us in a mood for breakfast. We took little time for the dry cereal and powdered milk, eager to put mileage behind us early in the day. This became our daily plan. Arriving at one of the open-face log shelters spaced conveniently along most of the trail, we had time to relax, explore, and talk over the day's events while our hot meal—soup—simmered on the campfire. For dessert we munched chocolate, as I made the daily entry in our red logbook:

We are camped beside a pond where a creek enters. Ice is around its outlet. Johnny and I took a swim bath about 3 p.m. when we got here. . . . Snuffy has been making it okay. He really wanted to take out after the deer we saw.

Snuffy's hunting instincts had to be stifled quickly. We had just passed through a game refuge and later would be crossing national parks, where even rattlesnakes have rights. But our six-year-old friend is a well-mannered canine. He soon learned to see, not stalk. We were grateful for that the morning we met a skunk feeding in the misty rain, and later when we came upon a bobcat eating its kill.

Junco, nuthatch, chickadee, pileated woodpecker, and raven enlivened the landscape. Late afternoon on the fourth day Johnny and I sat on an old log and listened to a turkey gobble. We saw a hawk dive on a flock of small birds and lift away with his prey. Grouse drumming in the forest sounded like muffled tom-toms.

MARTIN ROGERS

Blue Ridge Mountains. The range includes the Great Smokies, and marches north into Pennsylvania.

Pieced together from existing trails and following a plan proposed by forester Benton MacKaye in 1921, the highland path in part parallels an old lowland route—the Great Indian Warpath—which once led from Virginia into Pennsylvania. Indians generally shunned mountaintops, domain of gods who frowned on trespass. Pamola, wrote Henry David Thoreau, is always angry with men who climb Katahdin. Though I could not name the spirits of these southern summits, some high-level feathers did appear to be ruffled on our trek to Cheoah Bald and beyond.

Put on our ponchos and headed up Standing Indian. It thundered. It lightninged. The trail was like a running creek. . . . It started raining just as we started up Shuckstack. . . . Climbed Thunderhead. . . . Snow flurries this a.m.

Sullen spirits notwithstanding, the sun broke through on April 15 as we followed the crest of the Great Smokies and headed up 6,642-foot Clingmans Dome on the North Carolina-Tennessee border. The wind sang mournful ballads, shifting from one minor key to the next as we spiraled up the concrete ramp to the observation tower. From this eagle perch above the balsam-clad summit we gazed at the gentle grandeur of the Smokies rolling away toward a hazy horizon.

Gentle, that is, from a distance.

I have other adjectives for the contours of Charlies Bunion and the jagged crest of the Sawteeth. We explored this craggy stretch of country at greater length than we intended when we lost the main trail. By the time we got our bearings and

FIGHTING FISH LURE A LASS to frothing Straight Fork in Great Smoky Mountains National Park, where 600 miles of scenic streams teem with rainbow, brown, and brook trout. Appalachian Trail winds 70 miles through the park's famed balds and blankets of laurel.

JAMES L. AMOS, NATIONAL GEOGRAPHIC PHOTOGRAPHER

reached the shelter, we had put in 23 hard miles. A party of Boy Scouts had a cozy fire crackling. We made supper and fell into our bunks at 7 p.m. Our sheltermates must have taken us for a trio of tenderfeet.

They were not far wrong. The two of us who wear shoes were nursing monster blisters. And the hills were not yet through their spell of "weary dismals." Beyond rhododendron-clad Roan Mountain, thunderstorm after thunderstorm rolled over us. "Think of it this way," I said to Johnny as we stomped into cold boots still damp from yesterday's sloshing. "We're seeing mountains get patted down to size."

Rain, snow, wind, and hail that batter new mountains into old ones also ravage man and beagle. By the time we neared Roanoke, Virginia, and a long-awaited family rendezvous, trilliums and violets bloomed a quiet riot beside green-bowered paths. But we looked more like last year's desiccated foliage. After some 600 miles, I had lost 32 pounds, Johnny 29. And even though we had gotten haircuts, our

THOMAS A. DEFEO

RENDEZVOUS OF RIVERS, CROSSROAD OF HISTORY, Harpers Ferry poses for artists whose rocky easel overlooks the Potomac (above right) and the Shenandoah. Raided by John Brown in his 1859 prelude to civil war, the town was swept by battles as well as floods. Its buildings restored as a national shrine, it beckons hikers on the Appalachian Trail, which crosses the Potomac nearby and parallels Shenandoah National Park's Skyline Drive (right).

beards and lean look made us suspect. A filling station owner asked us to wait someplace else for my wife Brady and younger son Michael. We moved on to a trailer park. A deputy sheriff came to investigate us just as the family station wagon and trailer rolled into view.

The best of springtime beckoned us along the Blue Ridge. Breezes wafted the fragrance of azaleas through the forest. Hungry hatchlings—towhee and robin—clamored from their nests. A hen grouse trailed a fluffy brood behind her in a search for insects.

In May and June, Skyline Drive, riding the ridgeline through Shenandoah National Park, becomes a glory road for motorists. And though we walked every mile of the trail, we too made use of the wheel to ease our mountain marathon. We slept many nights in the trailer along the route. Rising before dawn, Brady drove Johnny, Snuffy, and me—and now Michael—to the spot where we had left the trail, arranging a pickup farther along. With lighter packs and

the prospect of home-cooked suppers to spur us on, we hurried toward the midpoint of our trek, regaining weight in the process.

Some days we hiked extra mileage, then took a day off. One busman's holiday the whole family climbed by moonlight up an extracurricular peak for a sunrise picnic. The trail offered fringe benefits—wild strawberries.

Songfests, gabfests, and lake swims lightened summer evenings, but during the day sweltering heat and insects stalked us across the ranges from Maryland to Massachusetts. To beat the midday heat, we used our own daylight saving time, starting as early as 3:30 a.m. Against insects we tried repellents and curses and devised weird contraptions. Johnny wore his hat on a pole as a gnat decoy. I resorted to a head kerchief that dangled to my collar. With my grizzled beard, I thought it gave me a bit of Bedouin dash.

Snuffy became adept at scrambling over stiles, but he got hung up on barbed wire fences, which caught his pack as he tried to duck under. I remember our crossing of the rich farmlands of Pennsylvania's Cumberland Valley as the day of the cottontail.

Trails etch New Hampshire's roof—the White Mountains. The Appalachian climbs distant peaks

We must have flushed 30 rabbits from brush heaps and old stone walls. Snuffy's nose twitched. His eyeballs hopped and jiggled. But his feet held fast to the trail, as though he understood that trail right-of-way does not always include permission to wander on private property.

Beavers had been busy along Connecticut streams; we detoured once when we saw that the next marked tree stood blaze-deep in a beaver pond. Porcupines abounded in Vermont; in one four-day period we met three of the bristly beasts, and each time the trail seemed suddenly quite narrow. Deer were plentiful, and we saw our first bear in a berry patch, the perfect excuse to belt out a chorus of "The Bear Went Over the Mountain"—when we had sidled safely past a possible hostile critic.

In mid-August, after paying our respects to the Old Man of the Mountain, famed granite outcrop in Franconia Notch that profiles a man's head, we broached the upper echelon of New Hampshire's White Mountains, the Presidential Range.

The day we meant to start, I woke to hear a steady patter of rain. Radio forecasts offered no encouragement. It was no go. Foul weather here endangers life. A gentle

of the Presidential Range, whose treeless summits culminate in lofty Mount Washington (far right).

KATHLEEN REVIS JUDGE

KATHLEEN REVIS JUDGE

rain can quicken to a raging electrical storm. Fiery pitchforks jab at trees. Torrents undercut rocks on the upper slopes, provoking deadly slides.

Next morning we hiked out of dense hardwood forest 3,000 feet up to the barren rooftop of New England. Wrapped in clouds and mist on most of the peaks, we groped from rock cairn to rock cairn, trail markers used above timberline. On one section Mike stopped suddenly, calling our attention to a sheer drop on the left side of the trail. Without a word Johnny pointed to the right—an equally abrupt descent.

Up there in the heights we met eight girls yodeling as they trooped along. . . . Mike took a bad fall on Zealand Ridge. Might have been tragic if his pack had not cushioned his head. . . . Wonderful views of Mount Washington.

Treeless gray tops of the mountains looked as benign as sleeping elephants on that rare clear day we headed up Washington's 6,288-foot cone. Cloud shadows like animated inkblots leapfrogged over the humps. Yet the weather history of these peaks is anything but benign. Snow lingers eight or nine months of the year. In 1934 the weather station on Mount Washington clocked a wind gust at 231 miles an hour, strongest ever recorded anywhere on earth. Blizzards strike in midsummer, and hikers have lost not only their way but their lives. But the Appalachian Mountain Club hut system—rustic lodges accommodating 36 to 90 guests each and spaced a day's hike apart—has absorbed some of the sting of storms.

Our overnight stay at Lakes of the Clouds Hut was like one big family reunion, Brady having chugged up on the Mount Washington Cog Railway. At supper, looking down

TRAINS AND TREKKERS PUFF TO THE PEAK OF MOUNT WASHINGTON, crown of the Northeast. Sightseers clack up on the Cog Railway, where engines began chugging in 1869. Cars ride uncoupled ahead of locomotives going up, behind coming down; skyline siding (above) eases traffic jams on the 6½-mile, three-hour round trip. Drivers and hikers also conquer Washington—in good weather. Men of its summit weather station dub it "Misery Hill," for temperatures can plunge to 30° below zero.

On another Presidential peak, Madison, girls pick their way up a slope like one Hawthorne limned: "masses and fragments of naked rock heaped . . . like a cairn reared by giants in memory of a giant chief." But amid such stern scenery blooms the beauty of New England's most unusual wild flowers. Creamy beds of arctic diapensia cling to rocks above the timberline. Tiny pink alpine azaleas rim one of Washington's Lakes of the Clouds. Pale laurel and dwarf cinquefoil grace rugged trails. Large-flowered trillium (opposite) glows like a sylvan star in moist woodlands.

DICK SMITH

INDIAN OLYMPUS, WHERE DWELLS THE SPIRIT OF THUNDER AND SWIFT LIGHTNING, Mount Katahdin shoulders the golden sky over 200,000-acre Baxter State Park, gift of former Governor Baxter. The peak, northern anchor of the Appalachian Trail, is his legacy: "Katahdin in all its glory forever shall remain the mountain of the people of Maine."

the red-checkered aisle at diners seated on the benches, I tried to guess their occupations. Lawyer, nurse, machinist? It was impossible. They were simply people enjoying the mountains. All I could be sure of was that they had mountain-air appetites and, from their animated chatter, felt they were among friends. A hootenanny rounded out the socializing before we headed for the bunkrooms.

At the end of August, Mike left for school and Johnny, Snuffy, and I marched into Maine, a land of lakes and streams. Here the trail threads wilderness.

Used ladders and a rope on Baldpate Mountain. . . . Saw three Canada geese and 30 minutes later a bull moose snorted and bellowed at me.

Many blowdowns and cut trees made for slow going. My 45-year-old kneecaps groaned from scrambling over fallen trunks. But I will always remember the sensation I had in the Maine woods of being inside a cavern of luminous green. Wall-to-wall on the forest floor lay a carpet of yellow-green moss. Overhead, trees locked branches to form a ceiling. As we sat there resting, I felt like something growing from the moist, black earth.

From Rainbow Lake on September 13, I could see with the naked eye the peak I had held in my mind's eye all the way from Georgia. Expecting frost, we had gathered enough wood to keep the fire going all night. Supper over, we stretched out before the fire, warm and content.

The sun went down—it always does. A breeze rippled the mirror surface of the lake. A beaver paddled to shore, sat on a log, and chewed a twig. A loon's wild laughter echoed across the lake. Swans floated near the far shore. Commonplaces? I don't think so.

Neither Johnny nor I had said much all evening. Words were something we really didn't need. I felt sure that our thoughts roamed a common ground, much as we had walked the trail these past five months—abreast or in tandem but never far apart. Just before he turned over to go to sleep, Johnny broke the silence. "Dad, even if my feet kill me tomorrow, I'm sorry it's almost over."

"I am too, son," I said.

By the flickering flames, I looked at the maps, reviewing the last 26 miles to Katahdin, now night-shrouded. Maybe Pamola of the stone eyebrows would not be too angry if a man and his son trod gently on his granite mountain.

Thoroughbred

 They're off at Churchill Downs, old Kentucky home of an American classic, the Derby; C. Thomas Hardin

By Peter T. White

Country— FROM START TO FINISH

BOLTING THROUGH THE BLUEGRASS, a prize stallion romps to his place in the sun—a spacious paddock on Darby Dan Farm, haven for horses and horse-loving tourists. From its Lexington hub bluegrass country rolls across 2,400 square miles. Thoroughbreds thrive on 250 farms with an annual crop of 3,000 foals. Rotting limestone enriches the grass to strengthen bones, also makes water ideal for the mash of Kentucky-born bourbon.

Henry Clay and other bluegrass patricians imported Arabian-blooded stock from England to begin the state's genteel industry. On estates graced by colonnaded mansions—another traditional feature (opposite)—they raised, raced, and revered their pride, The Horse.

Nowhere else, I thought as I scanned the restful, greening landscape of central Kentucky, does so much excitement underlie such calm. Amid the gentle hills, within the miles of white wooden fences and the spic-and-span barns, throbbed the high drama of a great sport and a multimillion-dollar industry: the breeding and nurture of thoroughbred horses.

No crowds roared, no bands blared, no tote boards blinked. That would come later, soon after May Day, when the prize three-year-olds now burning up the tracks in Florida, California, and New York gathered in Louisville for the fabled Derby that makes TV railbirds of us all. Here the spotlight focused on the broodmares, suckling spindly foals and soon to be served again by pampered stallions; on frisky yearlings months away from the strange press of girth strap, saddle, and exercise boy; on sleek two-year-olds rounding into shape for the grueling campaigns ahead.

DICK DURRANCE II, NATIONAL GEOGRAPHIC PHOTOGRAPHER

Before dawn one day I found myself watching them breeze past. Stablehands, dimly visible in the moonlight, yawned and stretched. A jockey waiting at railside with the rest of us told me why this hour: "Some horses run better in the dark. They can see all they need to; they don't get distracted." And then, suddenly, they were coming.

Even before the pounding of hoofs on the soft track you could hear a snorting, in rhythm—the horses were pushing, extending themselves. Why do they snort so hard? Because they're not yet in shape, the jockey explained. When they are, the snorting stops. Workout over, the gently steaming horses are led back to the barns, dried, washed down, dried once more, and walked around for half an hour or so to cool down. Success here in the bluegrass comes from meticulous care and training. But more than that, success—as all horsemen agree—comes from good breeding.

More big winners, including three out of four Kentucky Derby champions, are bred here than anywhere else, on the rolling fields of grass that everyone calls blue. And, indeed, when the grass is in bud and the light and the mood are just right, there are those who say they see a bluish cast in the green turf.

Here more visitors are permitted to come close to the idols of a major sport than anywhere else. Want to see Chateaugay at Darby Dan Farm? There he stands, winner of the Derby and the Belmont Stakes (a Preakness victory would have given him the Triple Crown). Want to hobnob with Tom Fool at Greentree or Bold Ruler at Claiborne? They piled up purses totaling well over a million dollars.

DICK DURRANCE II, NATIONAL GEOGRAPHIC PHOTOGRAPHER

You are welcome any day, from 10 to 4, at dozens of the great farms that spread in all directions within a 20-minute drive from Lexington. No smoking near the barns, of course.

At the 5,500-acre Spendthrift Farm, I passed within two feet of the nose of Nashua, the first stallion bought for more than a million dollars—$1,251,200 to be exact. Nashua had just been led into his stall, to stay in until late afternoon lest his glossy bay coat suffer sunburn. I paused before a brass plaque inscribed "Raise A Native." *He* had cost $2,625,000. He slid his chestnut head over his door, entrancing a lady from Cincinnati.

"How sweet," she said. "He wants to play."

His groom said, "He wants to get at my head."

"To lick it?"

"To bite it. Thoroughbreds usually like people and like to show off, but stallions sometimes can get mean. If you don't watch out, they'll hurt you."

Or hurt each other. That's why stallions graze alone, each in his own paddock the size of a football field.

Gentler and more gregarious, mares will come trotting over to a fence with their gangly foals to meet you. They probably spotted you from afar, for while their heads are down for grazing they can see in front, to the sides, and behind. Seeing things close up and straight ahead is harder because thoroughbreds have such wide foreheads. They can unite the vision of both eyes only by keeping the head

RACING HOPES RIDE HIGH on a spindly blueblood getting a blood test at Spendthrift Farm under his dam's watchful eye. Breeders brood over bloodlines, covet track-tested sires, mares worthy of the boast, "When she drops a foal, it hits the ground running!" They invest a small fortune in top stallions (or in stud fees that run to $20,000), in the end must hope for fortune's favor. Will the foal's legs hold up? In the Derby a force of about 16,000 pounds will pound each foreleg 350 times. Will he have heart, the will to win?

Odds against a Kentucky foal reaching the Derby: 400 to 1. Dropouts earn esteem in other fields; a racehorse turned hunter-jumper nimbly takes a fence at Tin-Dor Farm (above). Bluegrass horsemen also raise standardbreds for the trotting tracks, as well as show-ring saddlebreds with complex gaits and arched tails, a pleasure to ride and a joy to watch.

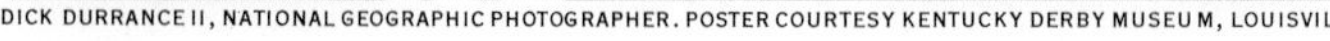
DICK DURRANCE II, NATIONAL GEOGRAPHIC PHOTOGRAPHER. POSTER COURTESY KENTUCKY DERBY MUSEUM, LOUISVILLE

DERBY WEEK: DAZZLING DAYS AND TWO MINUTES OF FRENZY. *Tootling steamboats racing on the river. Banjo zinging Stephen Foster tunes. Kentucky colonels trading fond memories mellowed in juleps. Louisville bursting, from posh hotel to rented back room. Then—*

The Day: prancing parade of long shot and favorite. Touts and tyros pondering bets. "They're at the gate! They're off!" *Pounding hoofs churn oval track; pounding hearts fill twin-spired Churchill Downs. No. 8, Majestic Prince, lunges to the finish line (below), winner by a neck of a $100,000 purse and a place on a golden roster dating to the Derby's beginning in 1875. Organized by the Louisville Jockey Club, the Derby grew from postered local renown to TV spectacular, the most famous horse race in America.*

slightly raised and in a straight line with the body. A playful foal, nuzzling you across the fence, may not see you very well but he smells you thoroughly.

These foals lie at the root of horse-country excitement. Long before the breeding season begins in late winter, owners talk bloodlines. Then the vans rush about, taking just these mares to just those stallions. Eleven months later, tired but tense breeders stay up all night with mares dropping foals. Whatever date he arrives, the foal's first birthday falls officially on the following January 1. Pity the poor foal born on December 31; at the age of one day he's a year old, fated to compete with horses nine or ten months older. If a yearling looks promising he may be auctioned off in July at the magnificent Keeneland racetrack near Lexington. There, on any morning, you can size up thoroughbreds at work, ask a question or two of the lady breeder in sweater and slacks, or of the trainer with the weatherbeaten face clocking his charges.

Derby Day! It's the first Saturday in May and the rush is on to Louisville. My wife and I set out in a bus chartered

by one of the venerable horse farms with a dozen other guests, three waiters, maid, and guitarist. A throng of 100,000 packs storied Churchill Downs—trading tips, sipping mint juleps, acting like winners. Tote board lights flash the pari-mutuel odds as seven preliminary races thunder by. Long lines at the bettors' windows feed in more than six million dollars. Shorter lines mark the payoff windows.

High school bands play, the National Guard marches, dignitaries make entrances. Excitement builds. National anthem, trumpet blasts. The crowd sings "My Old Kentucky Home." Eight three-year-olds file onto the track, five from Kentucky. The jockeys' silks shimmer, their mounts' ears prick up at the rustle and chatter of the milling onlookers. Each superbly honed horse looks like a champion as he ambles to the gate. They line up in the starting slots, dancing, tensed....

They're off! A rush, a blur of brilliant silks, bobbing caps, slender legs straining toward the clubhouse turn. Hoof-churned turf spatters the jockeys' faces. Loudspeakers blare the announcer's calls above the roar of a hundred thousand voices. The racers round into the distant backstretch, pacing themselves for the classic mile and a quarter. At the far turn the leader breaks from the pack but drifts wide and fades; another jockey spies an opening, drives to the fore. At the head of the stretch

In the summer twilight at Calumet Farm, rich in the glories of immortals like Whirlaway, Citation,

Number 3 takes over, a horse from Virginia. Number 8 forges ahead as they charge down the homestretch. Whips fly, the horses fight for the last few yards. It's Number 8—the favorite, true to form, that son of Raise A Native, Majestic Prince!

It's all over in 2 minutes 1⅘ seconds. In the next 3 minutes the winner is festooned with a 2½-yard garland of dark red roses (thorns carefully removed), led to the winner's circle, petted by his owner's family, and surrounded by squads of photographers. Then handlers spread a blanket over him so he won't catch cold. He'll race again—once, twice, twenty times? It's up to the owner: he wants him to win more, but there's a risk. The horse might injure himself so badly he'd have to be destroyed, and after today's triumph he's already worth millions as a stallion. Retired to stud, he may easily live to be 25.

The phenomenal Man O'War lived to 30. He was embalmed and lay in state in his barn for three days, in an open square casket. Now his grave near Lexington, surmounted by his larger-than-life bronze statue, draws hundreds daily. I stood there awhile in the afternoon sun. As I looked up at the great sculptured head towering above the bluegrass of spring, I imagined that the old boy was winking at me proudly. After all, he *was* one of 16 great-great-great-grandsires of Majestic Prince.

and five other Derby winners, broodmares roam the bluegrass, bearing the prideful hopes of tomorrow.

DICK DURRANCE II, NATIONAL GEOGRAPHIC PHOTOGRAPHER

By Ralph Gray

CANOEING KINFOLK RENDEZVOUS ON AN UNTAMED RIVER FOR AN

Ozark Odyssey

I'm ready to canoe any river almost anytime, so when Congress and the President of the United States get together and designate a free-flowing stream in my native state of Missouri as a National Scenic River, that's a bit of water I've got to explore. As a place-name buff I was doubly drawn to this particular river. It's called the Eleven Point. I wondered why.

Wife and daughter beside me, and canoe lashed to the car top, I coursed the highways toward the Ozarks, excitement rising with each mile at the prospect of once more wetting paddle and keel in fast water, once more escaping the encapsulated existence of home, office, and automobile, once more breathing the breath of the hills.

The hills. As a youngster from the flatlands I had often visited the Ozarks and came to know them as a green oasis of mini-mountains and giant springs and clear-flowing rivers in the midst of the Midwest's level farms and fields. But in the twenties I had moved away from the Ozarks and from Missouri. Now, after an absence, my wife Jean and I saw the hills afresh.

On an oak-wooded knoll near Alton, we rendezvoused with the families of my sisters, Carolyn Thornton and Ellen Massey. These two ladies, still lithe of limb and good canoeists, had chosen after college to live in the Ozarks; they had married men from the hills and now lead full lives as teachers and homemakers.

With chattering nieces and nephews and barking dog piled into truck and jeep, we lurched across open fields and along forest lanes searching for the infant Eleven Point River. Finally we came upon it nested in a deep fold of the Ozark hills, quiet and serene, gurgling a little tune

Paddlers and pet lead a fun-bound flotilla down the Eleven Point River in Missouri; Larry Nicholson

GLEAMING DRAGON ON A RUMPLED RUG, *Missouri's Table Rock Lake (below) writhes through the Ozarks. Erosion carved mountains in this tableland, underground water gnawed caves and sinkholes. On spring-fed streams moderns paddle for pleasure in a state whose name recalls Indian "people of the big canoes."*

Relics charm visitors amid hills that fill southern Missouri but rear highest in next-door Arkansas. In highland and hollow, where time turns slowly, a weathered well may gladden a thirsty Arkansas traveler; at Surprise, Missouri, an overshot mill wheel waits to creak again near the Eleven Point as planners dream of restoration.

to itself. Here we put in, a mile or two below Thomasville. In Indian style we shoved off a boatful at a time—good canoe cruising practice anywhere, but necessary here since the narrow headwaters could hold but one canoe. A few muscle-relaxing strokes swept me into the first run, a mild but exhilarating riffle at a sharp bend, complicated by a tree leaning into the current and by a barely submerged rock that had to be "read" from upstream to be avoided. My aluminum craft made almost lifelike response to my every nudge and urge, and we came through the dancing waters without a scrape or bump to disturb the primeval stillness.

When all the canoes reached the first eddy, as Ozarkians call the long flatwater pools between riffles, we floated alongside each other and exchanged notes. Nobody had shipped a drop of water. Having met the challenge of the sport we loved, we all felt a part of this new world where the signs—instead of "no left turn" and "yield" —were river birch greening on the banks, limestone outcroppings drifting past, and sandy beaches soaking up the sun. And in this different world of the Eleven Point even the places carried such gloriously distinctive names as Pigpen Hollow and Mary Decker Chute. The brawling days of Ozark pioneers and old-time loggers

BRUCE DALE, NATIONAL GEOGRAPHIC PHOTOGRAPHER. OPPOSITE UPPER: LARRY NICHOLSON

echo in those names—and come alive in the reconstructed hamlet of Silver Dollar City near Branson, Missouri.

As we paddled downstream a gorgeously plumed kingfisher patrolled overhead. Not 20 feet from us a smallmouth bass leaped free of the water. In a meadow beyond the woods a bobwhite paged himself with musical notes. Purple cliff brake and spotted touch-me-not flourished in crannies along the bank. All of a sudden we had a hard time remembering what bad shape the rest of the world was in. Or that we as a family had ever been apart.

Ahead lay a zigzagging course, 32 miles of riffles and holes, eddies and summertime shallows. The Eleven Point is not wild in the sense of tumultuous, frothing rapids, but wild as in wilderness—relatively unmarred by man, flowing in nearly pristine state. It demanded no great skill from us, but offered tests and tight places for paddlers who had tried Ozark streams before—the Niangua, the Current, and Osage Fork of the Gasconade. As on those, we navigated here by trying to figure out the pattern of ripples and slicks ahead. A slight misreading would send us aground, and one by one we occasionally found ourselves wading, leading our canoes like so many legless aluminum horses. The biggest challenge awaited us near the midpoint of our journey, at the fast run of Mary Decker Chute.

OLDEN DAYS, OZARK WAYS TAKE REFUGE FROM THE YEARS in havens like Silver Dollar City in southwestern Missouri. In a blaze of blanks a clan war rages anew (opposite) for visitors to this replica of an Ozark mining town of the 1880's. Feudin' over, vacationists pile into ore barges to tour the flooded silver mine. They ride shotgun as the Butterfield stage lurches on leather springs along trails cut by frontiersmen—even survive an ersatz ambush on a steam train chuffing through country where cutthroats and vigilantes fought. Back in town they watch a bearded smith bend to a sparking hearth (left), or sniff the fumes as a poke-bonneted matron concocts a kettleful of lye soap "as good for shampooing your hair as for scrubbing the hen house floor."

Mini-mountaineers in wood (opposite) coax a chuckle. Several thousand dollars will coax a carver to chisel out a full-size cigar-store Indian that wears the buyer's face. As of yore, craftsmen lighten their labor with whimsy. Deft fingers of Arkansas whittler "Uncle John" Findlay, whose work appears at Silver Dollar City, finish a model in a bottle—a model of a tiny Uncle John starting a model in a bottle!

More than a million visitors do the town and nearby Marvel Cave each year, many of them during October's National Festival of Craftsmen. Then grandmas gather here for the time-hallowed quilting bee; hardier lasses heft the menfolk's broadaxes in a log-hewing contest. Potter, basket weaver, glassblower, candy cook, rope and broom makers keep vanishing vocations alive and pass on their skills to young Ozark apprentices. Conestoga wagon builders proved so popular with festival crowds they now work here year round, crafting white-oak masterpieces that cost more than most new cars!

JAMES ROOT. ABOVE AND OPPOSITE: BRUCE DALE, NATIONAL GEOGRAPHIC PHOTOGRAPHER

BRUCE DALE, NATIONAL GEOGRAPHIC PHOTOGRAPHER

Before camping that first night at Cane Bluff we lifted our canoes over a low wooden bridge, recalling one theory about naming the Eleven Point—that the words were an anglicized form of *élevé pont,* or "raised bridge."

"I've never heard that one before," said my Ozarkian brother-in-law Lester Thornton. "But there are plenty of names in the Ozarks that go back to the early French explorers." He had heard that the river's name came from an early hunter who had felled an eleven-point buck. The namers of Lester's own home town, by the way, had curiously forecast its fate. They called it Protem (short for pro tempore). Today the old town lies beneath waters backed behind Bull Shoals Dam.

Preparing for sleep that night beneath beetling limestone cliffs, we took a last look across the murmuring river and saw a beaver cutting a V-wake in the crystal waters. Two whip-poor-wills had learned each other's area codes and carried on a clear if somewhat repetitious long-distance exchange. From my sleeping bag the Big Dipper seemed close enough to hang on our water bucket.

"Romp and stomp. It's daylight in the swamp!" bellowed Ned Therrien, one of the U. S. Forest Service men who had joined our flotilla. As Recreation Planner of Mark Twain National Forest, through which the Eleven Point flows, Ned was anxious to see whether the river's increasing popularity had disturbed its unspoiled look. The

VEILED IN LIQUID LACE AND BEAMING *like a bride, a Missouri maid romps in rapids at Johnson Shut-ins State Park. Here ridges of rhyolite a billion years old dam the Black River's East Fork; through channels it has carved in the rock the river foams to freedom—and the next "shut-in." Quiet pools, swift water, and a woodland net of nature trails bid the camper and picnicker tarry.*

Campers break out the skillets and tie on a likely lure (above) where Tomahawk Creek weds the Buffalo River in northern Arkansas. High esteem for Ozark streams—made to order for float fishing—draws anglers to crystal pools where they can spot bass lazing near the bottom eight feet down. Trout, walleye, and pickerel add zest to the sport—and the menu. Naturalists count more than 90 species of fishes in these waters. The campers mirror an ancient scene: On Ozark riverbanks archeologists have probed sites where Indians camped 90 centuries ago.

OLD MATT'S CABIN, A MISSOURI LANDMARK near Branson, welcomes throngs along "The Trail That Is Nobody Knows How Old." Here at the turn of the century the Matthews clan ground corn, hauled timber with wagon and team, foraged for food in the forest. Into their hills came Harold Bell Wright, seeking relief from tuberculosis in the clean air and rolling Ozark vistas (below). In 1907 Wright immortalized patriarchal Old Matt along with his kin and countryside in The Shepherd of the Hills, *a tale of faith and fury that became an all-time best seller.*

From ax-scarred beams of this homestead-turned-museum hang relics of a rugged life. Calloused hands drove in an iron auger by its T-handle, swung a heavy broadax, rolled logs with a pole through the ring of a hook-shaped "dog." A handled measuring wheel, rolled around a wagon wheel's rim, told how much strap iron to cut for a tire. Cradle on a scythe caught the grain it felled. These worn antiques whisper of times not quite bygone at Shepherd of the Hills Farm, where in rustic structures and summer theater Old Matt's workaday world lives on.

development plan calls for "peace, tranquillity, remoteness." It envisions float camps unreachable by road, accessible only by boat or foot trail. Larger camps away from the river will serve those who come by car. For us the plan was working beautifully; as we broke camp and loaded the canoes, the Eleven Point was ours alone.

It was already hot when we paddled off, hot as only a midsummer day in the Ozarks can be hot. But the river felt deliciously cool, and after Greer Spring added its immense flow it was downright cold. Greer more than doubles the Eleven Point's volume, turning it into a mature river. We dallied at the junction, wading in the frigid spring water and watching its aquamarine overcome the river's pewter.

On either side the hills rose into the humming summer air. Such a view, I thought, must have inspired Harold Bell Wright in the early 1900's when he wrote *The Shepherd of the Hills:* "When God looked upon th' work of his hands an' called hit good, he war sure a lookin' at this here Ozark country. . . . 'Taint no wonder 't all, God rested when he made these here hills . . . fer he done his beatenest an' war plumb gin out." Ozarkians have long since outlived that kind of talk but these hills still provide some of the Nation's beatenest scenery.

Next day we pushed off in early morning fog, the first canoe lost from view long before the last left shore. I had previously swapped turns at bow and stern with Jean, with our daughter Donna, and with my sister Ellen. This time I chose as my "front man" my sister Carolyn. Together we paddled under limbs hung with dew-pearled cobwebs.

OZARK WATCHER FINDS A ROCKY VIEWPOINT IN NORTHERN ARKANSAS. BATES LITTLEHALES AND (OPPOSITE) BRUCE DALE, NATIONAL GEOGRAPHIC PHOTOGRAPHERS

Before long the sun wiped away the pearls and the fog. We caught up with Michael Thornton, Carolyn's oldest, soon to enter the University of Missouri's School of Forestry. Then we pulled alongside David Massey, Ellen's firstborn, a student of landscape architecture at the university. Each had a common interest in talking forestry with Ned Therrien, but now they served as steersmen for two canoes full of bantering siblings and cousins—plus Buster, the Masseys' collie.

At times horseplay erupted, friendly insults flew: "It was easy to follow you, Michael. You left an aluminum blaze on every rock." At other moments we all felt simply a quiet appreciation of being together. Little was said, or needed saying. These waterborne reunions have been a mainstay of our family life for four decades. Much has changed in that time. Young men like David and Michael no longer have to leave the beauties of the Ozarks to find the futures they want.

When Jim Berlin, Supervisor of Mark Twain National Forest, joined us, I popped the familiar question about the Eleven Point's name. "We're looking into that," Jim replied. "Personally, I think it's because it rises in eleven sources."

If I kept at it, I would soon have eleven reasons for the river's name. Now, however,

Trailing wrinkled reflections, the Grays, Masseys, and Thorntons paddle into the low-hanging mist of

we were approaching Mary Decker Chute, a name known to stem from days when the safest passageway was a gap in a boulder dam timbermen had built for their logs. Here lay hunks of limestone, fallen from the cliffs above. We ran the tricky, rock-strewn stretch handily, thrilled by the surge of white water.

We stopped and walked up a ravine loaded with ripe blackberries—Ozark black gold—to the deserted community of Surprise. Then, as the Eleven Point straightened and widened on its way south to the Arkansas border, we paddled down to the grassy expanse of Bliss Spring Camp and an Ozark dinner of fried ham with navy beans and corncakes with honey. Under a full moon, around a fire beside the riffling river, we made our campground ring with song.

The Eleven Point held us to the very end. On our last day, before we beached for the final time at Riverton with its stacks of canoes ready for weekend renting, the river gave us an unforgettable show: a pair of great blue herons landing and flying, flying and landing ahead of us for miles before swerving high against the sun and heading back for the bit of stream they held deed to. When I added this to all the other good points of the Eleven Point, I no longer had to wonder about its name.

a new day, brought together by family ties and the free-flowing charm of the Eleven Point River.

LARRY NICHOLSON

By Ross Bennett

VACATION DRIVING TAKES A FASCINATING TURN—

Detour: America at Work

Molten torrent flows from a ladle at Bethlehem Steel's Sparrows Point plant in Maryland; Emory Kristof, National Geographic photographer

"They're slapping on the bumpers, Mom!" squealed six-year-old Barbara. Relieved at seeing a familiar object, she relaxed her armlock around my wife's neck and pointed to a pair of workers adding a shiny chrome bumper to a car frame in Ford's assembly plant in Dearborn, Michigan. Yes, we'd told her we were going to watch men make automobiles. But amid the jungle of conveyor chains and pneumatic hoses dancing to the hammer and hiss of machines, Barbara had sought her mother's arms.

"They don't just slap the bumpers on, dear," Vera explained above the racket. "They put them on with bolts."

Barbara cocked her head. "What's a bolt?"

In the days that followed, Barbara and teen-agers Nick and Anne and eight-year-old Patricia learned about bolts —and the men and machines that produce all those things Made in U.S.A. No better way to break up the miles on a trip from our Maryland home to relatives in Iowa, we had decided, than to drop in on industry. After poring over travel guides and thousands of listings in the U. S. Department of Commerce's *Plant Tours,* we set out on a zigzag route to see America with its sleeves rolled up.

Detroit. Automobiles. Chrysler, General Motors, and in suburban Dearborn, Ford's giant River Rouge complex, transforming iron ore into finished sedan and beckoning a quarter of a million visitors a year to see how a car is born. We fell in beside a conveyor-drawn car frame

WORKADAY FIREWORKS MAKE A GREAT SPLASH for the family touring a nation throbbing to the rhythm of 300,000 manufacturers. In Ford's mammoth River Rouge plant near Detroit, the Bennetts learned the recipe for a molten ton of steel: 1 1/5 tons of iron ore, 1/3 ton of scrap, 1/5 ton of limestone, 2/3 ton of coal, 165 tons of water, and 8 tons of air! They watched glowing 16-ton ingots, plucked from 2,500° ovens, squeezed through rolling machines into bars and sheets of steel. They gaped as great presses stamped out body panels like cookies, as welders joined frames (opposite), as skilled hands assembled a car in 54 minutes —ready for delivery, or a rough ride on the proving ground (below).

They traced America's industrial growth in nearby Greenfield Village; in Akron, Ohio, they saw how chance played a key role. In 1839 Charles Goodyear (opposite lower) put bounce and strength into rubber when he spilled a crude rubber-sulphur mix on the stove of his kitchen workshop. His discovery: vulcanization. America rolls on what resulted.

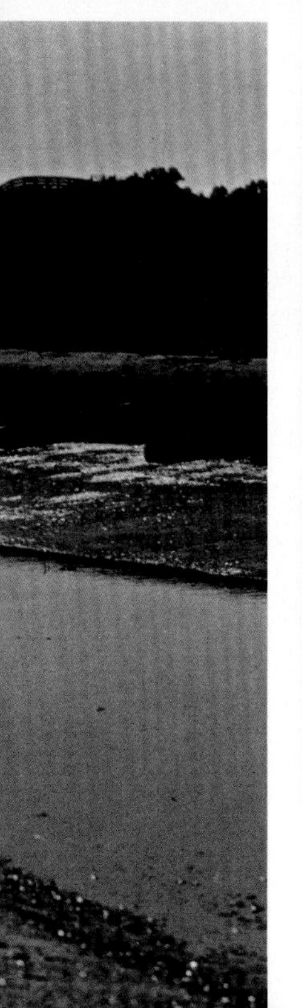

ROBERT W. MADDEN

BATS, BRASS, AND BUBBLES OF GLASS STILL TAKE THE HUMAN TOUCH in an age of automation. At Corning Glass Center in New York, where visitors witness an ancient art (below), sand, potash, and lead oxide fuse into molten glass at 2,500°. Coaxed into the form of a vase by blowing, swinging, and shaping, this Steuben crystal—when polished and engraved with a copper wheel—will bear the mark of craftsmanship no machine can match.

Framed by mellophonium bells and backed by saxophones at C. G. Conn in Elkhart, Indiana, an engraver in brass (opposite) etches a trombone bell with meticulous care.

Semi-automatic lathes spin out most of Kentucky's famed Louisville Sluggers. But a big leaguer wants a bat turner (left) as seasoned as his wood to chisel a finely balanced bat. Sensitive hands of a Ted Williams can tell if it's off a fraction of an ounce.

ROBERT W. MADDEN

on its 1,100-foot journey through a gantlet of United Automobile Workers. Stationed at bins brimming with parts and armed with an arsenal of tools, they swiftly attached springs, axles, shock absorbers, exhaust pipes, brakes, then "decked the engine," lowering it onto the frame as it moved ahead, a quarter of a mile an hour.

On went the wheels; torque wrenches tightened all five lug nuts at once. The body shell, painted and trimmed, appeared from above; men eased it into place. Suddenly the car took shape. "Hey, it's a yellow Mustang!" said Nick with admiration—and all the frustration of a newly licensed 16-year-old driver grounded by an arm cast.

The Mustang passed black, red, blue, and white fenders swinging like clothes on a line. As yellow ones clanked in from the paint area, workers took them down and fastened them to the body. Our guide explained that a coded teletype sent engine, body, fenders, and hood from subassembly areas, all timed to meet their frame. What about assembly-line breakdown? As if on cue a siren wailed and a boxy red cart with men clinging to the sides raced by. "Trouble in body trim," the guide noted wryly.

But our Mustang was complete, all 13,000 parts. An inspector turned the key and another car roared to life—55 every hour. And I thought of Henry Ford's first assembly line in 1913—a rope and windlass that dragged a Model T, started an industrial revolution, and put America on wheels.

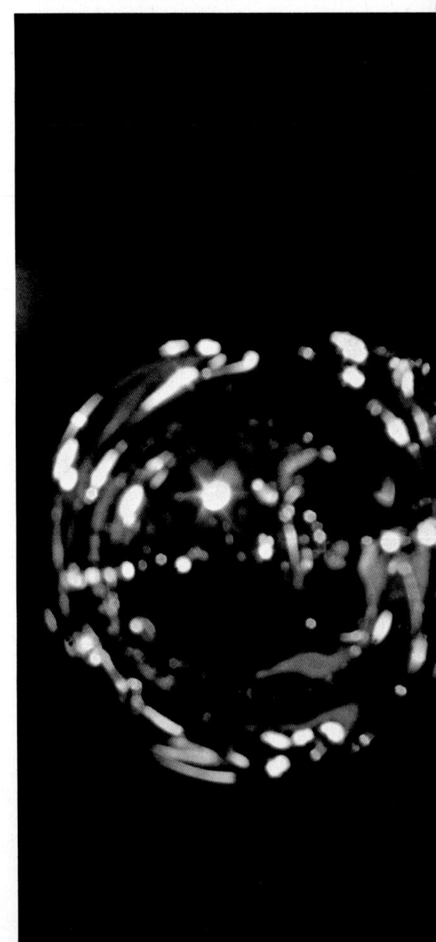

Elkhart, just off the Indiana Toll Road, conjured up images of the Music Man and John Philip Sousa. After the Civil War, cornetist Charles Conn split his lip in a fistfight. Impatient to play, he devised a rubber-cushioned mouthpiece. Soon he was making cornets. C. G. Conn, now one of the largest makers of band instruments, gave us a close-up of precision craftsmanship that weds music and science: the nimble fingers of a woman assembling saxophone keys, a Supermicrometer accurate to 50 millionths of an inch, the iron muscles of a bell-spinner shaping tuba bells with a wooden pole. In the casing section, festooned with polished euphoniums, trumpets, trombones, and clarinets, the air seemed ready to burst with E♭'s and C#'s crying for liberation by the final tester.

Before leaving Elkhart we freed Nick's arm from its cast, but his jubilation at being able to drive was short-lived. Next day he misplaced his license and crossed the Mississippi shrouded in gloom.

West of Iowa City we turned off Interstate 80 into the past at Amana Colonies, seven tidy 19th-century villages hesitant to enter the twentieth. Founded by German Pietists in 1859 as a religious communal society, Amana fought the Depression by switching to free enterprise and won a reputation for producing fine furniture, freezers, woolens, breads, meats, wines. We strolled quiet streets past 100-year-old houses framed by flowers and fruit trees, watched an old woman in poke bonnet and high-top shoes tend a grape arbor behind a home winery, sipped clear, anise-flavored *piestengel* wine made from rhubarb. We dined family style in the restaurants, slept amid antiques in the only motel, ate fresh-baked coffee cake from an open-hearth

ROBERT W. MADDEN

WAITING FOR WINGS TO WAFT THEM *into the wild blue yonder, fledgling fuselages shape up along one of Cessna's assembly lines at Wichita, Kansas. Workers daily transform 12 tons of aluminum into 30 planes, leading a mushrooming general aviation industry whose private planes outnumber airliners 60 to 1.*

Orange-suited Ted Hart, 23 years a test pilot, recalls barnstorming days for the author's family as they inspect planes ready to fly. It takes but 40 hours flying time to qualify for a private license. Today 280,000 Americans hold one.

oven, took an ear-splitting tour of the Amana Woolen Mill beside an old mill stream.

At the Amana Furniture Shop we watched artisans hand-craft tables, chairs, chests, clocks. "No mass production here," the foreman said. "We build to the buyer's design and use the time-proven method, hand-fitted dovetail with mortise and tenon." In the rubbing room a woman patiently worked a desk top to a soft, deep-lustered finish. "A factory might take five minutes to make a desk like that in veneer and sell it for a hundred dollars less. But we use solid walnut or cherry and spend 38 hours on it."

Most of rural Iowa lives the same unhurried way, growing corn, feeding cattle, hanging on newscasts that begin with the most important item, the weather. Nick joined the ranks of these working Americans, helping an uncle cut oats, while I visited Frank Gothier's mink ranch in Anthon.

Known to many as "Mr. Mink," the onetime homesteader and trapper snared his first mink at 15 and pioneered in breeding high-quality black mink. Still active in his 80's, he maintains a herd of 16,000. As his gloved foreman dragged a black bundle of fury from its cage, the tall old-timer explained that "ordinary pelts average $25 at auction, but an ebony like this fetches more than $100."

At 60 skins to the coat, I quickly calculated why Vera couldn't afford a black one.

Buckled up again, we headed south into Kansas, crossing the old Santa Fe Trail in country as quiet as when Coronado explored here in 1541. Tornadoes had played tag with us in western Iowa, and we cast a wary eye for twisters while crooning a chorus of "Over the Rainbow." After miles of nagging by the little girls, we pointed in desperation to an unpainted clapboard farmhouse whizzing by and cried in unison: "There's Dorothy's house!"

Wichita, "Air Capital of the World" and home of Beech, Cessna, and other aircraft companies, showed us Rosie the Riveter in slacks and kerchief and the highly mechanized business of building private planes. Sharp contrast to operations at the small pretzel company we searched out

HAMMER BLOW ON A BOX OF SALT GIVES A QUAINT TWIST to pretzel making in Indiana (below). Tell City's four pretzel workers join more than a million Americans who process our food.

Hickory-smoked meats tantalize eye and nose in the Amana Colonies (opposite upper), a cluster of villages amid the broad fields of Iowa. Young eyes peer into an 1858 smokehouse big enough to hang 3,000 hams, which would carry the old German religious community through the winter. Time is the essential ingredient, Amanites believe; they still cure bacon a month. Savory sausages made in the olden way include schwartenmagen, *a headcheese. In Middle Amana a century-old hearth oven supplies wayfarers with hot bread and rolls.*

A survivor of the scores of utopian societies that sprang up in 19th-century America, Amana turned from communal ownership to private enterprise in 1932. Its people formed a corporation, snuffed out lard lamps and tallow candles, switched to electricity and the making of freezers, and reaped dividends from their industry.

At the Battle Creek Sanitarium in Michigan, Dr. John Kellogg in the late 1800's preached "Biologic Living," banned meat, tobacco, and alcohol, served "vegetarian steaks" and "coffee" concocted from burned bread, bran, and molasses. Patients fed up with the regimen sneaked off to a "meat speakeasy" in town, puffed stogies at a nearby firehouse. Seeking a tasty, easily digestible substitute for bread, John and brother W. K. Kellogg ran boiled wheat through rollers and baked what came out—the first flakes in a blizzard that showers America with some six pounds of ready-to-eat cereal per capita every year. Today visitors tour the modern plant where a flake-flipping color inspector (opposite lower) and 4,400 other workers put the snap, crackle, and pop into breakfast food.

ROBERT W. MADDEN

in Tell City. Named for William Tell, national hero of Swiss immigrants a century ago, this Indiana town on the Ohio River comes alive at night with young folks driving up and down Main Street honking their horns at each other.

In the Tell City Pretzel Company's garage-size factory, Russell Kessler, great-grandson of one of the town founders, introduced us to his fellow employees, Mrs. Gertrude Glann on the bagging machine and young Norman Nugent at the glazing tub. He stepped over to what looked like a large meat grinder, stuffed in a huge wad of dough, and flicked a switch. Strips of dough came rolling out. All three workers twisted them into the familiar pretzel shape.

"You do it," said Mr. Kessler, handing Vera a strip. It seemed to come alive in her hands, jumping and wriggling. "That little twist," she frowned, "is harder than it looks."

With Mr. Kessler busy at his oven, setting screens of unbaked pretzels on revolving racks and extracting browned pretzels, we crowded around Mr. Nugent. He lifted a screen of pretzels from the steaming caldron of caustic soda, set it under a large wooden box full of salt, then picked up a hammer and gave the box a solid whack. Salt—just enough—showered from the sieved bottom, covering the pretzels. "How's that for automation?" he grinned.

Solid whacks on the baseball diamond are hopefully built into famed Louisville Slugger bats by Hillerich & Bradsby in Kentucky's largest city. The art of bat-turning, passed on from generation to generation, transforms a square, 40-inch-long billet of ash or hickory into a graceful round club. Workers then dunk it in a bath of wood filler, sand it smooth, and brand the barrel with a trademark. The Ty Cobbs, Babe Ruths, Musials, Mayses, and Mantles have taken over from there.

About the time the Hillerichs, father and son, began catering to the kings of swat in Louisville, up the Ohio in Cincinnati a different sort of batter had turned into something that would become as familiar to Americans as baseball—Ivory Soap. In 1878 a Procter & Gamble worker let a blender run too long and beat air into a batch of white soap. Customers who bought the bars weren't any more surprised than the company to find that "It floats!"

Since then Procter & Gamble has been repeating the mistake—on purpose. At the Ivorydale plant a machine whips the float into hot liquid Ivory, squeezing out an endless white rail that is sliced into bars, hardened in coolers, stamped, and wrapped.

Armed with gift packs of soap, shampoo, and toothpaste, we left Cincinnati to its lowering skies—a jump ahead of

BULLSEYE! THE PRACTICED HAND OF A QUALITY TESTER at Procter & Gamble squeezes off a silvery squirt as detergent ingredients come clean (opposite) in a Cincinnati plant. Quality control lapsed one day in 1878. The happy result: floating soap. Then a church-going Procter read in Psalm 45: "All thy garments smell of myrrh, and aloes, and cassia, out of the ivory palaces, whereby they have made thee glad." Next day he named the soap Ivory.

Sharp eyes, sensitive hands inspect threads (below) in Iowa's Amana Woolen Mill. Watchdogs of industry, inspectors crawl into half-finished cars, lather up on random samples of soap, set phones ringing nonstop to catch flaws.

Wise tourists invest a dollar in Plant Tours *(send to Supt. of Documents, Government Printing Office, Washington, D. C. 20402), and check ahead. Some plants—like Bethlehem Steel in Maryland—bar children; many close for vacation.*

ROBERT W. MADDEN

PYREX
500 ml

FORTY THOUSAND GOOD TURNS A DAY KEEP A RIDDLER BUSY at Taylor Wine Company in Hammondsport, New York. To send sediment to the neck for easy removal, he "riddles" or rotates each bottle of champagne a quarter turn; mask shields him from an occasional burst. In cool cellars the winery warms visitors with a welcome—and a sample.

a killer tornado—and pressed on to Akron. There we sought the story of a milky sap, first gathered by pre-Columbian Indians, that bounced into the 20th-century automotive age as the rubber on which we roll. For safety, the tire companies don't allow children under 12 in the factories. So after we had all explored the Goodyear exhibit hall, Anne turned baby-sitter while the rest of us peered over the shoulder of a man wrapping cord plies around a drum and mopped our brows in the 110° temperature as curing presses, like huge waffle irons, shaped, vulcanized, and labeled tires in one searing squeeze.

Glass matches rubber as one of man's most versatile materials, and nowhere I know of is its story told so graphically as at Corning, New York. In rolling land south of the Finger Lakes we let the sun burn off the morning mist from the meadows before losing ourselves in the wonders of the Corning Glass Center. In the Hall of Science and Industry the kids hammered glass pipe on wood, squeezed a glass coil, marveled at the artistry of a "lamp-worker" making delicate animal figures from glass rod over an open flame.

In the Steuben factory we watched workers move in a ritual about their glowing furnaces, shaping liquid glass into decanters, vases, and bowls. We followed the crystal to the grinders, the polishers, the engravers. An inspector lifted an elegant bowl—a $125 item, the catalog said. Turning it slowly before the light, he found a flaw. I flinched as he smashed the bowl to pieces.

Our final stop was Chocolatetown, U.S.A.—Hershey, Pennsylvania—and the kids could almost smell the candy 200 miles away. Chocolate mixing-vats large enough to swim in, rafts of warm bars vibrating to expel air bubbles, machines wrapping Kisses in foil, caravans of canned cocoa. Truly a wonderland of wishes—and frustrations. At one rhythmic, clacking conveyor, Anne, who at 15 is a waist-watcher, groaned, "Listen to that machine. It's saying calorie, calorie, calorie." And outside she generously divided her own gift candy bar between her little sisters, who have no waists, only middles.

Home at last, sunk in a deep chair, I stared in wonder as my wife industriously unpacked bags and put things away. In mid-stoop with a bundle of clothes for the washer, she caught my gaze. Raising an eyebrow, she asked softly: "Haven't you ever seen an American at work before?"

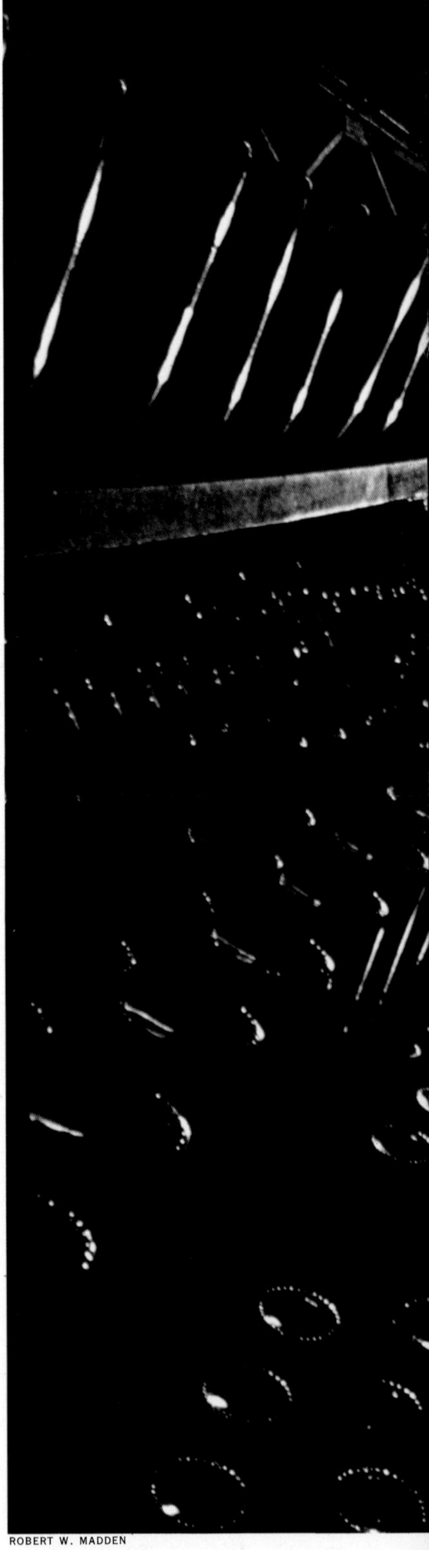

ROBERT W. MADDEN

EXPLORING CAVES FOR THE FUN OF IT, SPELUNKERS CRAWL TO

Underground Adventure

By Charles E. Mohr

Head to toe, cavemen squeeze through a slit at Longhorn Cavern State Park in Texas; Ted Spiegel, Rapho Guillumette

MARTIN ROGERS. OPPOSITE: JAMES PAPADAKIS

Descending the cool throat of Missouri's Blindfish Cave, Ken Dearolf and I came to a stream that fell away into a well-like chamber. Our flashlights showed water splashing on rocks 15 feet below. I posted Ken on the brink, tied a rope around a rock slab beside the waterfall, and started down, hand over hand.

The wall curved away, out of reach of my groping feet. Swinging like a pendulum, I arced over the falls, lost my grip, and fell to the floor of the pit. In pitch blackness, soaking wet, choking, bruised, I stood up and reached for the rope. It dangled just beyond my grasp.

Ken ran to the car to get a longer rope. While I waited, runoff from a sudden thunderstorm began pouring in through some unknown opening. The miserable little Stygian bathtub had no handle to turn off the shower; by the time Ken lowered a rope, water was lapping at my waist. I struggled up through a roaring waterfall.

We had violated basic rules of caving by embarking on a venture too complex for only two men and forgetting a standby safety rope. As a biologist, I had let my search for a rare blindfish block all else from my mind. I resolved never to let it happen again.

Such curiosity to learn how creatures survive in the lightless world below first drove me underground; but I do not endure the cramped miseries of playing mouse in a blacked-out Swiss cheese merely for the sake of science. I enjoy caving, along with thousands of others—teen-agers, housewives, businessmen.

Inner space—the nation's fabulous underground—is within a few hours' drive (and crawl) of most Americans.

GAPING GATEWAY TO A HIDDEN WORLD *leads a pair of spelunkers into Georgia's Blood Mountain. Caving's challenge—"mountaineering in the dark, upside down"—combines climbing and crawling, walking and wriggling.*

Beginners try "tame" holes, some 200 public caverns from Anemone Cave in Maine's Acadia National Park to Lava Beds National Monument at Tulelake, California. New Mexico's Carlsbad Caverns, king of caves, offers a three-mile hike with Park Service guides. Visitors boat on Echo River, 360 feet down, at Mammoth Cave National Park, Kentucky.

Seeping water at Crystal Ice Cave freezes into floor-to-ceiling icicles (opposite) 150 feet below Idaho sagebrush where lava fissures scar the earth. Such rugged caves demand hard hats and stamina, basic equipment for members of the National Speleological Society. Preservers and explorers—"Leave nothing but footprints, take nothing but photographs"—NSS spelunkers have probed 15,000 of the nation's estimated 50,000 caves, welcome newcomers primed for adventure in the winding depths (page 421).

BEAUTY, DWELLING IN DARKNESS, AWAKENS in the glow of cavers' lamps: Ribbons of rock festoon West Virginia's Probst Cave; a gypsum flower, its scale shown by a silver dollar, adorns an Ozark cave in Arkansas; in Endless Caverns, Virginia, stalactites glisten like stony icicles. Such formations, or speleothems, build from mineral-bearing water. Trickling through cracks and evaporating, it may form baconlike strips of calcium carbonate—the fat—and iron oxides—the lean meat. Droplets, dissolving limestone on their way down, deposit microscopic coats of calcite on cave ceilings to form stalactites; falling to the floor, the drops raise stalagmites. Seepage carrying gypsum oozes through porous rock like toothpaste, creating delicate floral patterns and needles that break at a touch.

In the Stygian fairyland of caves, spelunkers also find living wonders: creatures with the netherworld name of troglobionts. Most are blind and colorless. Some, such as insects and worms, eat food washed down from the surface. Or they feast on mushrooms sprouting from guano, the droppings of bats. Fish and salamanders devour their well-fed smaller neighbors. Scientists wonder what regulates life rhythms in a world unpaced by day and night or seasons. Some say cave tenants may respond to atmospheric or temperature changes that humans can't detect.

Exposed nerve endings on lips and head lead the eyeless cave fish (opposite) to its prey. The Ozark blind salamander begins life with eyes and plumelike gills; as it matures, eyelids fuse and gills disappear. The big-eyed cave salamander (opposite) lurks in the twilight zone just inside cave entrances—preying on the blind.

Every state except Rhode Island possesses known caves. All you need to begin is a hard hat, dependable light, and good company. And, if a past president of the National Speleological Society may reveal his bias, you'll discover the latter in any one of the society's 125 local chapters, which we call grottoes. You'll also learn to do your part in protecting our fragile underground realm, with its unique fauna, from misguided collectors, pollution, and litter. There are still towns and factories that dump waste into caves without realizing that seepage may eventually contaminate precious water supplies.

As a spelunker (from the Latin *spelunca,* cave) you will find your own reason for entering the underground. A chief attraction, I'm sure, is simply that cavern exploration is fun, an acceptable kind of hide-and-seek for grown-ups. But the true cave crawler also seeks adventure, the unknown, the thrill of discovery.

Discovery? Listen to spelunker Bill Varnedoe recall the 1961 exploration of Fern Cave in Alabama. He and his party had followed a stream 400 feet underground, then stopped. The stream plunged into a huge black well.

"There was so much mist we couldn't see bottom," Bill said. "The real puzzler, though—there was no roar as the water hit. We threw in some rocks. Not a sound! Finally we flung down a 40-pound boulder. Four or five seconds

LEFT AND CENTER RIGHT: ARLAN R. WIKER. BELOW: EARL H. NELLER. LOWER RIGHT: HOWARD N. SLOANE. LOWER LEFT: DAVID S. BOYER, NATIONAL GEOGRAPHIC STAFF

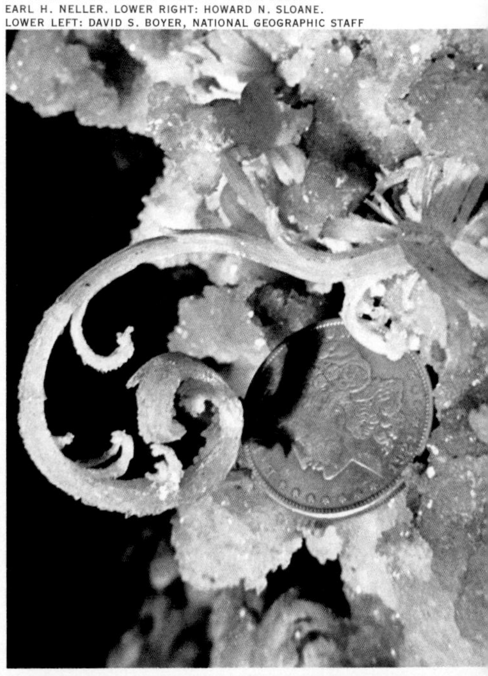

later we heard a thud." When finally plumbed, Surprise Pit measured 426 feet, the height of a 39-story skyscraper! It ranked as the deepest vertical underground drop in North America until the discovery in 1968 of 510-foot Fantastic Pit in Ellison's Cave, Georgia.

Spelunkers obey a cardinal rule: "Never go caving alone." They do not fear the collapse of a cave; the formations are remarkably stable. Dangers lie in human negligence and faulty equipment. The caver depends on nylon rope that will hold a ton. He backs up his carbide head lamp with a flashlight and fresh batteries, a candle and waterproof matches. He wears gloves, non-slip boots, snagproof clothes, and carries food concentrates and "spelunk junk"—pitons, mooring pins, sturdy wire ladders.

Bob and Bart Crisman of Abilene, Texas, tackled a sheer 220-foot pit in the Guadalupe Mountains of New Mexico using ladders. They linked four together with clasps to reach a shelf 130 feet down. Bob made it to the ledge and looked up to follow the slow descent of his brother, a firefly on a spider's web. When Bart was about 35 feet above the landing, a clasp parted. Reaching out, Bob broke the force of Bart's fall and kept him from rolling off the ledge to the pit floor 90 feet below. Bart, an ankle broken, was strapped to a wire-frame litter and hoisted out by rescuers.

Astute spelunkers, in the showery summer season, post weather watchers outside any cavern with a sinkhole or

HUMAN PENDULUM IN AN EERIE PIT, A SPELUNKER DROPS INTO DEVIL'S SINKHOLE, a Texas cave 310 feet deep. In parachute harness, he rides down a rope tied to a car bumper; a lighter line steadies him. Millions of bats live in the Sinkhole, emerging in twilight as "an undulating plume of blackness 75 feet thick and rearing 150 feet above the prairie." Emitting high-pitched, sonarlike beeps, they compute the echoes and swoop upon unseen insect prey.

Author Mohr, first U. S. scientist to band a cave bat, hunts other underworld creatures with a kitchen strainer (below) in Missouri's Piquet Cave. Beneath the Ozarks, rivers wind through a labyrinth of caverns formed by acid-charged water leaching away minerals.

Limestone, dolomite, or gypsum wall most American caves. Along coasts, waves sandblast cliffs, gouging holes. Molten rock flowing from volcanoes leaves blisterlike grottoes and sinuous tunnels like the Far West's lava caves. Nature's work takes time: 10 million years for Mammoth in Kentucky, one of the largest known cavern systems.

HOWARD N. SLOANE. OPPOSITE: ROBERT W. MITCHELL

Wall-to-wall stalactites spike the ceiling of Lone Hill Onyx Cave, Missouri, where a spelunker

valley-bottom entrance. Rain may bring sudden flooding. I remember how dry my mouth went in a wet Texas cave when a friend and I became conscious of a persistent noise. Starting as a whisper, it grew into a roar.

"Flash flood!" we exclaimed almost with one voice. There was no escape—nothing to do but stand and face our fate. Then around a bend came, not a racing wall of water, but a mass of flying bats. The whir of their wings, amplified by cavern echoes, sounded like a stream rushing through a tunnel. Things in caves are not always what they seem to be. And comical situations often pop up in the dark.

My friend Howard Sloane will never forget the day he went belly whopping through shallow water in New York State's mile-long Tri-County Cave near Albany. Howard felt a violent twitching beneath his body. He catapulted out of the water, slammed against the low ceiling so hard that he was stunned, and fell back on the wriggling

HARVEY R. JACKSON

stands in wonder. Lit by man, the cavern reveals the weird splendor that lurks in the underworld.

creature. His head clearing, he summoned courage, reached into the pool—and pulled out a four-pound catfish, washed in by floodwaters.

Hordes of enthusiasts, of course, enjoy caving without having to squirm through black alleyways. Many caves offer deluxe tours on lighted, manicured paths, on tramways, even in boats. Countless caves, including some developed as commercial attractions, have yet to be fully explored; and spelunkers will never stop shinnying, slithering, and clawing into that awesome silence and mysterious blackness.

Even in the Space Age the cave beckons. Rocket engineers like Bill Varnedoe find adventurous recreation and challenge in the hundreds of caverns that underlie the region around the Marshall Space Flight Center in Alabama. "Most of us," Bill once said, "can only dream of going into orbit. But tomorrow any of us could be standing where no man has ever been before—in a new cave."

By Bern Keating

ON HIDDEN BAYOU AND HISTORIC BYWAY A SHUNPIKER SAVORS A

Sojourn in the South

The shrimp boats were late, and by midmorning I nodded, drowsy from squinting into the wintry sun that glinted on the shimmering bayou at Lafitte. Cajun roustabouts sprawled on the dock, softly chatting in the French dialect of coastal Louisiana.

I had rented a shrimper's launch to explore Barataria Bay, once the haunt of Jean Lafitte and his band of corsairs, a land still hidden from the glitter of New Orleans. Most tourists who stroll the city's French Quarter do not realize that another fascinating Gallic world lies only 25 miles away. They can skim this world by taking a bayou cruise from New Orleans. Or they can plunge into it, as I did.

That's the way to see much of the South—shunpiking. Leave the turnpikes; take to the backwoods, the bayous. You'll meet amiable people. But you may have to go out of your way. I was musing on this as I watched the Lafitte watermen ignoring me, for my city clothes marked me as beneath their notice. They talked in what they fondly believed was a private language. But, with my French-Canadian rearing, I could eavesdrop shamelessly.

A big-eyed Cajun girl, a toddler of no more than three or four, tussled with a fisherman, punching him playfully on the biceps. The child picked up a stick and the playing got rough. I couldn't keep quiet.

"Lâche le bâton, méchante," I scolded.

The conversation stopped. All heads snapped around. A fisherman asked in English, "You speak French, mister?"

"Since I am a baby."

"But you not from Lafitte!"

Like figures in a poet's fantasy, children of the Acadians whirl through a dance at Longfellow-Evangeline Memorial State Park in Louisiana; Charles Harbutt, Magnum

"Oh, man, people speak French lots of places besides Lafitte," I assured him.

"Yes. I guess you right. Lafayette, Houma, Thibodaux, all them Loozeean places the folks speak French, so they tell me." Thus reminded of the widespread use of the Gallic idiom, the dockers resumed their drowsy hum, but now they amiably included me. I spoke French; ergo, I was a Cajun.

Cajunland (or Acadiana as some call it) is a strip along the Louisiana Gulf Coast running from the Texas border to the mouths of the Mississippi. It comprises a brackish marshland, plus a narrow band of drained farmland and a low-lying ridge just inland of the marsh. Some two centuries ago French colonists settled here after the British expelled them from their homes in old Acadia, modern Nova Scotia. Today descendants of the exiles preserve their piquant culture in a land that produces a wealth of game, rice, sugar, fur, oil, and cattle—some almost aquatic.

In Cameron Parish, just across the Sabine River from Texas, Cajun cowboys fasten hidalgo spurs on rubber boots to chase steers across soggy grasslands. But Cameron isn't Texas, and the people's accents show it. I arrived at the town of Cameron, the parish seat, during the annual winter fur festival. The waterfront teemed with merrymakers. On the flatbed of a truck a powerfully built man wielded an oversize jackknife, skinning a nutria in a race against time.

"What's in it for the winner?" I asked a spectator. "Championship of Loozeean," he answered, never taking his eye off the flashing blade. Later I watched an oyster-shucking contest, wild goose calling, and gumbo tasting. Always prepared for a

"FAIREST OF ALL THE MAIDS," *Evangeline in bronze sits atop the grave of Emmeline Labiche, the Acadian girl who may have inspired Longfellow's poem, at St. Martinville, Louisiana. Separated from her lover after the British drove French settlers from Acadia (Nova Scotia) in 1755, Emmeline later found him in Louisiana, wed to another —and died of a broken heart. Longfellow's tragic tale differs: Silver-haired Evangeline finds her Gabriel dying in an almshouse.*

Scions of tragedy, Cajuns find nature bountiful. Sunset frames a fishing boat on Barataria Bay bound for a harvest of shrimp from Gulf of Mexico waters. Crimson bouquet of crawfish gleams in a Lafayette restaurant; Cajun cooks serve this freshwater cousin of the lobster fried, baked in juicy patties, and simmered in bisques and gumbos.

CHARLES HARBUTT, MAGNUM

PELTS, POLE, AND PIROGUE MARK **A BAYOU SAUVAGE,** *a swamp rover. Acadians copied the Carib Indian piragua, hollowing a cypress log to make their "peashell in wood." Today Cajuns pole pirogues made from pre-cut planks, ideal for creeks choked by sedge, palmetto, and "bayou orchids," or water hyacinths. In bayous—swampy streams or side channels—Acadians tend oil rigs and cattle, raise sugar cane, and harvest pelts of mink, muskrat, otter, nutria. From Baton Rouge, Acadian Trail markers guide motorists down backroads to Cajun charms. Sportsmen find a paradise: bass abound, waterfowl darken the skies, deer browse on jungled isles. In a labyrinth with few landmarks, the wise hunter hires a guide.*

Bayou folk leaven hard work with hearty fun. At festival and fais-dodo (Saturday night dance) Cajun couples two-step to the tunes of accordion and fiddle. But the swamp is ever close; even the brooch at a beauty's throat recalls its denizen, the crawfish.

get-together, Acadians honor a variety of products with festivals. Adults and children alike jam the streets of towns to dance the Cajun two-step. Mardi Gras season provides more merriment: Masked celebrants raid chicken yards (with permission) seeking ingredients for huge gumbos. *Café noir,* the inky coffee Cajuns drink a dozen times a day, welcomes the raiders at each stop.

I found the marshlands as fascinating as the high-spirited people. In vast wildlife refuges wintering waterfowl form in great rafts half-hidden by marsh grass. Skeins of the wild geese and ducks crisscross the skies. Marsh wrens and yellow-throated warblers flit through the reeds. I scarcely needed binoculars to cram a notebook with sightings of species new to my bird list.

One night I helped capture an alligator for a wildlife study. Everywhere the swamp glittered with the silent fire of phosphorescent plankton. Minnows dashing for cover trailed wiggling darts of light. When we boated the gator, my companion tried to put me at ease: "That business about a gator's tail breaking your leg—don't you believe it. A gator's tail is no stronger than my arm."

Once a marsh dweller invited me to lunch—"A pot of gumbo with some nice young crab in it. Maybe a little fresh mullet to fill out the corners. You skin the fish, I brown the roux, and we both say some prayers the supper

FRANKE KEATING. OPPOSITE: FRED MAROON, PHOTO RESEARCHERS, INC.

don't kill us." When the roux—a mix of oil and flour for thickening—was ready, he added onion, bay leaf, Tabasco, and the fish. It was superb. A true gumbo, by the way, is not a French dish but a combination of African and Indian recipes, Spanish seasonings, and Cajun culinary genius.

Like their French cousins, bayou people talk interminably about pleasures of the table. At almost any restaurant I found gumbos, jambalayas, bisques, stews. Of the variety of game and seafood that goes into them, Cajun cuisine prizes above all else the little *écrevisse,* crawfish. Light, tangy, it delights the palate in its many guises.

How long can this exotic pocket of Gallic individuality last? Even the Cajuns wonder. But I think it will survive; it is made of tough stuff. Surely the American gumbo still needs the pungent flavor of the Cajun world.

North of Cajunland a manicured parkway invites shunpikers to another part of the Old South, also with its own flavor—the Natchez Trace. Winding some 500 miles between Natchez, Mississippi, and Nashville,

DENNIS J. CIPNIC, BLACK STAR (ALSO OPPOSITE). UPPER: CHARLES O. HYMAN, NATIONAL GEOGRAPHIC STAFF. LEFT: SLIM ARRONS

CLOPPING FEET, AN ANTIQUE STREET, A DIXIE BEAT, BON APPETIT! *Minutes away in time, a world apart in tempo from the Cajunland bogs, New Orleans enchants the visitor with Creole charm—part Spanish, part French, part Old South. A carriage ambles through the* Vieux Carré*—Old Quarter—where pirates and planters roistered, where the bygone beckons in antique shops and filigreed balconies. On Bourbon Street, named for kings, the music's sweet, the rhythm swings—and* laissez faire *reigns. Dinner: perhaps at Antoine's, with pompano and wine; or* al fresco, *with romance, at the Court of Two Sisters (left). Midnight: the French Market for doughnuts,* café, et bonne nuit?

Tennessee, the Trace (old French for "a line of footprints") played a turbulent role in America's westward expansion. Today a long strip of national parkland with a road down the middle—the Natchez Trace Parkway—preserves sections of old trail and a sense of frontier days. The Park Service has raised historic markers, added picnic areas and campsites, and stands ready to answer visitors' questions.

I began on the waterfront at Natchez, for that was where most old Trace journeys started. Beginning about 1785, "Kaintuck" flatboatmen floated into port to sell cargoes and rafts, have a little fun, then walk or ride home.

I felt their presence at Natchez-Under-the-Hill, bordered by riverbank and a 200-foot bluff. Here boatmen with a year's earnings in their pockets rubbed shoulders with gamblers, bushwhackers, thieves—the scum of the Mississippi Valley. Most of the old sin town has been swept away by the river. But a faded sign on a ruin advertises the Jesebel night club; nearby is the Blue Cat.

How different is the city atop the bluff, with its many ante bellum houses. Here in 1800, after the Trace was designated an official post road, dignitaries gathered to greet the first rider with the "Great Mail." He galloped into town, opened his pouch—and found a mass of pulp, all that remained after weeks of sloshing through swampland. For years the postmaster often had to announce, after waiting for the mail six weeks, that "the rider is presumed lost," a victim of the perils of the Trace.

Six miles east of Natchez lies Washington, capital of the Mississippi Territory during the Trace's heyday. At Washington in 1813 Maj. Gen. Andrew Jackson received the amazing order to dismiss his 2,070 Tennessee militiamen, bound for New Orleans to guard against the British. The redheaded frontiersman raged, then organized the long walk home, giving his horses to the sick and walking himself. His men marveled at their frail-looking commander and called him Old Hickory, a nickname that stuck. Two years later he finally reached New Orleans, whipped the British, and led a victory march up the Trace.

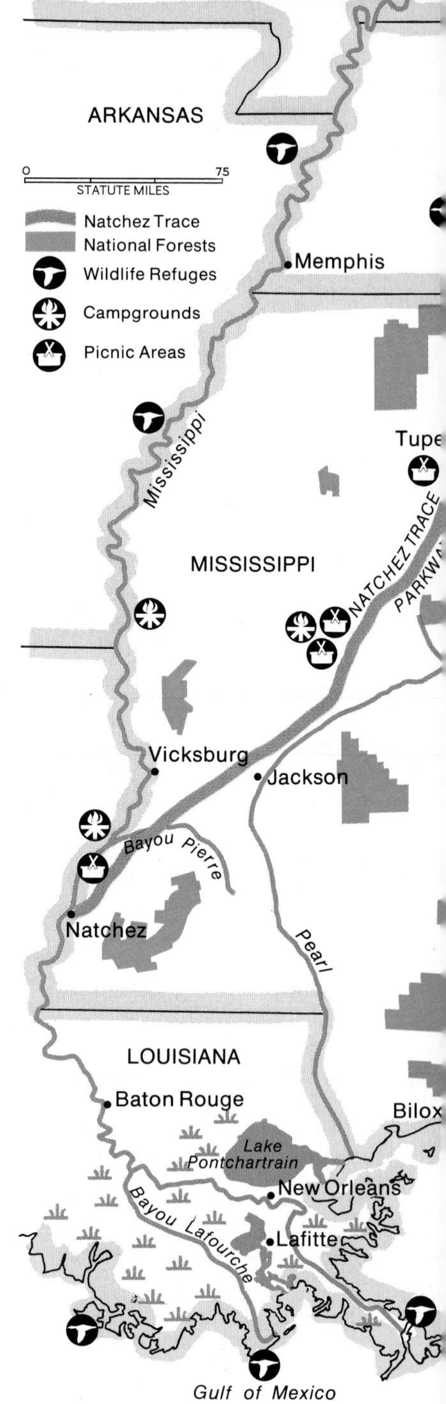

CHARLES HARBUTT, MAGNUM. OPPOSITE: WINFIELD PARKS, NATIONAL GEOGRAPHIC PHOTOGRAPHER. MAP BY MONICA WOODBRIDGE, GEOGRAPHIC ART DIVISION

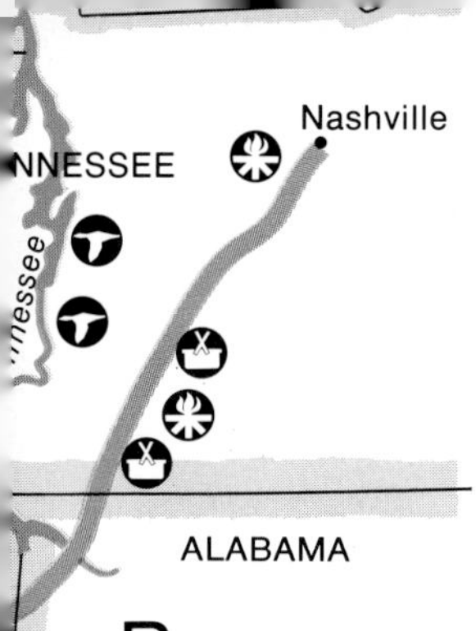

Nashville

NNESSEE

ALABAMA

Ribbon of legend across the heart of the Old South, the Natchez Trace Parkway tracks the footsteps of trailblazers and traders, preachers and footpads. In the late 18th century, as Acadians spread through the bayous west of New Orleans, flatboatmen floated down the Mississippi, sold cargoes at Natchez, broke up their boats to sell for lumber, and tramped the wilderness highroad toward Nashville and the Ohio Valley. Steam power came—and went. But in Natchez, intoxicated with its past, river bluffs still echo to a sternwheeler's toot (below), and each spring belles in hoop skirts welcome visitors to ante bellum homes and magnolia-scented gardens (right).

Near Natchez the Trace skirts Emerald Mound, raised by a vanished Indian people, and Mount Locust Stand, a restored inn where Trace travelers slept three in a bed. History's scenes haunt the woodlands: Aaron Burr fleeing treason charges; Audubon sketching birds; Andrew Jackson, dubbed Old Hickory for his toughness, leading his men during the War of 1812.

Today a National Park Service road threads the Trace for most of its 500 miles. Picnic sites, campgrounds, and nature trails provide glimpses of foxes, opossums, and quail that seek sanctuary in the protected areas beside the parkway.

Business deals, as well as military campaigns, kept Jackson shuttling along the Trace. Just north of Washington he built a log cabin and trading post. There he honeymooned with the irresistible Rachel Robards—both unaware that her divorce from her first husband was not final. They married again, but whisperings pursued Jackson.

Passing through Port Gibson, where the old trail serves as the main street, I came across a lonely grave near the parkway—the resting place, it was said, of a "ride and tie man." One ride and tie man, the story goes, was a Kaintuck who lost his money at Natchez-Under-the-Hill and joined another boatman to split the cost of a horse. The first man rode till noon while the other walked. After lunch the morning rider tied the horse to a tree, and, leaving it for his partner, walked till the afternoon horseman caught up with him. According to local gossip, one member of this team, tired of walking, dissolved the partnership with a knife.

SUNLIGHT HALOES A HORSEMAN in a shadowy world where the Natchez Trace still ruts the land near Port Gibson, Mississippi. Buffalo hoofs, Indian moccasins, watermen's boots, and horseshoes wore down the trail. In places riders could not see the ground above—nor the cutthroats lurking there. President Jefferson in 1806 called for a road "twelve feet in width, passable for a wagon." Today's parkway opens vistas, takes driving out of the rut. With speed limits strictly enforced and a ban on trucks, antique auto buffs (opposite) find the road ideal.

The treacherous murder—if it really happened—was only one of thousands of bloody deeds along the Trace. The money carried by boatmen on their way home attracted gangs of cutthroats. At Jackson, once a tiny trading post and now the capital of Mississippi, I read the original court record of the trial of the Samuel Mason gang. They had terrorized the Trace until, at last, the severed heads of two of Mason's henchmen were hoisted on poles by the trail as a warning to other transgressors.

Ten miles northeast of Jackson a dam across the Pearl River has created a 30,000-acre lake. It flooded the Trace—old and new—and required rerouting the parkway. On weekends it seems that the entire population of Jackson has taken to the water for fishing, sailboat racing, or poking around in the inlets. I was tempted to join them.

In this area I came across a remnant of the Choctaw nation that once owned two-thirds of Mississippi. In 1830 the tribe signed away its rights and trekked to Oklahoma. About a thousand elected to stay and farm the tract of ancestral land promised them. Few got any land. Today most of their 3,600 descendants work for planters around Philadelphia, just east of the Trace. There they hold their annual fair and dream of the planned Indian pleasure park that will attract visitors with plenty of wampum.

Half-tame deer ramble across the parkway around French Camp. I saw one old jalopy make a skidding 180-degree turn to avoid a magnificent buck. In the 70 miles to Tockshish I spotted three kinds of hawk, a Mississippi kite, and a red fox. Once a covey of quail forced me to stop until they decided which side of the road they preferred!

FRANKE KEATING. LEFT: B. ANTHONY STEWART, NATIONAL GEOGRAPHIC STAFF

At parkway headquarters in Tupelo, rangers showed me how to approximate the old Trace route by car where the parkway has not yet been built. In the northwest corner of Alabama I rolled on across the mighty Tennessee River—harnessed by dams and a popular recreational waterway—and into the state of Tennessee. In Meriwether Lewis Park I paused at Grinder's Stand, an old Trace hostelry. Here in 1809 the explorer stopped on his way to the Nation's Capital to report on his activities as governor of Upper Louisiana. Only three years earlier he had returned in triumph as co-leader of the Lewis and Clark Expedition. But now, accused of financial irregularities, he was deeply depressed. On the night of his arrival at the inn he was found shot. He lingered painfully for hours, begging his servant to end his life. At the time it looked like suicide. Decades later came talk of a murder scholars still debate.

Beyond Duck River, where the parkway remains unfinished, you can drive 24 miles on the old Natchez Trace—if, warns the Park Service, "you are venturesome and curious, willing to risk getting stuck or lost." In this hilly region the Trace split

In the "Notchey" Trace backcountry of Mississippi and Tennessee, tilled fields spread like golden

CHARLES HARBUTT, MAGNUM

corduroy, the mule still has his place, and faces mirror the strength and character of the pioneers.

into a lowland route for the dry season, a ridge road for times of flood. I rode the delightful ridgetop by horseback, pausing at the occasional clearings to gaze down on rich bottomland. After a day in the saddle I fell disastrously off my diet with country ham, grits, red-eye gravy, biscuits, and molasses—real Tennessee cooking, much the same sturdy fare that fed Trace travelers in the old days.

Vestiges of the Trace rut suburban lawns in Nashville, where an aged oak that once shaded a blacksmith shop marks the end of the old road in Centennial Park. But Trace country does not really end there. It ends at the Hermitage, east of the city, the home of the Trace's greatest hero.

At Andrew Jackson's quiet mansion the turbulent frontier days seem far away—but only because rugged warriors like Jackson tamed the wilderness, and their devoted women brought gentleness and civilization to the raw new country. Here, at the end of my Southern sojourn, I felt closer to those old pioneers—and to their descendants in the bayous, backwoods, and hills.

THE TRACE ENTWINED THE LIVES OF ANDREW JACKSON and his Rachel. He married her near Natchez and took her up the trail; when scandal marred their union, his love remained as steady as the pistol he drew defending her honor. The Trace terminates in Nashville, but history lovers continue on to the Hermitage (left), Old Hickory's home 13 miles east of town. There in his later years he read Scripture by candlelight, his dead Rachel's image always near; in 1845 he went to rest by the side of the light of his life.

B. ANTHONY STEWART, NATIONAL GEOGRAPHIC STAFF. PORTRAIT OF ANDREW JACKSON, COURTESY OF THE HERMITAGE. OPPOSITE: CHARLES HARBUTT, MAGNUM

60 Nevertheless, as the will of
God is in heaven, so let him do.
CHAP. IV.
THEN took Gorgias five thousand
footmen, and a thousand of the best

 Carefree houseboaters dock for a dip in Old Man River near McGregor, Iowa

LIFE ON THE MISSISSIPPI: A RAFT OF FUN IN A

Home, Sweet Houseboat

Story and photographs By Albert Moldvay

You can drive a houseboat if you can drive a car, river people say. They're right. My family and I, landlubbers all, proved it on the Upper Mississippi. At McGregor, Iowa, a ferry landing that became a town, we rented a house that bobbed on the twin hulls of a 39-foot catamaran. After a short shakedown cruise skippered by our landlord, I took the wheel. We loafed upriver against a three-knot current and charted a carefree cruise to anywhere.

The houseboat seemed to have the same idea. In those first few hours, while I taught myself how to drive a boat, it seemed as if we were going anywhere but in the middle of the buoy-marked channel. "Don't worry," a veteran houseboater had cheerily advised us. "At eight miles an hour you're not going to hit anything very hard." But worry I did: Was it red buoys to starboard, black ones to port. . . ?

A few miles above McGregor I felt confident enough to steer out of the channel. I aimed for an inlet that, according to our charts, led to a boat ramp. Nearby loomed a site to explore, Effigy Mounds National Monument, a prehistoric Indian burial ground humped by heaps of earth in the shapes of bears and birds.

S-c-r-a-a-p-e! Some Indian spirit or the eternally restless Mississippi had put bottom where the chart makers had put water. Our 40-horsepower outboard churned sand. I cut the motor, rushed from the pilothouse, and, suddenly realizing I was a

RIVER ROAMERS SET A CAREFREE COURSE WHERE THE UPPER MISSISSIPPI *keeps on rollin' along. At bluff-browed Lansing, Iowa, a marina crooks a beckoning finger downstream. In such havens houseboaters sign aboard rented craft for a taste of Old Man River's history, solitude, and fun.*

Young Andrew Moldvay takes a turn at the helm, chart at one elbow—and perhaps at the other the shade of young Sam Clemens whose "one permanent ambition" was to pilot a riverboat. In a craft Clemens never knew, an outboarding Odysseus steers his mates past a sunning siren, the author's daughter Susan, whose home floats astern while she visits the neighbors.

captain, began barking orders over the shouts of Susan, 13, and Robert, 12. Andrew, our 14-year-old, took my place at the wheel. My wife Bernice manned an oar and I grabbed a boathook. While we pushed off against the bottom, Andrew cautiously started up and shifted into reverse.

We eased back into the channel and back into the spell of the Mississippi—Mark Twain's "shining river, winding here and there and yonder, its sweep interrupted at intervals by clusters of wooded islands threaded by silver channels." It was as tranquil as he had known it, with "nothing to hang a fret or a worry upon."

Late in the afternoon we found a silver thread to a lake on one of those islands. We anchored near shore, making neighbors with another houseboat. Installed in my captain's chair on the roof deck, I contentedly ended a captain's day. My first mate and her apprentice cook went on duty in the galley. (With its gas range and refrigerator though, they insisted it was a kitchen.) My deckhands, taking well-earned liberty, piled aboard the 14-foot dinghy we towed, and with a growl of its six-horsepower motor put-putted off to explore the marshes.

The sun lay low and golden in a sky as wide and still as the water. A flock of mallards dipped overhead and I heard the rustle of their wings. Then I was one with Twain, enraptured by his river and "the unobstructed splendor that was flowing from the sun."

After dinner I turned from the river's splendor to its challenge as a watery highroad. In the glow of our cabin

"ENGINE ON A RAFT WITH $11,000 WORTH OF JIG-SAW WORK AROUND IT," scoffed critics of ornate steamboats in the 1800's. Wary Indians called the first one "fire canoe" in 1811; river folk who heard its hiss feared a comet just sighted had hit the water. Soon multi-decked palaces on hulls so shallow they would "float on dew" touched wharves in a blaze of music. Locals gaped at marble statues, cut-glass chandeliers, lavish menus (one offered 24 imported wines, another 36 desserts), and shows: animal acts, melodramas, minstrels.

Showboat tradition lives aboard the University of Minnesota's Gen. John Newton *(opposite). Cast of* The School for Scandal *waves from the renovated sternwheeler. One port of call: Stillwater, where logrollers (below) evoke lusty days of Paul Bunyan and Whisky Jack. Other legends live 1,000 miles south; on the Lower Mississippi Mark Twain's keelboatman bellowed as he brawled: "Whoo-oop! I'm the old original iron-jawed, brass-mounted, copper-bellied corpse-maker. . . . I'm the man they call Sudden Death. . . . I take nineteen alligators and a bar'l of whisky for breakfast."*

JOHN

light I studied the U. S. Army Corps of Engineers' instructions for "locking through" the Mississippi's massive stairway of locks. Ahead, I knew, lay my next test as a river captain: the barrier of lock Number 9.

We had not given much thought to the locks we had seen as we looked down on the river during an earlier tour of the Mississippi's realm. On bluff-hugging roads and bridges alive with wind-song our charts were highway maps; our buoys the green-and-white pilot-wheel markers of the Great River Road. It twists along both banks of the Father of Waters, from the source at Lake Itasca in northern Minnesota to the Gulf of Mexico.

Motoring alongside the Upper Iowa River, a tributary of the Mississippi, we got a warm *velkommen* at the Nordic Fest in Decorah, Iowa. Norse Americans in Old World garb served up a smorgasbord of music and folk dancing. Nimble-footed logrollers dazzled us at Stillwater, Minnesota, where we joined in celebrating Lumberjack Days. In St. Paul, where the Mississippi drops 74 feet down the Falls of St. Anthony, we climbed aboard the old sternwheeler, *Gen. John Newton,* showboat stage for drama students.

Now, on our houseboat, we were in a drama of our own: *Open Sesame,* Act I. The lock towered before us like the walls of a fortress, its massive gates closed. We had spied the traffic signal atop the lock as we neared the lower approach wall that paralleled the river. A red light meant "stand clear"; a green one, "enter lock." What greeted us was an amber light: "approach lock." We did, as close as we dared. Nothing happened. We circled, plaintively blowing our horn. The gates stayed shut.

Enter another houseboat. It passed us, glided confidently up to the approach wall, and pulled alongside a line dangling there. A passenger tugged the line, a horn blared, and

GOOD TIMES GALORE AWAIT ASHORE *when the Nordic Fest explodes in Decorah, Iowa. Then boaters let the waters roll on without them as they munch* varme pølser *— Norwegian hot dogs — and watch children of the Norsemen dance in the streets (above left). Folk tunes flow from a lanky* lur *(above), wooden horn of shepherds who tooted to hail comrades or shoo predators in the old country. When the sun retires, square dancers (opposite) swirl by storelight far into the night.*

Fairs and festivals and shrines of pioneer days tempt sailors to swap helms for steering wheels along the Great River Road. Beribboning both sides of the river, it spans 10 states from palm to pine country, extends beyond the Mississippi's source to link with the Trans-Canada Highway.

Touring the river afloat offers sterner challenge — and always has. Keelboats struggled upriver by sail, oars, poling, or bushwhacking — crews pulling on riverbank shrubs. In 1811 the New Orleans, *first of the steamers, left the Ohio and ran a gantlet of snags and sandbars. She made it to New Orleans but lacked the power to return north. Boaters still respect Old Man River and stick to the safer stretches.*

the gates swung open. *That's* the horn you're supposed to blow, I told myself. Sheepishly, we followed the leader into the lock pen. The gates ponderously closed behind us and we found ourselves bobbing at the bottom of a concrete bathtub 110 feet wide and 600 feet long.

Enter the lockkeeper, some 20 feet above us on the pen wall. He dropped us two lines so Bernice and I could steady the boat during lockage. Rapidly, water started to fill the lock, and Act II began. A gust of wind caught our towed dinghy, which wedged itself between the wall and our houseboat. Bernice teetered; only her desperate grasp of the line saved her from a dunking. Susan coaxed the dinghy aft. Robert jumped into it, holding it astern by grabbing another line on the lock wall.

Rising closer to the lockkeeper's smiling face, I felt obliged to explain. "Our first lock," I shouted up to him. "That's easy to see," he laughed. Then came the curtain line. "But don't feel bad. I've seen worse."

Tons of fish filled the tightening seine dragged through acres of river by a crew from the Iowa State Conservation Commission. Men in chest-high waders plucked out the specimens they wanted. The boys and I had never seen such a haul: crappies and bluegills by the thousands, walleyes, saugers, and northern pike. Up from the bottom, the Mississippi's vast catfishery, came flatheads, channel cats, bullheads. Buffalofish swarmed amid leaping carp and living fossils: the toothless, long-beaked paddlefish, and the air-gulping bowfins that can live all day out of water. When the conservation crew released their bouillabaisse, we needed no urging to try for keepers.

Fishing from the houseboat, we didn't have the outlandish luck of Huck Finn, who claimed a 200-pound catfish—"as big a fish as was ever catched in the Mississippi, I reckon." But we could honestly say we catched a hefty string of crappies and scrappy bluegills.

We cruised for days through the Upper Mississippi River Wildlife and Fish Refuge, a 284-mile swath of hills and bluffs that hem the river with wilderness from Wabasha, Minnesota, to Rock Island, Illinois. Great blue herons ruled tall river-bottom trees. Patches of white—common egrets—took wing in the green marshes. White-tailed deer lapped the water of ponds, the gifts of busy beavers.

Some days the Mississippi was a great lake buffeted by winds that whipped up whitecaps. I struggled to hold a heading. Even with binoculars I had trouble finding the wave-washed buoys. Once, leaving the channel, I luckily heard the frantic shouts of a fisherman on shore: "Wing

"A LONG, RUFFLED TRAIL THAT SHONE LIKE SILVER"—*Mark Twain's river flows through another night of "soft distances . . . dissolving lights" and a campfire's glow. The Moldvays and houseboat neighbors make a midstream sandbar a Shangri-La. Some 500 named islands dot the Mississippi between St. Paul and St. Louis, a stretch where 27 lock-and-dam barriers tame it for traffic. Misnamed towboats push packs of barges; a string's 30,000-ton load would fill 600 railway cars. A pack may find scant clearance in lock No. 9, but floating homes and pleasure craft (opposite) can ease through—seeking days and nights Huck Finn knew on his raft: " . . . they slid along so quiet and smooth and lovely."*

dam! Wing dam!" These rock jetties were built long ago to drive Old Big Strong's gnawing current from the banks and deepen the channel for navigation. But, lurking below the surface, the dams also rip hulls.

Houseboaters flock like gulls to the midstream beaches of sandbars created by river dredging. On one we had ridden out a storm in snug solitude, dozing off to the howl of wind and the pelt of rain on the roof deck. Now it was night again, a bright, starry night, and we had neighbors; Dick Kresin, his wife Frances, and five of their children, longtime river rovers, had anchored nearby.

We huddled around a driftwood fire, old friends in hours, because that's the way of the river. The kids made plans for a day of water-skiing and fishing. The adults drank in the glory of the night.

Passing boats winked in the darkness like fireflies. Once a blinding beam stabbed our sandbar as a barge train, pushed by a chugging towboat, rounded a bend. Then, suddenly, the river was still and dark. We leaned back like Huck Finn and gazed into a sky "all speckled with stars."

"You know," Bernice whispered, "I had forgotten there was a Milky Way."

"And I remember. . . ."
Iowa born and bred, a poet finds America's heartland at the fairgrounds. Share the sights and sounds and smells of the Iowa State Fair with

Paul Engle

Swirling lights of the midway begin a photographic tour of the fair by National Geographic's
Albert Moldvay

"I like the roundness of those shoulders, the graceful head, the strong set of the legs, and the alert eyes." An amplifier booms a man's voice from a wide-open door. "She's not too attractive in the hindquarters—and that udder isn't carried out to the corners the way it should be." Intrigued, I enter the building to see for myself. I agree. The Jersey cow has a graceful head.

I'd be surprised if she didn't have. For this is the Iowa State Fair in Des Moines, one of the best fairs in the land, a living museum which renews itself every August, as wholesome as home-baked bread. Nowhere else in the U.S.A. is there such a variety of perfected animals, such homesickness for the loved rural past combined with such ready acceptance of the mechanical present. Come to the fair. It's the most all-American thing you can do.

The nature of the fair is in the smells that tease your nose: baled hay in the horse barn, butter on popcorn, the many manures of many animals, grease of hamburgers, gasoline and diesel exhaust fumes, flowers in the horticulture building.

The fair is in its sounds, in the solid chunk of horseshoes against steel post and wet clay, in the whip cracks of the harness racers as they come down the stretch, horses' hoofs pounding, rubber tires zinging on the hard dirt track.

The fair enchants the eye. By day the Ferris wheel, both single and double, makes swinging circles over the ground, with the panorama of moving masses of people tilting under you. By night it spins a circle of glittering lights in the heavy midwestern darkness of late summer. Sometimes, when it stops, there will come from a swaying seat near the top the cry of a frightened child. In the poultry exhibit two roosters threaten each other, crowing their anger, the Barred Rock with his precise black and white markings like a pen etching, the Rhode Island Red glowing and ruddy.

No longer do I see the dust-covered buggies or the horses that munched hay under trees full with summer. In those days we came to look at animals, but arrived by animal too. I remember my boyhood chores, watering the horses and draping them with fly nets.

My uncle raced trotters, shouting at them, pleading with them—for they responded to human voices. Nowadays people in cars talk to other people, but back in buggy days we talked to horses. And when we tied up next to a strange steed, there was jostling and whickering among the high-strung animals.

Draft horses today show better. In the old days before a fair we took them right out of pasture and tried to get the harness marks off. Today they seldom know the touch of a rein. The gaited horses lift their quick feet as if the ring were burning. The ponies are fiery, accusing the air itself of being in their way.

In the cattle barn a girl in blue jeans, curlers in her hair, twists a curry comb to shape precise waves in the glossy coat of a black Angus steer. Tonight she'll be swinging in the dance at Teen Town.

Every breed of livestock shown has its queen: Miss Jersey,

Come to the Fair!

Judging hands feel for mutton as hopeful hands steady their Suffolk sheep.
Solid but not square teen-agers—one a queen, the other a winner—ribbon a champion.

Miss Guernsey, Miss Ayrshire, each from a family that raises the breed. Miss Holstein sweeps her eyes over her charges and sighs, "Aren't they beautiful! I'm so glad daddy didn't go into Shorthorns."

A row of sheep quietly awaits a judge's eye. His long fingers plunge quickly into the fleece and then, as he steps back for a final look at length of rump and depth of "twist" (where the hind legs join together), he sticks his fingers into his wide leather belt, its huge buckle decorated with a steer head and boots.

I watch a judge of hogs stoop to inspect the underside of a boar.

"What are you looking for?"

"Teats," he replies.

"Not very useful for a boar, are they?"

"Oh yes they are," he assures me. "If he doesn't have them, he may not transmit them to his offspring. Unless he has a full set, I disqualify him."

The fair has a language you won't hear in the ordinary business of your life. "That guy's got barn blindness," they say of a cattleman

Self-crowned ruler of the roost, a Black Minorca cocks an eye for his competition.

Step right up! It's only money, midway money—tossed for trinkets and spent for show.

who can see virtue only in his own animals. "That steer is gutty," an exhibitor says of an animal with an excess of stomach, "and if they keep on overfeeding it, the poor critter won't be able to walk across the slaughter yard." A huge man, no beauty, ambles by with a button on his shirt which reads: "Hogs are Beautiful."

The midway has its own raucous sounds: "The crowned heads of Europe and the bald heads of America could admire these girls." At the call of the barker the girls in the girlie show come out of the tent to tempt the customers. How can they possibly express temptation in the glare of the noonday sun, the tired faces, the bored hands and legs doing their endlessly repeated dance?

The games of chance put all the chance on the side of the visitor. "You win something every time!" The familiar cry is true, however insignificant the trinket you get. But there is always the chance that you

Fling a coin to win your best girl a prize she may treasure only for its memories.

might be so unlucky as to win one of those stuffed animals, dolls, or lamps on display. Along the midway you sometimes see a burly farmer, face tanned from the fields, uneasy in his away-from-home clothes, carrying a doll awkwardly under his arm, not knowing where at the house he can put this creature with her flamboyant dress, her flaming cheeks, her parted lips.

The greatest quality of the fair is its amazing variety. There is hardly a human interest which cannot find something here worth its time. Fashions? Here are the 4-H farm girls, each designing something with only her own figure in mind, not to be duplicated for anyone else.

The girls come from rural Iowa, from Gravity, Osceola, Morning Sun, Wapello. They produce attractive and contemporary clothes, but the judges also consider the entire background emphasized by 4-H: a girl's health, posture, her record book of all her activities, what

In the ring, a Tennessee Walker high-steps. Under the sun, a draft team pulls for prizes. Under canvas, the Toby Show teases slickers. Straw-hatted Toby: "Got to go oil the hogs." City Girl: "Yes, I heard them squeaking." Laughter: farm folk know oil's a remedy for mange.

her outfit cost and how she made it. The winner goes to the 4-H Congress in Chicago the weekend after Thanksgiving. How many models of high fashion today could appear wearing garments they had designed and made with their own hands? The girls look younger and more beautiful now—or else I am a lot older.

The boys and girls of the 4-H Clubs (Head, Heart, Hands, Health) are the most unknown and the most attractive, the hardest working and the most community minded in the land. What a variety of things they do! Two boys invented a "flushing bar" that would scatter pheasants ahead of a hay mower to avoid injuring the birds. Another spoke on the pollution of streams. A girl studied guinea pigs to see whether rock music played at the usual decibel level had any effect on hearing. It did; after prolonged exposure the guinea pigs couldn't even hear the call for dinner!

The newest thing is "Clover Power"—the spirit, symbolized by a gay pink and green button, that says it "isn't carrying home a blue ribbon," but "being satisfied only with your best."

When 4-H steers are sold, there are tears. The youngsters have fed their animals, tended them through illness, washed them, trimmed their hoofs. Even if an owner gets $1.30 a pound for a blue-ribbon winner instead of 27 cents, there are tears when a pet is led away to slaughter.

The boys judge meat animals on the hoof and as carcasses. Trained eyes look for conformation, trained hands touch the hide to estimate the meat underneath. Then the judgments are confirmed or rejected by

Miss State Fair graces the bounty of "the largest cornfield on earth"—Iowa.

"See yonder fields of tasseled corn . . . Where Plenty fills her golden horn, Iowa, in Iowa."

an examination of the slaughtered animal. In a sense, this is the single most important activity at the fair. All the wild rides that throw the young bodies (the older ones can't take it) up into the air and revolve or bump or swing them are a traditional part of the fair and change only in mechanical cleverness. But the fair began in the 19th century as a place for people who raised food—meat or plant—to exhibit their best. In a hungry world, that is still the basic fact here.

The first exhibitors wouldn't recognize the development in the things they raised. The corn is now hybrid, with yields five times greater. Growers covet awards for the best ears, for this is where it all begins, the primary feed that produces the meat we sink our teeth into. The marbling in beef, which indicates tenderness, comes from the corn and commercial feed consumed by the animal.

The old-timers would stare in amazement, too, at the intricate machinery—combines which can harvest any crop with hydraulic-powered levers moved by a man in a high cab equipped with a radio and air conditioning. Farmers whose fathers husked corn ear by ear with a metal-edged glove can sit in a cushioned seat in total comfort and pick six rows at a time, with a stream of golden grain pouring out of the spout.

The fullness of American life past and present is at the fair. Barbershop quartets sing out the old songs. The singers are young, but their audience is old and on its faces you can see the joy of anticipating the next line.

Some are city people of farm origin, back to look at the rural life they no longer live. Many are regulars, farmers who come year after year and camp on a hill that overlooks the grounds. Among the campers you hear the old banter as people renew friendships formed at the fair: "Hey, Joe, I see you didn't winter-kill!"

Tractors chug by, hauling loads of manure, bedding straw, high-protein feeds for livestock, more cunningly blended than the diet of a human baby. The miniature train puffs by, a gray-haired grandfather having more fun than the blond boy he holds.

Over at the old fiddlers' contest they're swinging out the tune of an old favorite:

On a Ferris wheel, a boy and his girl slowly round out the day.

I asked her, would she have some dance,
Have some dance, have some dance;
I thought that I might get a chance
To shake a foot with her. . . .
Buffalo gals, won't you come out tonight
And dance by the light of the moon?

Down at the barns, cows are lowing at their calves, pigs are grunting in disgust at being prodded out of pens and into show rings by farmers with canes, the hilarious pigtails twisting tightly in outrage; horses are whinnying from their stalls as other horses walk out to the ring, sheep are bleating in their strange voice which always sounds as if there were a little fear in it.

That uninterrupted whine, rising to a roar as you approach the grandstand, is the stock car race, the modified engines screaming as the wide tires throw out clods of dirt on the turns. Under the grandstand the ladies exhibit their jellies, pickles, crocheted shawls, cakes (one in the shape of a grand piano!). Anything done by hands is here—the map of Iowa worked out in seeds; the blacksmith with his leather apron pounding out cherry-red horseshoes; the art exhibit where some of the paintings are as bad as the worst calendar art and some are on their way to New York galleries.

The ladies' sewing looks very modern; I miss the bloomers which fascinated me as a 10-year-old. Another notable disappearance: the classes for the hand-painted nut sets. I remember when people sat around cracking and eating nuts from wooden bowls on which the womenfolk had painted flowers.

Do you want to know how to smoke fish? The Iowa State Conservation Commission, whose exhibit displays turtles, snakes, raccoons, pheasants, and skunks, has a pamphlet which will tell you.

Do you like barbecued meat? The men's cookout contest is smoking up a storm between the grandstand and the food tents. One man is cooking steak marinated overnight in lime juice, cherry brandy, and corn oil. There's turkey, pork, pheasant, lamb, each barbecued with the contestant's special formula. A downpour can't dampen the chefs' enthusiasm. They break out umbrellas—for the meat; the cooks themselves get soaked.

On the track, screaming stock cars speed round and round.

Judges skip breakfast to keep their taste buds in shape for the cookout. Watch their faces light up with a satisfying *Ahhhhh!* as they sample each offering.

The great time is the last evening. The circling rides stop. The sentimental music of the merry-go-round dies out, and the carved horses end their galloping. The cries of the barkers are stilled, the garish lights of the midway go out, and the city bands cease playing for the country kids. But lights still blaze in the barns. Down in the straw a foal born that day sleeps, its mother standing over it protectively.

Men walk our dead moon. Life walks in its many forms at the many-sided state fair. The fair is life. We live in it.

Going Places West

"America is West and the wind blowing," Archibald MacLeish's *American Letter* sings. ". . . in the eddy of clean air the smoke goes up from the high plains of Wyoming: The steep Sierras arise: the struck foam flames at the wind's heel on the far Pacific." The West wind sweeps a land of giants. Here we crane at trees 300 feet tall, 2,000 years old, spot a landmark rock a hundred miles away, explore a mile-deep canyon or a desert that spills over the brink of sight. We can drive all day in a single state or, standing, touch four. We can mount the Rockies on our highest auto road or cross Death Valley on our lowest. Parklands preserve the West's grandeur, her immense forests, her matchless mountains. The call to "Go West!" raised towns now ghostly, cities that dazzle, meccas of make-believe. On a Texas plain, computers guide flights to the moon. In a sun-baked pueblo, Indians keep sacred their living past. Beyond old frontiers new ones beckon—glaciers bathed in eerie northern lights, volcanoes smoldering over balmy isles of lei and luau.

"Vacationland" design by Tasi Gelberg Pesanelli, Inc. Sculpture by Don Turano, photographed by National Geographic's Robert S. Oakes

Going-places signposts spike Western peak and plain: With tent or trailer, stake your claim to a campground . Match wits with wily Western whoppers , or make your own splash in water sportlands, fresh or salty . Meet the first Americans at Indian reservations . Say "Howdy!" to the Old West in ghost towns, at rodeos, in storied outposts of badman and marshal . Stalk a wildlife refuge . Hike  or bike  on trails to adventure. Clamber up mountains   for breathtaking fun. Snow-time means go-time in white-mantled realms  where winter is king.

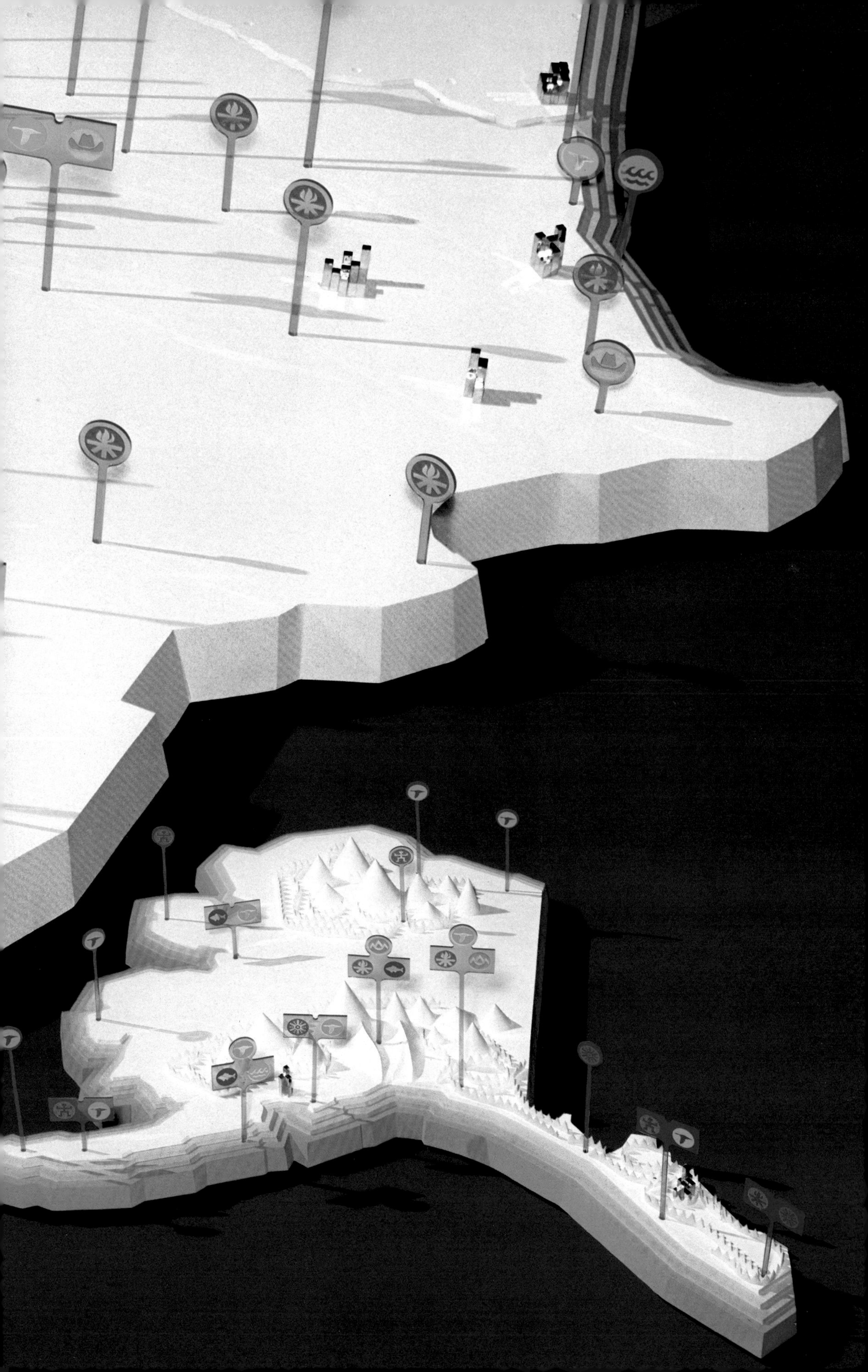

HAPPENINGS WEST

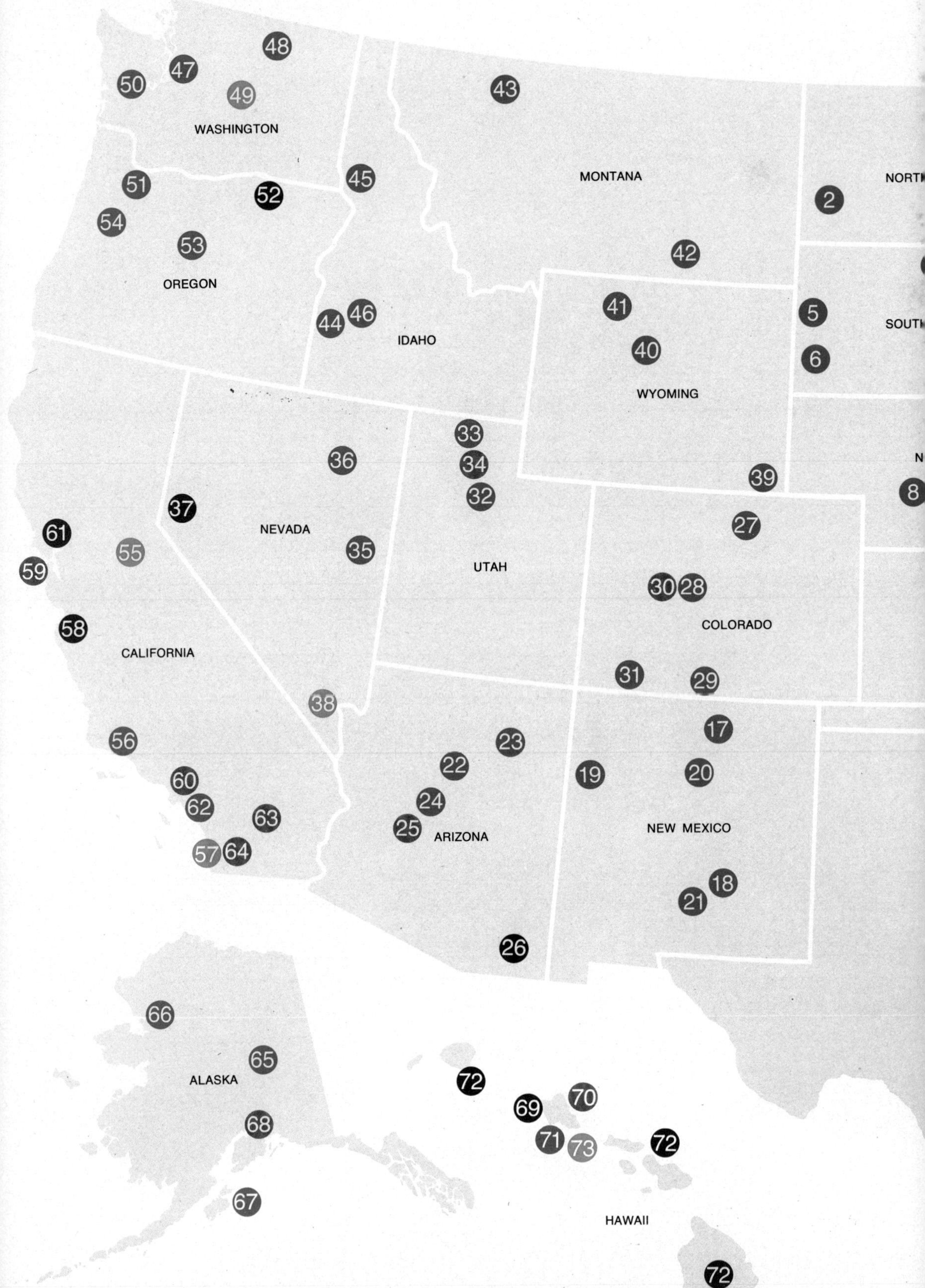

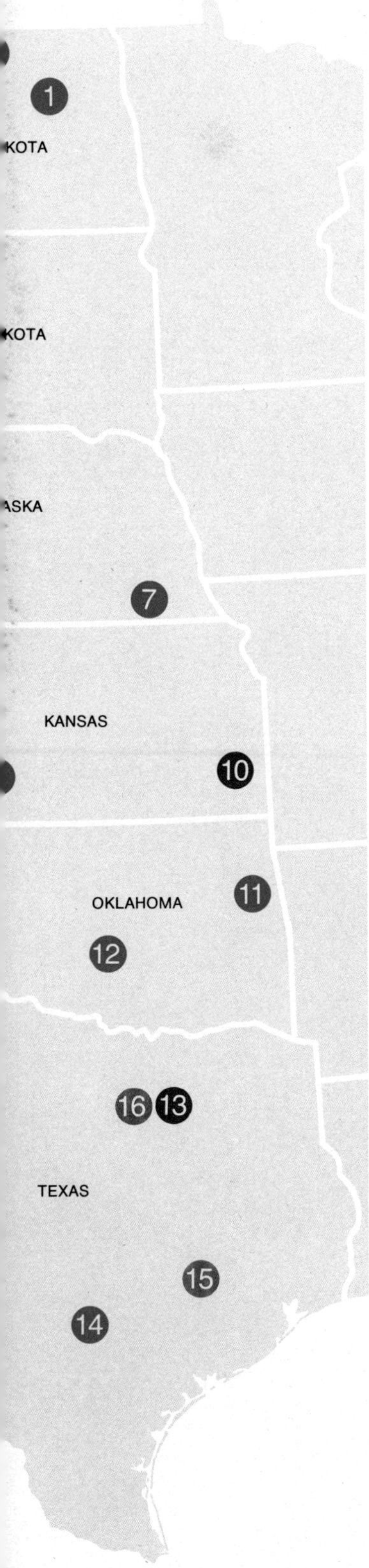

West is best—for roping and riding, barbecue and bear meat stew, Spanish fiesta and Chinese New Year, cowboy pageant and Indian powwow, Hawaiian hula and Eskimo hijinks. Name the season; somewhere out West you'll find fun and games: tribal dances in Oklahoma in summer, panning for gold in Arizona in winter, rodeo in Nevada in spring, winery tours in California in fall. Check state agencies on page 422 for exact dates.

NORTH DAKOTA: 1 Fort Totten Days, July; rodeo, Indian dances.
2 Ranch-O-Rama, Medora, July-Aug.; calf roping, bronc riding, branding.
3 Chippewa Pow Wow, Belcourt, Aug.; Indian rituals, rodeo.
SOUTH DAKOTA: 4 Sitting Bull Stampede, Mobridge, July; Indian powwow, parade.
5 Black Hills Passion Play, Spearfish, June-Aug.; drama of the Crucifixion.
6 "Hanging of Fly Speck Billy," Custer, June-Aug.; justice triumphs on saloon stage.
NEBRASKA: 7 Czech Festival, Wilber, Aug.; carnival, craft displays, old-time food.
8 Nebraskaland Days, North Platte, June; Buffalo Bill Rodeo, barbecues, shooting meet.
KANSAS: 9 Dodge City Days, July; Old West recalled in parades, rodeo.
10 Biblesta, Humboldt, Oct.; Bible times parade, group singing, free bean feed.
OKLAHOMA: 11 "Trail of Tears," Tahlequah, June-Aug.; drama of Cherokee exile.
12 American Indian Exposition, Anadarko, Aug.; tribes gather for dances, games, parade.
TEXAS: 13 Texas State Fair, Dallas, Oct.
14 Fiesta Noche del Rio, San Antonio, June-Aug.; Mexican rhythms at riverside.
15 Salt Grass Trail Ride, Brenham, Feb.; four-day, 85-mile horseback trek to Houston's Livestock Show and Rodeo.
16 Southwestern Exposition, Fort Worth, Jan.; rodeo, steer auction, milking contest.
NEW MEXICO: 17 Corn Dances at Taos, Acoma, and Cochiti pueblos, July.
18 "The Last Escape of Billy the Kid," Lincoln, Aug.; outdoor drama.
19 Inter-Tribal Indian Ceremonial, Gallup, Aug.; dozens of tribes take part.
20 Santa Fe Fiesta, Sept.; commemorates 1692 reconquest of town from the Indians.
21 Apache Gahan Ceremonial, Mescalero Reservation, July; dances around fire.
ARIZONA: 22 All-Indian Rodeo, Flagstaff, July; wild-cow milking, bareback pony races.
23 Hopi Snake Dance, Hopi Reservation, Aug.; live rattlers used in prayers for rain.
24 Frontier Days, Prescott, July; the country's oldest rodeo, with picnic, parade.
25 Gold Rush Days, Wickenburg, Feb.; panning for gold, Pony Express races, parade.
26 Helldorado, Tombstone, Oct.; historic town re-enacts its early days.
COLORADO: 27 Rock Hounds' Gem & Mineral Show, Fort Collins, June; collectors buy, sell.
28 Aspen Music Festival, July-Aug.
29 Mormon Pioneer Days, Manassa, July; street carnival, rodeo, dance.
30 Winterskol Festival, Aspen, Jan.
31 Navajo Trails Fiesta & Racing, Durango, Aug.; Brahman bull riding, quarter horse racing.
UTAH: 32 "Promised Valley," Salt Lake City, July-Aug.; drama of Mormon settlers.
33 "Uniting the Nation by Rail," Promontory, May-Aug.; golden spike pageant.
34 Utah Winter Carnival, Salt Lake Valley, Jan.; sled dog races, jeep hill climbing.
NEVADA: 35 Pony Express Days, Ely, Aug.; quarter horse and thoroughbred racing.
36 Basque Festival, Elko, July.; sheep "hooking" contests, costume parade, picnic.
37 National Championship Air Races, Reno, Sept.; aerobatics, closed-course racing.
38 Helldorado, Las Vegas, May; fair, barbecue, rodeo, beard-growing contest.
WYOMING: 39 Cheyenne Frontier Days, July; rodeo, chuck wagon breakfasts.
40 "Gift of the Waters," Thermopolis, Aug.; drama of Indian healing waters.
41 Buffalo Bill Cody Stampede, Cody, July.
MONTANA: 42 Custer's Last Stand, Crow Agency, July; Battle of Little Bighorn.
43 North American Indian Days, Browning, July; Blackfoot pageant, Sun Dance, parade.
IDAHO: 44 Snake River Stampede, Nampa, [illegible]; horse show, rodeo, parades.
45 Pi-Nee-Waus, Lapwai, Aug.; displays of Indian artifacts and crafts, friendship feast.
46 Basque Festival, Boise, July; dance the *aureska* to accordions, tambourines.
WASHINGTON: 47 Seattle Seafair, July; aqua show, hydroplane race, parades.
48 Stampede and Suicide Race, Omak, Aug.; horseback race over hill and river, rodeo.
49 Apple Blossom Festival, Wenatchee, May.
50 Bear Festival, McCleary, July; don your coonskin cap and eat stewed bear meat.
OREGON: 51 Portland Rose Festival, June.
52 Pendleton Round-Up, Sept.; rodeo, chuck wagon races, stagecoach rides.
53 Rockhound Pow Wow, Prineville, July; swap rocks, hunt agate, petrified wood.
54 World Championship Timber Carnival, Albany, July; tree climbing, ax throwing.
CALIFORNIA: 55 Jumping Frog Jubilee, Angels Camp, May; frogs hop for cash prizes.
56 Old Spanish Days Fiesta, Santa Barbara, Aug.; mission times evoked.
57 Kite Festival, Ocean Beach, March.
58 Butterfly Parade, Pacific Grove, Oct.; paraders welcome butterflies' return.
59 Chinese New Year, San Francisco, Feb.; gongs, fireworks, dancers hail lunar new year.
60 Tournament of Roses Parade, Pasadena, Jan.; floral floats precede the Rose Bowl Game.
61 Valley of the Moon Vintage Festival, Sonoma, Sept.; wine tasting, winery tours.
62 U. S. Surfboard Championships, Huntington Beach, Sept.; surf's up for the experts.
63 National Date Festival, Indio, Feb.; date delights, ostrich races, parade.
64 Pacific Coast Mid-Winter Soaring Championships, San Diego, Feb.; glider events.
ALASKA: 65 Golden Days Celebration, Fairbanks, July; parades, dancing, pageant.
66 Eskimo Games, Kotzebue, July; dances, kayak races, blanket-toss, muktuk eating.
67 "Cry of the Wild Ram," Kodiak, Aug.; outdoor drama of Russian colonization.
68 Fur Rendezvous, Anchorage, Feb.; sled dog race, parade, trappers' ball.
HAWAII: 69 Aloha Week, Oahu, Oct.; heritage in song, dance, pageantry, canoe race.
70 International surfing contests, Oahu, Dec.
71 Kamehameha Day, Honolulu, June; parade, public luau, hulas, pageantry.
72 Makahiki Festival, all islands, Nov.-Dec.; honors god Lono, celebrates harvest.
73 Lei Day, Honolulu, May; judging of floral garlands, sunset hula pageant.

MAPS BY SNEJINKA STEFANOFF AND VIRGINIA BAZA, GEOGRAPHIC ART DIVISION; ALASKA AND HAWAII OUT OF SCALE.

PARKLANDS

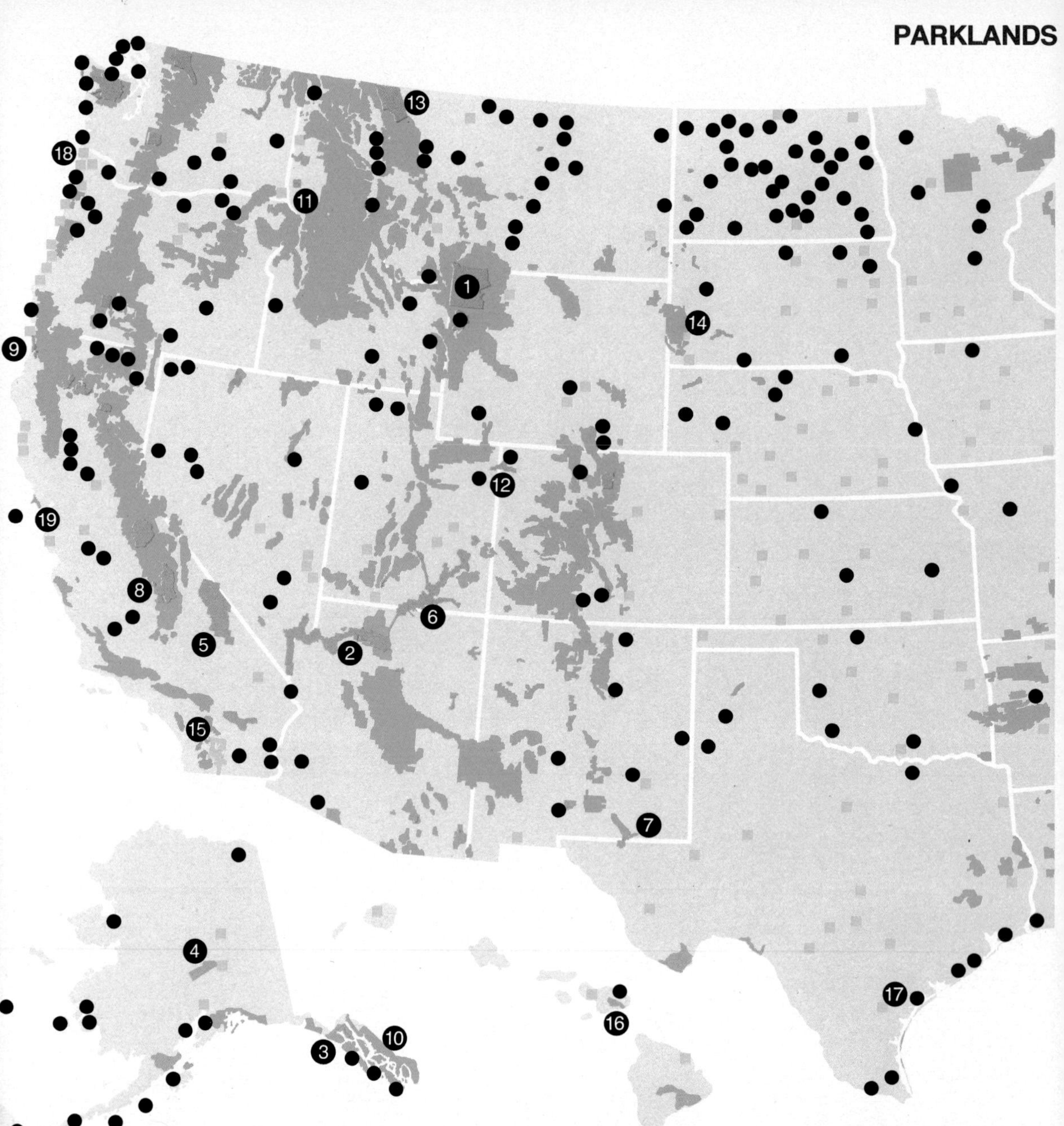

Western parklands and wildlife refuges ● feature superscenes, from the vast California desert to the icy roof of Alaska. Old Faithful reigns over geyser-dotted Yellowstone ❶, our first national park. The Colorado froths through earth's mightiest gorge, the Grand Canyon ❷. Ice cliffs crash to sea in Alaska's Glacier Bay National Monument ❸, and Mount McKinley National Park ❹ enshrines North America's loftiest peak at 20,320 feet—20,602 feet higher than the lowest point in Death Valley ❺. Rainbow Bridge ❻ boasts earth's largest natural span; Carlsbad Caverns ❼, largest underground chamber. Giant sequoias, the world's biggest living things, thrive in Sequoia National Park ❽; the tallest living things, in Redwood National Park ❾. Tongass National Forest ❿, the Nation's largest, offers 16 million wild acres. History comes to life on the battlefields of Chief Joseph and campsites of Lewis and Clark at Nez Perce National Historical Park ⓫. Prehistoric animals come to light at Dinosaur National Monument ⓬. Grizzlies live in Glacier National Park ⓭, buffalo in Custer State Park ⓮, bighorn sheep in Anza-Borrego Desert State Park ⓯. Vermillion iiwis wing in safety at Haleakala National Park ⓰; whooping cranes winter at Aransas Refuge ⓱. Clam diggers can scrape up their supper at Ecola Park ⓲ in Oregon, a state that preserves nearly all its coastline for the public. And Golden Gate Park ⓳ insists "Do walk on the grass.

National Park System
National Forests
State Parks, Forest Preserves

WATERWAYS

Westerners wrought engineering marvels to store precious water and harness its power. Man-made lakes may drown scenic land, but they spawn spacious playgrounds like that at Coulee Dam (1), a water-sports center of the Pacific Northwest. In the shadow of Mt. Shasta, vacationists pan for gold or water-ski at three sparkling lakes of Whiskeytown-Shasta-Trinity Recreation Area (2). Red sandstone canyons hem Lake Powell (3) behind Glen Canyon Dam. Lake Mead (4) jewels the desert; Lake Texoma (5) adorns the once dusty Red River Valley. Bighorn Canyon (6) and Flaming Gorge (7) offer wilderness boating; moose and elk patrol the slopes around Palisades Reservoir (8). Padre Island (9) and Point Reyes (10), national seashores, preserve unspoiled ocean beaches; surfers find the ultimate challenge off Hawaii's shores (11). And the Wild and Scenic Rivers System protects the free-flowing waters and natural charm of rivers like the Salmon (12), Rogue (13), Feather (14), Clearwater (15), and Rio Grande (16).

Water recreation areas

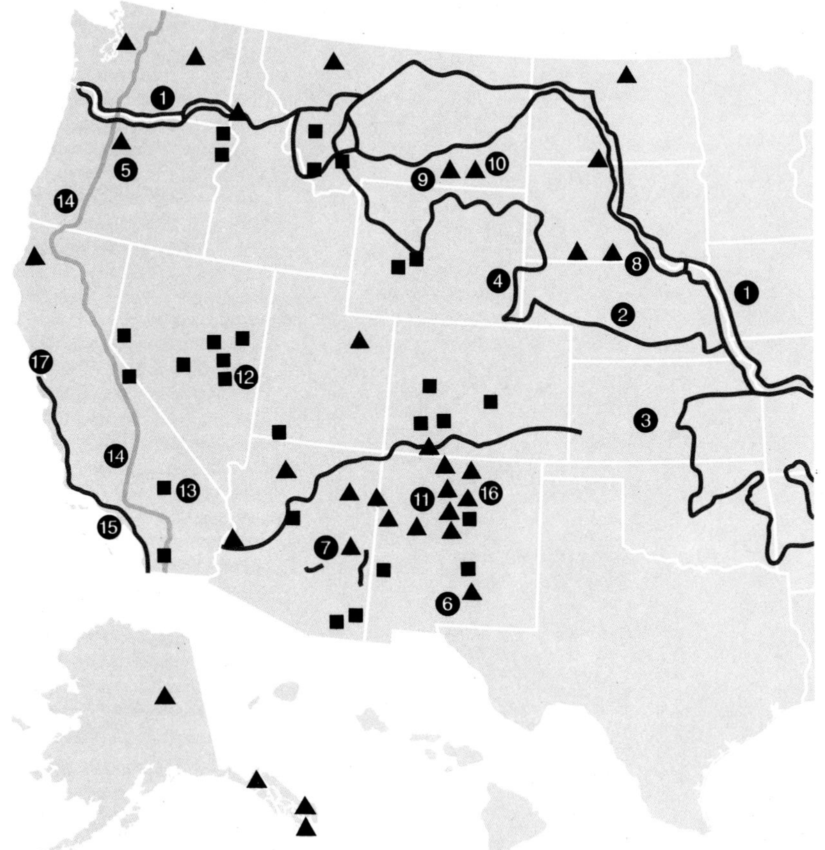

THE OLD WEST

Pile into the station wagon and follow the covered wagons to learn the West's lore and legacy—in silent ghost towns ■, in Indian communities ▲, along historic routes. Markers steer motorists over the Lewis and Clark Trail (1), to famed sites on the Old West Trail (2). Old forts (3) and wagon ruts (4) dot stretches of the Santa Fe and Oregon Trails. In Indian country you can sleep in a tepee at Warm Springs (5), ski with the Mescalero Apache (6), camp at Fort Apache (7), hunt or fish with the Sioux (8), the Crow (9), or the Cheyenne (10), explore 19 pueblos in New Mexico (11). Dig for old glass in ghostly Treasure City (12) or ride a burro and tour a silver mine in restored Calico (13). Rugged mountain scenery? Hiker and horseman take the highroad to beauty on the 2,350-mile Pacific Crest Trail (14), part of the National Trails System. Cyclists flock to bikeways at Azusa (15), Taos (16), and San Francisco's Golden Gate Park (17).

Wilderness Trails

Heritage Roads

Fiesta!

The river sleeps in darkness. Suddenly, spotlights lance the night and a brilliant stream of color pours out on the riverbank stage—gowns of scarlet, yellow, and green, sombreros of gold. Throbbing guitars blend with cricketing castanets, slim brown legs flash, skirts swirl in a fresco of music and motion.

It's *Fiesta Noche del Rio*—Party Night on the River, on the sinuous San Antonio, in the sprawling town that grew from the frontier Mission San Antonio de Valero. Mexican voices rise in lilting songs of love and laughter. *Olé!* Flamenco dancers burst upon the stage, stamping and snapping and whirling to the surging rhythm. *Olé!* Cheers in Spanish ring out from the grassy tiers as tourists succumb to the Latin mood, enchanted by the Old World flavor of a city deep in the Mexican heart of Texas.

Four nights each week in summer the river sparkles with fiesta at Arneson Theatre. By day the meandering waterway casts a quieter spell. Then visitors can see for themselves why Indians characterized it as a "drunken-old-man-going-home-at-night." And why old-timers, confused by a maze of streets that followed cattle trails, dubbed the town a "skillet of snakes."

Wandering river and serpentine streets weave together a city of steel skyscraper and adobe hut, of stetson and sombrero. Here come shoppers from south of the Rio Grande to see the latest in United States wares, and tourists from the north to walk amid shrines of history that stir memories of pioneering padres and proud conquistadors—and a bloody siege that Texas can never forget.

Along colorful streets, Mexican shops offer an array of exotic items: candy made of cactus, pumpkin, pecans, and loaf sugar; jerked meats; handmade tallow candles hung in bunches; cakes of charcoal for cleaning teeth. Peddlers hawk bundles of dry corn shucks for wrapping tamales—and roll-your-own cigarettes.

Before dawn the silence outside a downtown hotel gives way to a burst of laughter and bawdy song as sanitation men begin their rounds, beating out rhythm with trash-can lids. Roused by this raucous reveille, the visitor sets out to explore what boosters call "one of America's four unique cities." (So it seemed to the late Will Rogers. If pressed, San Antonians will name the others, "each with a flavor and character all its own"—Boston, New Orleans, and San Francisco.)

Inevitably the visitor is drawn to the river, the silvery thread hardly 50 feet wide that makes San Antonio a kind of one-canal Venice. In its leisurely course, it manages to travel 15 miles

A ROSY SWIRL AND MARIACHI MELODIES BRIGHTEN SAN ANTONIO'S "FIESTA NOCHE DEL RIO"; DEAN CONGER, NATIONAL GEOGRAPHIC STAFF

while crossing only six miles of city. Along one charming stretch, steps lead down from hot pavements to a cool river walk—the *Paseo del Rio.* Shaded by oaks and cypresses, low-hanging banana trees and bougainvillea bowers, strollers reflect the river's mood—slow, peaceful, quiet.

Bang! Bang! At times members of the Bexar County Gun Slingers shatter the calm with mock gunfights for the tourist trade. The bullet-pocked past comes less vividly alive on a plaque placed near a sycamore: "Legend says Mexican snipers used the fork of this tree as a vantage point from which to shoot Texans who came down to the river for water."

Tour boats glide on the river, some serving dinner by candlelight. Enchiladas, tamales, tacos? Diners can sample the peppery fare at restaurants that line the Paseo. Or they can zoom to the top of the 622-foot Tower of the Americas (symbol of the 1968 HemisFair), take in a 100-mile sweep of Texas, and eat in the highest revolving dining room in the Western Hemisphere.

San Antonio spent millions beautifying its river walk and the nearby *La Villita.* "The little village" dates from the 1700's, when San Antonio stood at the center of a Spanish realm that stretched from St. Augustine to San Diego. Amid the adobe walls of the restored La Villita, French scrollwork and a church built by Germans recall the immigrants from many lands who clustered here when Spanish power waned. In shops, some open to the square, weavers, glassblowers, and leatherworkers keep old arts alive.

During springtime's festive Night in Old San Antonio, La Villita opens its wrought-iron gates to masqueraders—businessmen squeezed into tight-fitting *charro* suits, their ladies in mantillas and lace. With a smiling *gracias* they take a taco or a steaming tamale cooked over charcoal and served by lantern glow.

Long ago, when it housed the families of the soldiers of imperial Spain, La Villita was called "Town of the Alamo." The remains of that historic mission-fort lie but a few blocks away. On an April Monday each year a reverent procession

AIRBORNE DANCERS AND WATERBORNE TOURISTS LIVEN FIESTA NIGHTS AND DAYS ON THE SAN ANTONIO RIVER; DEAN CONGER, NATIONAL GEOGRAPHIC STAFF

GOVERNOR'S PALACE FOUNTAIN AND MEXICAN MARKET REFLECT THE STYLE OF THE OLD SOUTHWEST; DEAN CONGER, NATIONAL GEOGRAPHIC STAFF

arrives at the hallowed site to begin the city's grandest festival, the Fiesta San Antonio. Mission bells toll as floral tributes are heaped high on the Alamo Plaza, scenting the air of the sun-dappled square. Thus the Lone Star State keeps fresh the memory of those days in 1836 when Davy Crockett, William Travis, Jim Bowie, and some 180 others held the Alamo against the 4,000-man army of Mexican dictator Santa Anna.

"I shall never surrender," wrote Travis. "Victory or Death." The defenders died to the last man. Not two months later, rallied by the cry "Remember the Alamo!", Texans defeated Santa Anna at San Jacinto and won their freedom.

Other San Antonio missions stand as shrines of peace, earliest links in the chain of churches Spanish priests forged in America. San Jose Mission, founded in 1720, is a national historic site. Its sisters grace the Mission Trail, where visitors can see a dam whose mortar (waterproofed, some say, with goat's milk) still holds, more than two centuries after it dried in the sun. A mile south, the only Spanish aqueduct in the United States carries its shining flood through *acequias*—irrigation ditches—to the mission fields that Indians once tended.

San Antonio's most beautiful building, the Spanish Governor's Palace, rose around 1749. History remembers it as the residence of the captain of the presidio. Tradition makes it the home of royal governors. Civic pride restored it. Once more utensils gleam, and corn and chili peppers hang from beams in the *cocina.* Intricate candelabra adorn a white stucco bedroom; at the foot of the bed sits a copper basin of Aztec design. His Excellency would enjoy the shade of his garden (above).

Three blocks west, the Mexican market beckons. Here women shawled in black *rebozos* offer tortillas, cafe singers strum guitars at tableside, shops display woven baskets, steer horns, clay pots, stone vessels, pungent herbs.

What to buy? Perhaps a chubby clay *piñata.* Take it home, hang it high, and whack it open. Down will come a shower of candy, sweet souvenirs of a fiesta city.

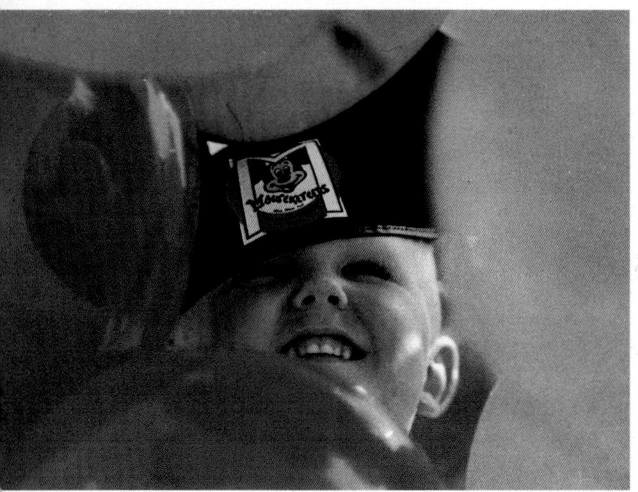

Disneyland... and Extra Added Attractions

A*rggahh!* The gorilla growls, pounds his chest, threatens to leap into our boat. A crocodile knifes past as we round a bend. Ahead, snorting hippos pop up, jaws agape. "We may not make it!" shouts the captain, emptying a pistol at the menacing menagerie.

Where are we? On a river in Africa? No. We're in California, 27 miles southeast of Los Angeles, in a town called Anaheim, in a state of mind called Disneyland. Doubt turns away at the turnstile. In this made-to-order world a teeming jungle, a pirate galleon, an Alpine peak are real; the past is nostalgic, the future hopeful. Outside? All make-believe!

Here a Soviet cosmonaut, fresh from the wonders of space, gets down to earth. He dons Mickey Mouse ears, takes a lunar-rocket ride, and exclaims, "I feel 25 years younger!" Millions of others know the feeling—four out of five who come here are adults. World renowned VIP's troop through this Very Incredible Place in such numbers that one observer called it "almost an instrumentality of American foreign policy." Faces furrowed by cares of state break out in smiles. For Mickey Mouse—Topolino in Italy, Mik-kii Hiiri in Finland, Mik-kii Ma-u-su in Japan—speaks the universal language of laughter. All visitors pass him at the entrance, limned in living flowers, grinning at his feat: He built a better man-trap.

Hop on the Santa Fe and Disneyland train to circle six wondrous realms. The steam engine chugs off from Main Street, U.S.A., whistles past Adventureland's jungle of live rubber trees, giant bamboos, brilliant hibiscus. As New Orleans Square flashes by, the sun glints on a pirate's cutlass. Suddenly it's Frontierland, and the steamboat *Mark Twain* answers our toot. Sleeping Beauty Castle heralds the happy realm of Fantasyland. Overhead, a monorail zips past a mighty Matterhorn of concrete, all 146 feet of it, to Tomorrowland.

We arrive back at Main Street, to the turn of the century. Kids in a horsecar wave at a white-haired man lost in reverie. But memory trots away, muffled. The horse wears rubber shoes.

Down gaslit streets we stroll to the Opera House, just in time to see its curtain rise on a familiar figure who sits and gazes in monumental majesty. "He blinked!" a boy whispers. "His hands

MOUSEKETEER REIGNS IN A MAGIC KINGDOM; THOMAS NEBBIA. OPPOSITE: MATTERHORN LOOMS ABOVE FANTASYLAND; DEAN CONGER, NATIONAL GEOGRAPHIC STAFF

CASEY JONES Jr. R.R.
CASEY Jr CIRCUS SPECIAL

moved!" says another. "He's getting up!" Hush. Mr. Lincoln speaks. . . . Sure, we know, an electronic effigy. And yet. . . .

A pair of ladies peer intently at the live swans patrolling the moat of Sleeping Beauty Castle. "Not real," one lady says. The other nods. Who knows where Disneyland's "illusioneers" draw the line, especially in Fantasyland.

Fluted columns and ornate grillwork draw us to a mansion. Haunted, they say. In small cars we plunge into darkness. Silence. Then the glow of dim lights—and screams, some from lips, some (hopefully!) from tapes. We pause at a great empty room. Out of the gloom a specter emerges, wispy, silent. His bony fingers ripple the keys of an organ, wrenching from it eerie groans as vaporous skulls float overhead. Phantom dancers whirl amid swooping bats in a cobwebbed ballroom. The cars grind into a black, creaking attic. A coffin grates open. Invisible fists pound on the door.

HOAX HIPPOS HARASS A SAFARI IN ADVENTURELAND; THOMAS NEBBIA. PHANTOM OF THE ORGAN (OPPOSITE) PLAYS GHOUL MUSIC IN THE HAUNTED MANSION AND (ABOVE) THE BIG BAD WOLF AND A LITTLE PIG FLANK A FRIGHTENED FRIEND; DEAN CONGER, NATIONAL GEOGRAPHIC STAFF

Sunlight dispels the wraiths, and we watch kids twirl like tops in the cups of the Mad Hatter's Tea Party. Nearby, the Mad Hatter himself, surrounded by squealing true believers, trembles rubbery jowls in mock fear.

The Matterhorn challenges us. Wedged in a bobsled, clutching the children, we surge up, around, and through the mountain. Now we zoom down the slope to splash to a stop in a glacial lake.

What next? An aerial romp with Dumbo? A whirl in Flying Saucers that bounce on air? Lured by a Jolly Roger, we pick piracy. Diners at the Blue Bayou watch as we board a flat-bottomed bateau to cruise through grottoes menaced by buccaneers. As we swirl into the dank underworld, shafts of lightning silver the sabers of skeletons clashing on a spectral ship. Wind howls in the rotten rigging. Thunder crashes like a salvo of cannon. Off to starboard a pirate's bones guard glittering piles of treasure.

We glide into a Caribbean port under assault by corsairs. Leering captors lead captive damsels past a sign: "Auction. Take a Wench for a Bride." Brigands gulp liquid loot, sack the town, finally put it to the torch. "Avast there, landlubbers! Hold on!" Dynamite kegs explode and our bateau lurches *up* a waterfall.

Marvelous actors? Marvelous robots, life-size dolls of valves and wires, created by what the illusioneers call Audio-Animatronics. Robot pirates,

TEACUPS WHIRL, ELEPHANTS FLY, SLEDDERS SHRIEK IN THE SHADOW OF THE MATTERHORN; DEAN CONGER, NATIONAL GEOGRAPHIC STAFF

robot damsels, real passengers.... *Really.*

A *live* Tinker Bell, harnessed to a cable, wings out of the pages of *Peter Pan* and soars over Sleeping Beauty Castle. Through a night lit by fireworks we also fly—in an aluminum gondola of the Skyway, aerial link between Fantasyland and Tomorrowland. There, in a sub of the Disneyland fleet, we hear "Dive! Dive!" (tape-recorded in a U. S. Navy submarine in action), and illusion takes us under. Don't expect mermaids, the skipper says, as we sail serenely through treacherous reefs ablaze with animated tropical fish. But somehow we nose impolitely into a mermaids' boudoir, where they don necklaces plucked from sunken treasure chests. Finally we pass what may be the largest sea serpent in the world. Certainly the largest cross-eyed one.

A voyage to the moon—by Apollo, it's still fantastic!—ends our sojourn in Walt Disney's land, a land of the future, past, and never-never. At the gates fantasy fades, doubt rejoins us; the kids are sleepy, their whining real. We're back in our world again.

Disneyland sprang from the brow of Hollywood, the hamlet that invented the dream factory. From one of its first film studios—a barn—came *The Squaw Man* in 1913; a year later D. W. Griffith produced *The Birth of a Nation,* and Hollywood, too, was born. Movieland lured the starry-eyed and turned a few into stars. Their fans followed, eyes bright as marquee bulbs, to glimpse glamor in the flesh. Hollywood soon had a word for itself: Colossal.

Today, usually in bumper-to-bumper traffic, movie buffs grind through the heart of the town that spangles their

BOGUS BUCCANEERS MIME THE PAST AND (OPPOSITE) TOMORROWLAND'S MOON ROCKET BLASTS INTO THE FUTURE; DEAN CONGER, NATIONAL GEOGRAPHIC STAFF

HOLLYWOOD BOULEVARD GLITTERS AND (OPPOSITE) CONCRETE BILLS THE STARS; THOMAS NEBBIA. LOWER: FRANKENSTEIN MAKES FRIENDS; DEAN CONGER, NATIONAL GEOGRAPHIC STAFF

dream world. On Hollywood Boulevard, they crane in vain to see the stars. Dad and mom, remembering, make the pilgrimage to Grauman's Chinese Theater. "Who's Ritz Bros?" a youngster asks, gazing down on three sets of hand- and footprints preserved in the sidewalk cement. Parents smile, perhaps a little sadly. They look for John Barrymore's concrete profile, step in the shoes of Rita Hayworth, trace Jimmy Durante's schnozzola and Joe E. Brown's mouth.

North of Hollywood Bowl the family finds common ground: Universal City,

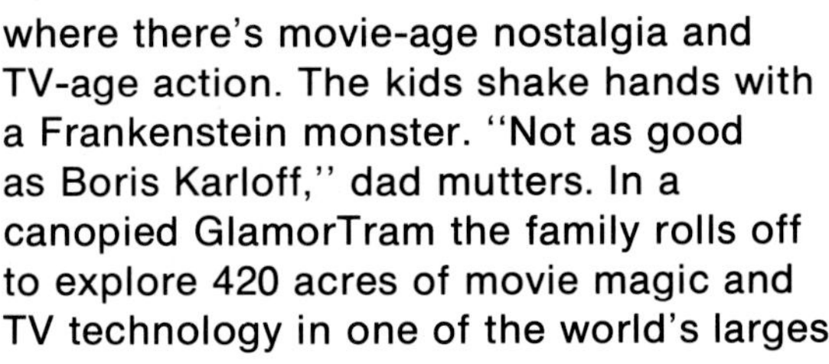

where there's movie-age nostalgia and TV-age action. The kids shake hands with a Frankenstein monster. "Not as good as Boris Karloff," dad mutters. In a canopied GlamorTram the family rolls off to explore 420 acres of movie magic and TV technology in one of the world's largest

GLAMOROUSLY GUIDED, MOVIE FANS MARVEL AT MAKE-BELIEVE IN UNIVERSAL STUDIOS; DEAN CONGER, NATIONAL GEOGRAPHIC STAFF

film studios. *The Phantom of the Opera* still stalks Sound Stage 28; on another set cameras grind next season's TV fare.

The tram guide, pretty enough to have stepped out of a big or little screen, gives her opening line, "Good morning!" —and the show begins. Special-effects admirals shell a sub that looks tiny to eyes but not to cameras. High-noon stillness haunts a town that launched a thousand Westerns. The tram goes thataway, to another era. A medieval tower looms ahead. Someone recalls *The Crusades.* A bleak Gothic dwelling grips a lonely hill. "That's the *Psycho* house," says the guide. "You remember—where Tony Perkins stuffed his mother?"

The tram passes a parked locomotive, a horseless stagecoach. "We're entering

Six Points, Texas," warns our hostess. "Watch out for flying lead!" Tom Mix made his first Universal movie here, and the six streets that give the set its name still echo to six-guns.

Mexico lies ahead. Across the way, Russia's onion-shaped turrets peer down on adobe walls. In minutes, the tram visits Lapland, Paris, India, San Francisco.

Off the tram now, we file through Lana Turner's dressing room. On a sound stage a technician quips, "We make our own weather in California," and rain showers down from overhead pipes. Lilliput comes alive. A biplane darts out of a painted sky. A stern-wheeler splashes across a lagoon.

Recall that roaring avalanche scene, boulders bounding down a hill? The roar is recorded, the boulders foam rubber. A child can toss them; in movieland he does. Some cutting-up goes on at the Visitors' Entertainment Center: "Paleface, you die!" cries an Indian leaping at a tourist. Gunfire erupts, and a well-drilled outlaw topples from a roof ... to a cushioned pad. And then it's

THE END

But no bill is complete without short subjects—and in California, aquatic animal acts provide some of the best. From Crescent City in the north to San Diego in the south, major aquariums net millions of sightseers.

A splashing sea circus erupts in the giant fishbowls at Marineland of the Pacific, 25 miles south of Los Angeles. Sea lions and dolphins perform in one arena, whales in two others. Some 4,000 creatures—from sharks to goldfish—glide past portholes encircling a 540,000-gallon tank.

In San Diego's Sea World, a two-ton killer whale named Shamu shows off before spectators with all the talent of her cousin the dolphin. Netted in Puget Sound in 1965 and fed regularly, Shamu grew tame and friendly.

AT UNIVERSAL STUDIOS' ENTERTAINMENT CENTER, FAKE ROCKS AND OUTLAWS TUMBLE; DEAN CONGER, NATIONAL GEOGRAPHIC STAFF. RIGHT: AN INDIAN TAKES MOCK REVENGE; THOMAS NEBBIA

"Reinforcement" trained—rewarded with fish—she leaps straight out of the water, gives a ride to a trainer who signals commands with a whistle (below), gives him a kiss. One description of *Orcinus Orca* bestows on it "the appetite of a hog, the cruelty of a wolf, the courage of a bulldog, and the most terrible jaws afloat." Yet into Shamu's jaws—studded with thumb-size teeth—her trainer puts his head!

Sea World lies in Mission Bay Park, a 4,600-acre aquatic playground created from marshland and offering a special place in the sea for every player: sailor, powerboat racer, swimmer, water-skier, fisherman. To the north, surf's up at La Jolla's Boomer Beach. The big ones are breaking, and body-surfers catch combers far from shore and ride them in.

In the heart of San Diego spreads Balboa Park, whose Spanish-style museums and art gallery reflect the city's origin. In 1769 Father Junípero Serra founded the Mission San Diego de Alcalá, first of a chain of 21 Franciscan missions in California.

The park's most famous attraction, the San Diego Zoo, boasts the largest animal collection in the world—5,500 mammals, birds, and reptiles. Nearly all live outdoors year-round in lairs tucked away among wooded canyons and mesas. Buses and an aerial tramway take visitors through and over the zoo.

In a section reserved for them, children fondle cats, ducks, chicks, or push through a turnstile into a corral filled with baby hoofed animals (exiled when they grow big enough to kick or bite). Youngsters may romp with a guanaco (a llama's relative), feed a fawn, or gaze into picture-window burrows of ground squirrels. Attendants teach the children not to squeeze the lamb or feed chewing gum to the tapir. The courageous take turns aboard a giant tortoise (opposite). Sometimes a shaggy kid butts in.

SEA WORLD'S SHAMU CARRIES A RIDER AND (OPPOSITE) A PYGMY GOAT SLOWS A TORTOISE AT THE SAN DIEGO ZOO; BATES LITTLEHALES, NATIONAL GEOGRAPHIC PHOTOGRAPHER

A Swing Through San Francisco

Want to swing in swinging San Francisco? Take a wild, dizzy, eye-popping ride on a cable car. And hang on tight! If you don't, you'll fly off a slippery wooden seat as the car right-angles to plunge down a side street. Listen! As you near the next street corner the gripman grasps the bell rope and clangs out a brassy, syncopated rhythm that lets everyone know *his* car is clanking through.

The gripman reigns over a noble San Francisco institution invented by Andrew Hallidie, who pitied the horses struggling up the steep hills. On the first trip in 1873 Hallidie took over after the gripman eyed the hill and the fog—and quit. Ever since, gripmen have kept a grip on themselves. They control speed by tightening or loosening a pincer that grabs an electric-powered underground cable pulling at nine miles an hour.

Bristling with hangers-on, the brightly painted cars clatter up hills and down as if propelled by a benign local genie. Their defiance of gravity fascinated Rudyard Kipling: "They take no count of rise or fall, but slide equably on their appointed courses . . . turn corners . . . cross other lines, and, for aught I know, may run up the sides of houses."

From the top of a hill, look at the city's spectacular bay. Few harbors in the world are more beautiful, or more beloved. Every visitor who has seen it cherishes his own particular vision: of a great caldron seething with fog pierced by the lofty towers and graceful arcs of Golden Gate Bridge; of Victorian houses climbing up an incredibly steep street, their gingerbread gewgaws glistening in the morning light; of a solitary ship steering westward through the Gate at dusk, outward bound in the copper wake of the sinking sun.

Or at night watch the lights glitter and pulse on the encircling cities and hills—a galaxy of more than four million residents. At the center of it all stands San Francisco, queen city, born of the sea. Beneath the fringe of her waterfront lie hulks of ships that brought roistering forty-niners around the Horn. Indeed she looks, from a distance on a clear morning, like a becalmed windjammer, sails squared, motionless in the sun.

Gold built her and an earthquake tore her down. Four-fifths of the city was destroyed by the quake and fire of 1906. "The old San Francisco is dead," mourned a newspaper. "Don't talk earthquake. Talk

SWINGERS START YOUNG IN SAN FRANCISCO; JAMES L. STANFIELD, NATIONAL GEOGRAPHIC PHOTOGRAPHER. ABOVE: RIDERS CLING AS CABLE CAR CLANGS; ANDRES PRUNA

SPANGLED STREAMS OF TRAFFIC SPAN DOUBLE-DECKED SAN FRANCISCO-OAKLAND BAY BRIDGE

business," replied billboards sprouting amid four square miles of ashes. The rebirth of the city was phenomenal —and the building never stopped. The gutted Palace Hotel (here, they said, the chef sprinkled the entrees with gold dust) came back in gilded elegance. Over the old carriage entrance vaulted a roof of iridescent glass, hung with crystal chandeliers. San Franciscans bask in the glow of yesteryear, dining under that dome (page 306). Modern towers of steel rise from a peninsular downtown with nowhere to go but up. Gold-rush gusto blends with Nob Hill sophistication, producing

an architecture that fits the city's split personality: pride in a frontier past, passion for the new and revolutionary.

Where else but in San Francisco would you expect to hear and see the latest in mod styles, campus protests, nightclub poetry? Precocious movie-makers make the scene with loaded Super-8's; roving theater troupes improvise in city parks; rock bands blare the San Francisco Sound; blossoming poets—and faded ones—take root in this literary greenhouse that nurtured Robert Louis Stevenson, Bret Harte, Ambrose Bierce. Kipling called it "a mad city—inhabited for the most part by perfectly insane people whose women are of a remarkable beauty." Novelist Herbert Gold calls it "still the great city in America where a walker can experience nostalgia for the place while still there."

Few walkers can resist the pungent appeal of Fisherman's Wharf, where diners feast on the bounty of the bay. "Nice big crabs, live or cooked!" cry wharf vendors. Succulent crabs boil in sidewalk kettles. Strollers buy "walkaway cocktails" of shrimp and crab, munch on sourdough bread. Oysters overflow baskets in hosed-down passageways. Fishermen in rubber boots

DUNGENESS CRABS DELIGHT A SMALL DINER; THOMAS NEBBIA.
LEFT: BOATS BOB AT FISHERMAN'S WHARF; JAMES L. STANFIELD, NATIONAL GEOGRAPHIC PHOTOGRAPHER (ALSO UPPER LEFT)

and aprons make change in English while making jokes in Italian. For those who savor history, it awaits in the *Balclutha,* a wharfside square-rigger with a maritime museum as cargo. For treasure-hunters, oriental imports crowd the shelves of shops in nearby Ghirardelli Square, an urban oasis of fountains, cafes, and gardens.

For people-watchers, San Francisco offers special treats. In Aquatic Park (below), a swinging musicale pulls spectators to their feet. Professionals and amateurs perform; admission's free. And a short cable-car ride from the waterfront lies that city within a city, Chinatown, largest Chinese settlement outside Asia and focal point for an estimated 60,000 Chinese-Americans. Grant Avenue, with its pagoda rooftops, dragon-twined streetlamps, and garish rows of shops (opposite), runs like a strip of tinsel through the heart of Chinatown. Along this "Street of a

IN OAKLAND, A MAJORETTE TURNS ON THE RAIDERS' FOOTBALL FANS; IN SAN FRANCISCO, A FLUTIST TURNS ON A PARK

CHINATOWN DAZZLES SIGHTSEERS IN A MOTORIZED RICKSHA; THOMAS NEBBIA. OVERLEAF: GRANDEUR GRACES LUNCHEON IN THE SHERATON-PALACE'S GARDEN COURT; JAMES L. STANFIELD, NATIONAL GEOGRAPHIC PHOTOGRAPHER (ALSO OPPOSITE)

Thousand Lanterns" a dragon romps on Chinese holidays. Spitting electric fire, the 60-foot monster is borne by shopkeepers who know that "where the dragon dances, prosperity follows."

On Grant Avenue and in its maze of alleys, visitors find displayed the strange pharmacopoeia of Chinese medicine: tiger bones, dried lizards, ginseng roots. A temple, bells tinkling under its curved eaves, opens off the Passageway of Peace; not far away shoppers throng a Chinese supermarket. In the Lotus Fortune Cookie Company women stuff sayings (usually from Ben Franklin) into 40,000 cookies a day.

Even Chinatown cannot compete with San Francisco harbor, a magnet night and day. In an endless parade you may spot a Japanese ore carrier, a dazzlingly white Swedish cruise ship, an ancient, rust-splotched tramp flying the star and stripes of Liberia. Around the giants scurry lesser craft: On a sail-spangled day sloops with bright spinnakers billowing race home (opposite). Above their rainbow sails stretches the wind-humming harp of Golden Gate. Soon the bridge will snare the sun, setting in a gull-graced sky as golden as the city that rises on the bay.

BEAUTY ON WING AND WIND ADORNS THE BAY; JAMES L. STANFIELD, NATIONAL GEOGRAPHIC PHOTOGRAPHER

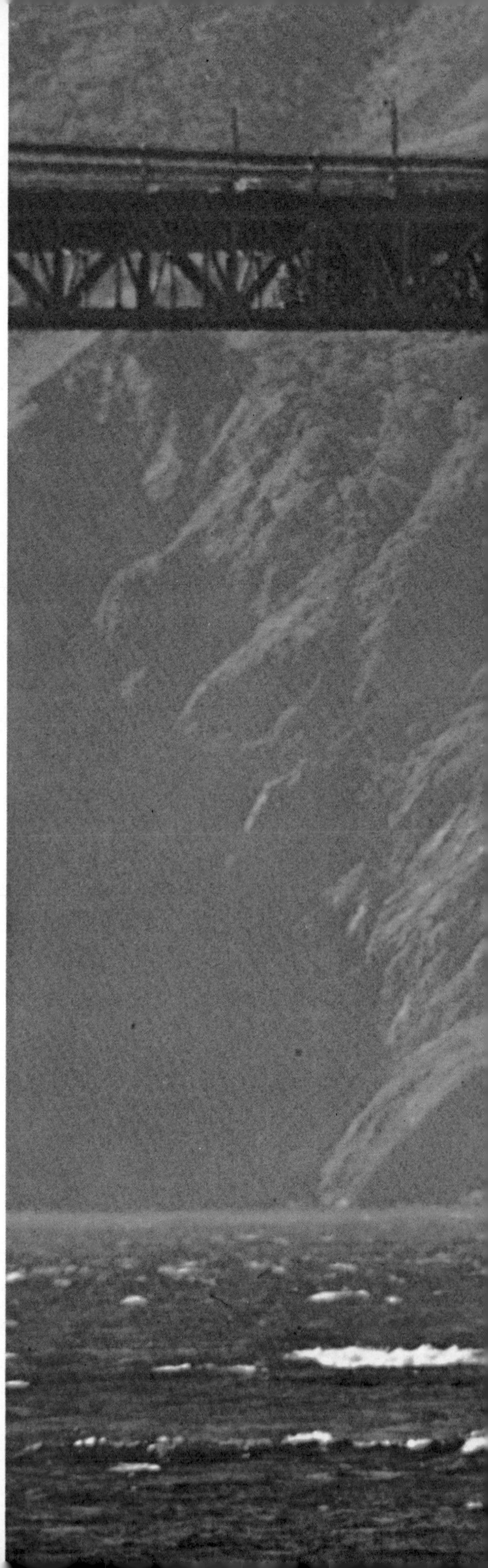

7485

Aloha!

Smiling *wahines* in *ti*-leaf skirts sway like the palms that fringe the glittering beach. Breezes ruffle a blue lagoon, and music drifts on the perfumed air: tinkling ukeleles, pulsing drums, clacking wands of split bamboo. From the stands comes an answering chorus of clicks and whirring—cameras of *malihines,* newcomers, filming a hula show at Honolulu's Kapiolani Park.

Aloha oe . . . Aloha oe . . .
I ke ona ona no I ka lipo . . .

Hawaii's haunting song of welcome greets customers of a leading state industry, tourism. But the islanders prefer to call them visitors, these mainlanders who have journeyed 2,250 miles from the West Coast to call on their countrymen in our 50th—and most exotic—state.

In the language of the hula the visitors can read Hawaii's lures. Fingers open to suggest flowers blooming; rippling, rustling movements evoke the sweep of surf, the curve of a wave. Hands in tandem, pointing upwards, pantomime mountains. In dance and in spirit, this land knows two vistas: *mauka,* toward the mountains, and *makai,* toward the sea.

Hawaii's seven inhabited islands span some 400 miles of ocean, gracing the Pacific with their beauty and the map with their melodious Polynesian names: Niihau, Kauai, Oahu, Molokai, Lanai, Maui, and Hawaii. Tips of mountains thrust up by volcanic eruptions, the islands still seethe, with "a smell of sulphur . . . a sound of crackling as if the surface of the earth were being torn apart . . . the sight of fire ebbing and exploding in the dark night. . . ."

The fire pit of Kilauea on the island of Hawaii, in Hawaii Volcanoes National Park, flamed thus for James A. Michener, author of *Hawaii.* Not all visitors get such a spectacular. Once, though, hoping to lure tourists to Volcano House on the crater rim, the innkeeper tossed a bottle of gin into the pit to bribe Pele, goddess of volcanoes. She thanked him by making a ripsnorting spectacle of herself. Haleakala National Park, on Maui, offers a tamer wonder: a crater half a mile deep and almost wide enough to swallow Manhattan.

Visitors need not leave Honolulu, on Oahu, to explore Hawaii's enchanted past. The war god Kukailimoku (above), with dog-teeth snarl and pearl-shell stare, guards the Bishop Museum. Feathers of the iiwi and oo plume him. Royal treasures—crowns, capes of feathers from 10,000 birds—recall Hawaii's monarchy. It lasted a century after Kamehameha I consolidated a kingdom in 1795. Hawaiians remember

GRINNING DANCER AND A GRIMACING GOD GREET VISITORS TO HONOLULU; BATES LITTLEHALES, NATIONAL GEOGRAPHIC PHOTOGRAPHER

him each June 11 with Kamehameha Day—start of a festival of parades and pageants—and the draping of 40-foot leis on his bronze statue. It stands across from Iolani Palace, Hawaii's former capitol.

Beach buffs who jam the world-famed strand of Waikiki follow regal precedent. Here kings and nobles feasted, swam, and pursued the royal sport of surfing. A chief might bet all he owned, including his wife, on a contest. Today surfboards dot the waves off the mile-long strip; beachboys and visitors paddle outrigger canoes, and twin-hulled catamarans sail out beyond the reefs past Diamond Head. On days of high tourist tide Waikiki offers sunbathers less room than Coney Island in August.

The world's highest rideable waves—30-foot winter giants—roll in at Oahu's Sunset and Makaha beaches. Catching a swell at its crest, a surfer drops down the towering face (left), then braces for a 30-mile-an-hour trip to shore.

SURF BATTERS, SUN BRONZES AT OAHU'S BEACHES; ROBERT B. GOODMAN AND (LEFT) DR. DON JAMES

On lesser combers, body-surfers shunning polished boards scoot down the billows belly-first. Poor timing can catch them in a curl for a jolting "trip to the bone yard."

The days are filled with fragrance as tourists browse in scented shops and watch lei-makers at work in Kapiolani Park (below right). "Memory imprisoned on a chain," a poet called the lei. The exquisite necklace breathes the spirit of aloha with all its meanings: love, friendship, welcome—and farewell.

Night weaves its spell: a moon so bright it sometimes paints a glowing lunar rainbow on cloud and mist; outriggers torchlit to greet the twilight; Honolulu gleaming against the brooding backdrop of Diamond Head (right). On the beach mouths water at a luau fit for kings: succulent pigs roasted in a rock-lined pit; poi, a taro-paste dip. (One-finger poi is thick; three-finger, soupy. Two? Finger-lickin' fun!)

Like lei flowers that quickly wilt, Hawaiian holidays end all too soon. But in the spirit of aloha lingers always the promise of return.

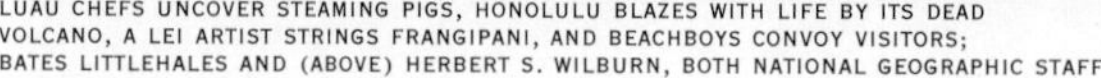

LUAU CHEFS UNCOVER STEAMING PIGS, HONOLULU BLAZES WITH LIFE BY ITS DEAD VOLCANO, A LEI ARTIST STRINGS FRANGIPANI, AND BEACHBOYS CONVOY VISITORS; BATES LITTLEHALES AND (ABOVE) HERBERT S. WILBURN, BOTH NATIONAL GEOGRAPHIC STAFF

N2659U

Wings Into the Wilderness

By W. E. Garrett

Bush plane whisks campers into Alaska's Tongass National Forest; W. E. Garrett, National Geographic staff

As a child I played a private game, the opposite of follow-the-leader. From this make-believe exploring grew a lifelong pursuit to put my feet where no man had walked before. In two decades of wandering the world I never felt nearer fulfillment of my dream than when I stood with my wife and two sons above the shores of a lake we own in Alaska.

No smog thickened the air we breathed; no pollutants scummed the still inlets; no mechanical cadence drowned the subtle sounds of nature. Virgin spruce and western hemlock bristled on the slopes that cupped our lake. Only our presence betrayed man's existence on this planet.

We own this lake called Ella—in partnership with more than 200 million other Americans. For Ella lies within one of our national forests set aside "for the permanent good of the whole people."

At this moment, though, all the other people were elsewhere and we had the lake to ourselves, reserved with the district ranger of Tongass National Forest in Ketchikan. In the 16 million acres of Tongass, foresters have scattered more than 130 cabins, some with a dock and a skiff and a supply of firewood. For a couple of dollars a day you can reserve any of these one-room resorts for as long as a week. Like most of the camps, ours could be reached only by floatplane or boat.

In Ketchikan we booked our trip with Pete Cessnun, a veteran bush pilot. Once bush planes were dubiously regarded as broncos for airborne cowboys. Today the planes serve as the safe, dependable trolleys of Alaska's vast transit system of the air. But to my wife Lucy, who won't go up in a Ferris wheel, Pete's little single-engine craft, perched high on its floats, looked like an ungainly water bug, frail and perilously inadequate. "It won't even hold all of us and our things, let alone fly," she predicted.

If sons Mike and Kenny had any qualms about their first bush flight they concealed them. Lucy sat rigidly as the plane roared and splashed across the harbor, eased up onto the choppy swells, and then leaped free. It flew, but Lucy was partly right—we did have to leave behind a few nonessential items.

Alaskans measure distance in minutes of flying time, not miles; Pete told us our campsite lay 20 minutes east of Ketchikan, which stretches along the edge of an island in the Alexander Archipelago. Here southeast Alaska hangs under the main body of the state like the tail of a treed raccoon. The Tongass mantles most of the tail.

Pete took longer than 20 minutes to fly us in. With typical Alaskan pride, he gave us the bonus of a short

W. E. GARRETT, NATIONAL GEOGRAPHIC STAFF

***CALLED TO THE WILD, ALASKAN ADVENTURERS** stake a claim to a cabin on Ella Lake in Tongass National Forest. Bush pilot Pete Cessnun helps Lucy Garrett set up her outdoor kitchen. He'll leave the family on its own—but not alone: Mink, marmot, beaver, land otter, marten, fox roam the vast forest. Wolverines, largest and strongest of American weasels, hunt along streams teeming with salmon and trout. Black bears and great "brownies" tread age-old paths. Moose bulls and cows claim river valleys.*

The Tongass, marching some 250 miles northwest of Ella, sweeps past Haines, where Kenny Garrett bottle-feeds moose calves adopted by human parents.

W. E. GARRETT, NATIONAL GEOGRAPHIC STAFF

"HEAVEN TO LOOK AT AND HELL TO NAVIGATE," *Klondikers cursed as they climbed Chilkoot Pass. In their footsteps, the Garretts trek the gold-rush trail. Below them spreads Crater Lake in British Columbia. Bivouacked on a ledge during the four-day, 35-mile hike, Lucy Garrett worried that the boys might sleepwalk. Mike vowed: "I'm not walking anywhere tonight." At Lindeman they slept in a ghost-town cabin. A narrow-gauge train shuttled them back to Skagway, gateway to Yukon gold from 1897 to 1905 when thousands struggled over the pass, a few to prosper, countless to die. Now tourists head for Skagway and hit the trail; planners hope it will thread a two-nation park.*

Alaska offers visitors plenty of excitement, with brown bear cubs that pop up on Kodiak Island (opposite) and fighting salmon like the 13-pound beauty landed by Kenny Garrett near Juneau.

course in wilderness lore. Seconds out of town Pete banked tightly around an eagle's nest built in the top of an old snag of a tree. As if afraid a movement might tip the plane even more, Lucy looked with a sidelong glance. The two eaglets didn't turn to look at us either.

"It's been there for years," Pete shouted over the engine's growl. "Babies in it almost every summer. They tell us we have more bald eagles in Alaska than anywhere else in the world." Rangers require loggers to spare trees with nests and leave around them a buffer zone of uncut trees.

As we flew over the gray waters of Tongass Narrows, Pete pointed to fishing boats circling to set purse nets around migrating salmon. In late spring and summer the salmon return from the sea to spawn and die in Alaska's creeks and rivers. A good crew working a 1,500-foot net can haul in 12,000 fish for processors in Ketchikan.

Pete nosed the plane toward the coastal range whose glaciers and snow-clad peaks trace the Canadian-Alaskan border. Breakfast grew heavy in our stomachs as Pete fulfilled his promise to show the boys some mountain goats. He twisted and swooped among jagged ridges and snow-filled clefts where he knew the sure-footed goats grazed.

"Right there!" Pete shouted, pointing past our right wing tip. We only saw more rocks and snow. He made a second, then a third turn past the mountain face before the goats materialized among the crags. In the next few minutes we saw more of these shaggy white acrobats with black spike horns, but never before Pete pointed them out.

"Used to go on a hunting trip once a year," Pete said.

PLYING THE WORLD'S LONGEST FERRY ROUTE, *the* Malaspina *with her cargo of vehicles and voyagers cuts the molten gold of the Inside Passage near Wrangell. The 986-mile nautical highway from Seattle to Skagway on Alaska's panhandle skirts snowy peaks, icy fiords, calving glaciers. Travelers bed down in snug staterooms, dine on fish caught in Alaskan waters.*

"The last twelve years I haven't shot anything. I'd rather see wildlife in its natural habitat. Flying up here and being around the back country—you get to appreciate it."

We flew over a ridge, Pete cut the throttle, and we banked in a descending spiral. Below lay Ella Lake.

Our floats shattered the glassy surface. Then we eased alongside a small dock on the north shore and tied up. At the edge of the forest we could see our cabin. After we had unloaded our gear, Pete took a last look around to make sure we were settled. Before climbing into the plane he said, "In case of trouble build a fire and throw on lots of wet wood. Someone flying in the area will probably see the smoke and check." And off he roared, circling high to clear the western ridge.

Probably see the smoke, he had said. Lucy and I could not disguise our uneasiness: a city-bred family suddenly isolated in the wilderness. It wasn't like exploring alone. What if one of the boys got sick? And what of the animals? We knew Tongass abounded with wolves and brown bears, largest carnivores that walk the earth. There was also the realization that we were utterly out of touch. The nearest town was the one we had left, across mountains and stretches of salt water. We had no radio. Until Pete returned for us we would have only each other.

The boys, though, showed no concern, and we all set about enjoying camp life. Or trying to. City habits rushed the pace: Hurry up and fix a fire. Hurry up and go for a boat ride. Hurry up and catch some fish.

Slowly the hurry-ups left us, and our moods blended with Ella's. We began to feel the beauty instead of the fear of the forest. We walked the animal paths and explored. Mosses festooned the lower branches of trees along the shore and bulged as thick as pillows on the damp floor of the Tongass. In its luxuriance grew starflowers, goldthreads, violets, bluebells, lilies of the valley. We enjoyed lying out in the open at night and counting shooting stars—or not counting them, as we chose.

When the sun shone through the towering conifers, we cooked our meals over a campfire behind the cabin; when it rained, we stoked up the cabin's wood stove. Lucy fast learned to cope with the stove's eccentricities: slow to heat, then furnace-hot, then slow to simmer down.

Only Ella Lake's trout could possibly enjoy swimming

W. E. GARRETT, NATIONAL GEOGRAPHIC STAFF

AIRBORNE ESKIMO BOUNCES AT POINT BARROW, *northernmost tip of the U. S., 335 miles above the Arctic Circle. A standing landing earns cheers: "Aazigaa—good!" Walrus-hide blankets once may have lofted sharp-eyed scouts looking for game. Now the sport hails a successful whale hunt and entertains visitors from Fairbanks, 500 miles south.*

An Eskimo woman (above) on Little Diomede, tiny isle in the Bering Strait, cuddles a freak three-tusked walrus skull. Visitors, rare here, see a chunk of the U.S.S.R.—Big Diomede, only 2½ miles away across the Date Line.

Far to the south, tourists can see the results of a renaissance in the nearly lost art of totem carving. A raven (opposite), created by Tlingit Indians, leers from his perch on a pole near Ketchikan.

in its cold, clear water. To us a swim proved a merciless test of endurance. Mike and Kenny, ever resourceful, splashed into a shallow, sand-bottomed pool heated by the sun to a barely bearable temperature. Accepting their challenge, I joined them for a few painful moments. Then I fled to a warm beach and watched the boys try to hand-catch the minnows that nibbled around their toes.

We found the wily trout almost as hard to catch as the minnows. But we persisted, even when it rained in chilling torrents. Maybe it was because we worked so hard to catch them, but no trout ever tasted sweeter than those served crisp and hot from the skillet. And no sleep was ever sweeter than the sleep that came as the rain dripped through the sheltering trees and onto the roof of our snug little cabin.

In the summer in southeast Alaska you fish in the rain or you may not fish at all. For the Tongass is rain forest, kept lush around Ketchikan by 150 inches of precipitation a year. When the glaciers retreated in the last Ice Age, vegetation took hold. Animals began trickling in. Then, some 8,000 years ago, man arrived, lured by the relatively mild climate and an abundance of berries, fish, and game. The forest also provided wood for shelter and canoes. The Indians who came here—the Tlingit, Haida, Tsimshian—attained what we sought, a oneness with the forest and its creatures. Some of these creatures, like the trout, sustained us. Others, like the deer we watched swimming across the lake, enriched our eyes. We used film to perpetuate what we saw; the Indians used trees, perpetuating their legends with carvings of the eagle and the raven, the bear and the wolf. We had marveled at their totem poles in Ketchikan and neighboring Saxman and Totem Bight.

Too soon we left Ella. But *Alashka*, the "Great Land" of the Aleuts, casts a great spell: We would come again. In a motor home we rolled down an Alaska road and camped at a lake of glacier melt. We drove our home aboard the ferries that ply the Inside Passage from Prince Rupert, British Columbia, to Sitka, Juneau, and Skagway. Standing at the rail, we watched porpoises vaulting from the water—and occasionally

GEORGE F. MOBLEY (ALSO OPPOSITE) AND W. E. GARRETT, BOTH NATIONAL GEOGRAPHIC STAFF

spotted the "blow" of a whale traveling the Passage. Once an otter scampered up a bank as we passed. On another ferry we rolled and pitched through the night from Seward to rugged Kodiak Island, home of a giant race of brown bears. There, armed with a camera for offense and a .30-06 rifle for defense, I came upon two cubs and a mother eight feet tall. She looked ten to me until she and her youngsters vanished into the brush.

We have explored Katmai National Monument's awesome Valley of Ten Thousand Smokes and camped amid the peaks and glaciers of Mount McKinley National Park. Twice we have flown to Skagway to hike over the gold-rush trail of 1898. Once, only 12 miles from the state capital of Juneau, we looked out upon Mendenhall Glacier from the wide windows of a Tongass visitor center. We stood on ground that had been covered by ice up to 1941. A naturalist told us that within decades the ice could advance again and crush the building. Mike and Kenny promised to bring me back to witness the event.

In a way, we do keep coming back. The days of our lives in the city dissolve and run together in a smoggy blur. But those days and moments our family has shared in the wilderness stand as clear and untarnished in our memories as the peaks we saw around our lake called Ella.

"AND THE NORTHERN LIGHTS IN THE CRYSTAL NIGHTS CAME FORTH with a mystic gleam." Sun-spawned aurora borealis dances over Fairbanks, shimmering "with a ceaseless ebb and flow," as in the ballad by polar laureate Robert Service.

A magical sky backlights the grandeur of Alaska, our biggest state. Its Aleutian finger reaches toward the Date Line, nearly touching tomorrow. It wears the white crown of North America, 20,320-foot Mount McKinley.

Alaskans don't boast about size (more than twice that of Texas and big enough to hold 21 other states); they merely define claustrophobia: "How we feel in the heart of Texas."

Place names bespeak four tongues. Mitliktavik, Chakachamna Lake, Point Romanof, Goodnews Bay echo the Eskimo-Indian-Russian-American heritage that shaped Alaska.

Here visitors gaze at the past in Saxman Totem Park (below), roam a lonely realm that holds a fourth of our national parklands. The 49th star guides us to our last frontier.

W. E. GARRETT AND (OPPOSITE) GEORGE F. MOBLEY, BOTH NATIONAL GEOGRAPHIC STAFF

By Ralph Gray

STEERING NEOPRENE STEEDS DOWN THE WILD COLORADO, RIVER RIDERS BUCK GRAND CANYON RAPIDS THAT CHURN TORRENTS OF

White Water!

Hard-pressed jockey reins a runaway raft in Upset Rapids; Ralph Gray, National Geographic staff

Let me try to tell you how it feels to float like a leaf on a roaring river at the bottom of a mile-deep canyon. You buck and plunge, borne by a current as irresistible as a runaway freight on a downgrade. The water looks black and glassy, but your eyes stay glued to the spot ahead where a taffy-smooth curl drops 10 or 15 feet and breaks into a mad white froth of standing waves.

This is the moment of truth. You can't go back. In dream-like slow motion you approach the brink, not really hearing the pounding roar between canyon walls. The front of the raft tips down into the hole. You hold your breath and grab a firm handhold. Your speed increases. And an almost unbearable moment ends as you smack into the standing wave that rises in the Colorado River like a wall.

The raft trembles and buckles upward, and your neck snaps back. Impossibly, you have climbed the wall of water, and now you're looking down into the next trough. You've made it. You realize you haven't breathed for quite a while. You can't recall when you got soaked to the skin. And your friends—are they still aboard? They are—and amid the roar you now can hear their whoops and hollers as the raft gallops through a half-mile of choppy runout.

Paria Rapids, Badger Creek Rapids, Soap Creek Rapids: boom, BOOM, BOOM! The first day after setting out in rafts from Lees Ferry below Glen Canyon Dam, Arizona, we were veterans of some of the wildest water in North America—each rapid rougher, louder, better than the last.

They more than fulfilled my youthful dream. As a young man I had hiked with my friend Caleb Hathaway down from the Grand Canyon's rim to the rampaging Colorado. When we reached its banks, night overtook us; we unrolled our blankets and slept to the water's deep-throated music. That throbbing sound haunted me for years. Now, with other friends, I was riding those very waves. Clinging to our flimsy-looking rubber rafts, we surged into the thundering gorges, wondering what kind of pummeling to expect next on the 226 miles of our Grand Canyon run.

Between rapids our outboards chugged through flatwater stretches that offered unlimited peace and quiet for canyon-watching. Here you can bail out your rafts, stretch out on your back, and drink in the constantly changing panorama of pink and purple cliffs that drift past your eyes. And on the shores, campsites of surpassing beauty tempt you to pull in and linger awhile. Ahead lay such havens as Redwall Cavern, an open-mouthed cave large enough to dome an entire football field. But on our first night, we beached at Brown's Rock, just below Soap Creek Rapids. Shucking our life jackets, we hurried to make *(Continued on page 336)*

WALTER MEAYERS EDWARDS, NATIONAL GEOGRAPHIC STAFF

FLOATING THROUGH TIME, *raftsmen thread Marble Canyon, 60-mile corridor of the Colorado into Grand Canyon. This Wall Street of the West rears its cliffs ever higher as river runners bump down a staircase of rapids into the abyss of the ages. Each stratum of stone marks a page in earth's biography. Along placid stretches of the imprisoned river lie beaches and driftwood for campfires where fellowship blazes amid Stygian blackness at the bottom of time.*

Thread of life through the parched Southwest, the Colorado zigzags 1,450 miles from snow-crested peaks of its namesake state to Mexico's Gulf of California. Float trippers and hikers marvel at nature's variety—lizards, mule deer, the unique Kaibab squirrel, the sweet-singing canyon wren, the wild flowers—in four climatic zones encompassed by vacationlands along the river's dammed but not tranquilized middle course. Probing a seam in Marble Canyon cliffs, river runners discover a limestone sanctuary (opposite); cactus yields prickly pears, wild burros startle picnickers, boys find goatsbeards to blow to smithereens. Most Grand Canyon tourists crowd the South Rim. Some descend on muleback to Phantom Ranch, or visit the Havasupai Indians in their side-canyon Eden. Backed-up waters invite water-skiers to Lakes Mead and Powell, turn generators, irrigate California fields, feed Los Angeles faucets, fill San Diego swimming pools.

WALTER MEAYERS EDWARDS, NATIONAL GEOGRAPHIC STAFF. MAP BY BETTY CLONINGER, GEOGRAPHIC ART DIVISION

Moab
CANYONLANDS NATIONAL PARK
UTAH
Lake Powell
GLEN CANYON NATIONAL RECREATION AREA
BRYCE CANYON NATIONAL PARK
NEVADA
ZION NATIONAL PARK
Glen Canyon Dam
RAINBOW BRIDGE NATIONAL MONUMENT
Lees Ferry
KAIBAB NATIONAL FOREST
MARBLE CANYON NATIONAL MONUMENT
GRAND CANYON NATIONAL MONUMENT
Lake Mead
Las Vegas
Colorado
GRAND CANYON NATIONAL PARK
Grand Canyon
Hoover Dam
LAKE MEAD NATIONAL RECREATION AREA
ARIZONA
Lake Mohave
National Parks, Monuments, and Recreation Areas
National Forest
Needles
0 100
STATUTE MILES
CALIFORNIA

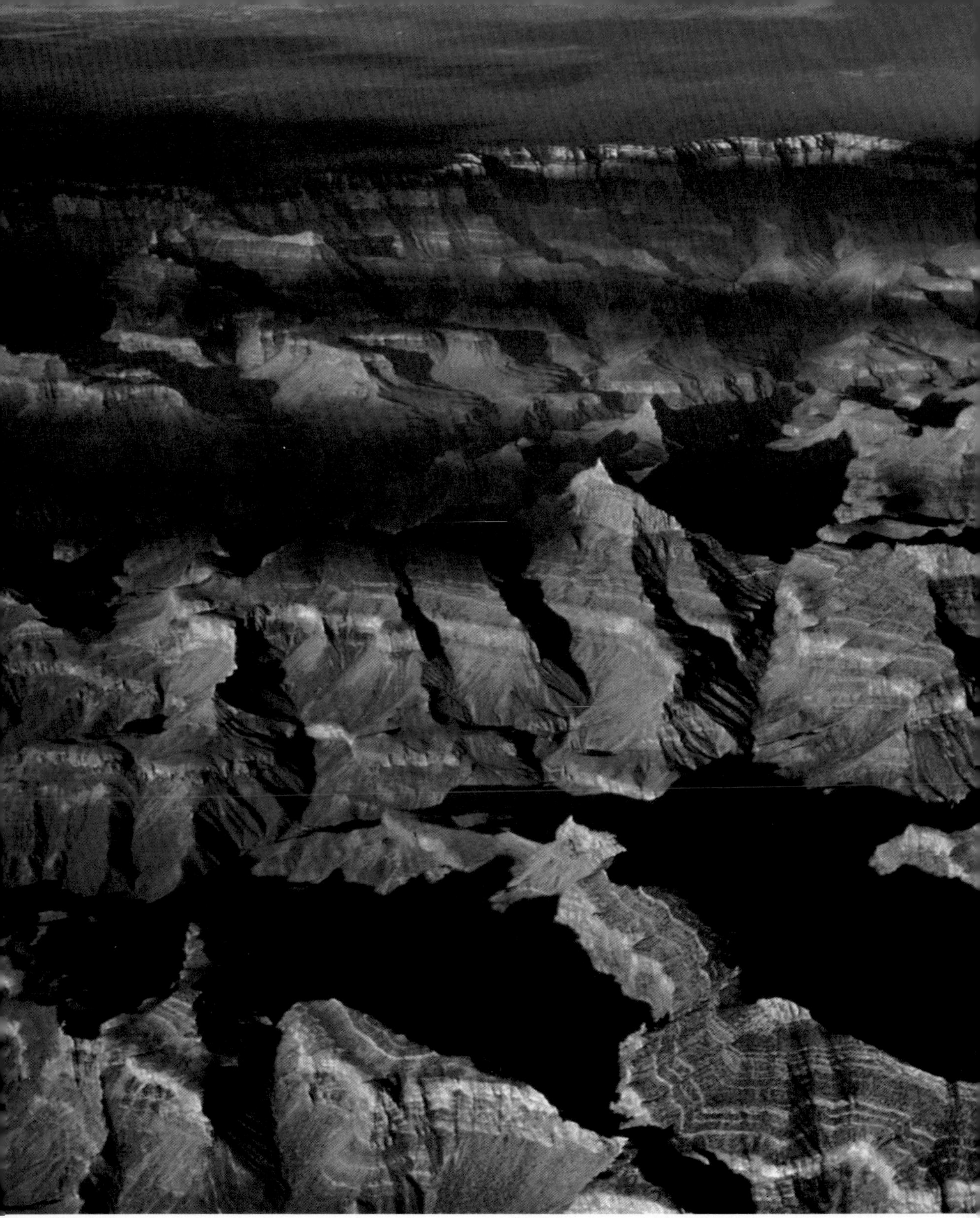

"THE WORLD'S MOST WONDERFUL SPECTACLE, EVER CHANGING, ALIVE WITH A MILLION MOODS."

Naturalist John Burroughs' words leap to mind as we look southwest over the Grand Canyon to the South Rim from 23,000 feet. Purple isles looming out of early-morning shadows reveal bands of pink and gold to the climbing sun. Imagination fills the water-sculptured gorge with temples to Venus, Vishnu, Wotan, Zoroaster. Novelist E. M. Forster

WALTER MEAYERS EDWARDS, NATIONAL GEOGRAPHIC STAFF

described "sphinxes draped in crimson shawls." Barrier to gold-hungry Spaniards in 1540, magnet to jet-age tourists, this 217-mile gash in the plateau, 4 to 18 miles wide, amazes all by its immensity. Pinnacles that seem man-size tower 30 stories high.

Reading earth's record in the rocks, scientists say that for 600 million years thick layers of sediment spread over remnants of mountains. Geology's layer cake then rose against the cutting edge of the Colorado River, formed 10 million years ago, after the seas retreated from Arizona. Limestone layer at top holds fossil sponges; ancestral starfish rest in lower, Cambrian beds. A mile below the rim the river still gnaws at rock two billion years old.

camp before the sun set. I buddied up with my brother Vernon, who spread his groundcloth on a spot where the sand couldn't blow in our faces. We inflated air mattresses and placed our bedrolls side by side.

"Come on over and join the group," Doug Dewar sang out above the sound of the river. Doug was the dean of our party, the best storyteller, and the first to get a round of socializing going after we all had pitched in to unload the boats and set up the camp.

Over a driftwood fire, steaks sizzled and coffee bubbled. Coffee! I dug into my gear—and found that, of all things, I had forgotten to bring along a metal cup. Most Western rivermen carry a stainless-steel Sierra Club cup that hangs on the belt; it serves for soup, stew, and fruit desserts, as well as coffee. Always handy, too, for dipping a drink out of the river as you ride along.

"Don't worry, Ralph," said a companion who had just discovered he'd lost his cup. "Here's what we'll do." We took two empty beer cans, cut out the tops with our hunting knives, pressed down the jagged edges with pliers, and wrapped cord around them for insulation (camp coffee is *hot*), leaving a length for tying to the belt.

I poured myself a cupful, dug into a steak, and joined in the fireside talk that relived the day. When talk and fire faded, we turned in, tucked between canyon walls whose glorious hues had faded into night's blackest black.

As we hefted our gear down to the boats in the morning, Joe Munroe, organizer of our trip and a riverman who loves the Colorado and its history, led us to a nearby ledge. There we read the weathered, rock-carved inscription to F. M. Brown, who was sucked under by a whirlpool and

WALTER MEAYERS EDWARDS, NATIONAL GEOGRAPHIC STAFF; ENGRAVING FROM POWELL'S "CANYONS OF THE COLORADO," 1895

***FIRST TO MASTER THE FURY** of the Colorado through Grand Canyon, John Wesley Powell unveiled the West's greatest wonder. On May 24, 1869, 10 men and 4 wooden boats set out from Green River, Wyoming. "What falls there are, we know not," Powell wrote; "what rocks beset the channel . . . what walls rise over the river, we know not." Ninety-eight days and 1,000 miles later, 6 men and 2 boats emerged from the unknown. A National Geographic expedition rode rubber pontoon rafts and a plastic skiff (opposite) to mark the centennial of Powell's feat.*

drowned here while leading a survey for a proposed rail line through the Grand Canyon to San Diego.

"A friend of Brown's scratched these words in his memory and later *he* was drowned," Joe told us. "After that it was considered bad luck to mark the site of misfortunes. So no one knows how many have drowned in this river."

Brown's railroad plan had been inspired by the first major exploration of the Colorado, the 1869 voyage of Maj. John Wesley Powell, a one-armed veteran of the Union Army, later a founder of the National Geographic Society.

We launched into the roar of Marble Canyon, northern gateway to Grand Canyon. A scene from Powell's journal flashed by: "Now the scenery is on a grand scale. The walls of the canyon, 2,500 feet high, are of marble, of many beautiful colors . . . polished below by the waves."

For a novice navigator following in the wake of Powell, the Grand Canyon run could be suicidal. If you were enthusiastic enough to try it yourself, you would have to apply for permission from the Superintendent of Grand Canyon National Park. He would demand proof that your equipment, skill, and knowledge of the river were adequate to assure a safe ride. But if you sign on as a passenger with any of the 15 or more commercial outfitters for hire on the river, you need only pay your fare, grab tight, and enjoy 9 to 15 days of adventure.

You will probably ride a G-rig or a J-rig. The first is named for Georgie White, a lady pioneer of Colorado rafting who began experimenting with inflated pontoons shortly after World War II and is still guiding trips. Her typical rig consists of three 33-foot-long neoprene pontoon rafts lashed side by side. The J-rig, named for Jack Currey, links five pointed-prow "sausages."

Both kinds are powered and guided by outboards. Too large to tip, the rigs can be fitted with decks for carrying 30 or more persons plus all their iced-food hampers, camping equipment, cameras, radios, cushions, and the extra clothes they never get around to wearing.

We bounded safely down the rapids guided by the able hands of Dick McCallum, a registered Western riverman qualified to lead parties on this roughest of rivers. Ron Smith's Grand Canyon Expeditions, which supplied a single 33-footer for our trip, also provided my favorite Colorado River float—three 10-man GI assault rafts that look like puffed-up rowboats lashed together. In this motorless rig, guided by two oarsmen, you ride lower, get more splash and a lot better feel of the river. Aboard it I soon became intimate with the Colorado, with the sweep of current and the slap of spray as we caterpillared over and through the ranks of house-size waves.

We bounced, glided, and bounced again through clear water. In the turbulent stretches, the gleaming flood of white froth shattered into sunstruck crystals of purest sheen. Luckily we had found the Colorado in a white-water mood. Often silt muddies the water, making it "too thick to drink and too thin to plow," as the rivermen say. (Actually, it is drinkable, but the National Park Service recommends adding a drop of iodine per cup.)

Glen Canyon Dam, which bridled the Colorado and created the great jewel of Lake Powell, holds back much of the upriver sediment. But streams cascading down the canyon's sides still sluice red and brown mud into the Grand Canyon run. Powell named one such side creek Dirty Devil; another, sparkling as it tumbled down from the North Rim, he named Bright Angel Creek. At its mouth we camped. Here Powell and his party had paused a century earlier. And this happened to be where my own love affair with the Colorado had begun with a rugged hike three decades before. Today most tourists ride in by muleback on switchback trails that snake down from the South Rim.

Sodden, sun-tinged survivors of rapids with such marvelous names as Kwagunt, Unkar, Sockdolager, Grapevine, and Zoroaster, we pushed off into the lower depths of the canyon and went slamming on to more—Horn Creek, Granite, Waltenberg, Dubendorff. In one of them (I forget which) we plowed into a wall of water so rambunctious that it doubled back the whipping prow of my 33-footer, smashed it down on the top of my head, and knocked me out. The kayo punch missed shorter Joe Munroe, hanging on beside me. He held me aboard and kept intact his no-loss record as a trip organizer.

But the river offered more than perils. We exulted in its wildness as much as we did in our own isolation—"a concept of sublimity," as Powell said, that cannot "be equaled on the hither side of Paradise." In such grandeur we often tarried, hiking into side canyons and hidden glens, probing the mouths of tributaries, seeking the sources of streams so deeply imbedded in rock they seemed almost subterranean.

From the mouth of Tapeats Creek, Joe, Vernon, and I started one morning for Thunder Falls, high on the North Rim. A climb in the mile-deep gorge is like

CANOE RACING: NEW FUN IN ANCIENT CRAFT

Through a bath of spray the kayak shoots the chute on the foaming headwaters of the Potomac. The racer "reads" the rapids ahead, flips his double-bladed paddle to avoid a deep sousehole, to skirt a boulder, and heads for the slick that flumes between rock walls.

A haystack slaps him over. The slender fiberglass kayak bobs along upside down in the West Virginia gorge as spectators gasp.

A paddle blade surfaces, sweeps in a downward stroke. Sealed in his kayak by a waterproof skirt, shielded from rocks by his crash helmet and from the river's chill by his wet suit, the racer flips right-side up with an Eskimo roll and continues his rodeo ride on the singing waters.

Fun? You bet. Thrills of white-water weekends lure ever more paddlers to rampaging streams for races over measured courses and weaving slalom runs (adapted from skiing, with gate poles hung from wires)—flashy young sports with boats of ancient design.

With the Indian's canoe, explorers, traders, and trappers opened North America. Settlers followed river corridors that veined the virgin land. But river-nurtured settlements have become river-killing cities. Pristine streams are dammed, diverted, polluted. Fewer and fewer rivers run clear and free.

One saved by the Wild and Scenic Rivers Act of 1968, the St. Croix that divides Wisconsin from Minnesota, leads canoeists by the Dalles (lower), cliffs that echoed to voyageurs' chants. The law preserves other waterways (pages 101, 197, 277, 421), as do local enthusiasts. The Ozark Wilderness Waterways Club ends a year's fun with a cleanup. Results of a September romp on the Current River: 283 sacks of trash, and a sparkling stream for next spring.

W. E. GARRETT AND (LOWER) JAMES L. STANFIELD, BOTH NATIONAL GEOGRAPHIC STAFF

a hike through the four life zones of the North American Continent, for each 1,000 feet up is equivalent to a 300-mile hike northward; it was as if we could stride from the deserts of Mexico to the forests of Canada in giant steps. Our four-hour climb began on blistering rocks and ended at the base of the falls. Bathed in its mist, shaded by cottonwoods, we stood, if not in Paradise, at least in Eden.

Back on the river, we braced for one of the roughest spots in the final stretch of the canyon run—Upset Rapids. As Dick McCallum bucked into the churning water, his one motor (Hance Rapids had smashed the other) conked out. He spun into Upset's deepest "hole," a maelstrom roiled by submerged rocks (page 328), and punctured a pontoon. Dick hung on but lost his treasured Navajo hat. Safely ashore, he found two skilled scavengers among the passengers, who helped him get a motor to sputter. The battered raft coughed through Lava Falls and the rest of the way to Diamond Creek—66 major rapids, 226 miles, and 12 days from where our run had begun.

We pulled the rafts ashore for the last time, deflated them, packed our gear into a truck, and headed back to civilization. Yet I could hear louder than ever before the boom of the rapids, the voice of the Colorado resounding in the echo chamber of the Grand Canyon. The river's roar has yet to fade away.

Probing upstream from the Gulf of California in a prefabricated iron steamboat in 1858, Lt. J. C. Ives could not foresee millions of Americans coming each year to enjoy its waters and bordering parklands.

Campers, who spread sleeping bags beside Lake Powell, greet the dawn with the aroma of sizzling trout (below). Airdrops of fingerlings by the million stock the waters rising here behind Glen Canyon Dam. The lake's 1,800-mile shoreline beckons boaters to nature's wonder, Rainbow Bridge, and to Hole in the Rock, where Mormon pioneers braked wagons down a 45° cleft, then rafted across the Colorado.

As the sun completes another passage over Grand Canyon (opposite), visitors may well reflect on words of President Theodore Roosevelt: "The ages have been at work on it, and man can only mar it. . . . keep it for your children, your children's children, and for all who come after you, as one of the great sights which every American . . . should see."

WALTER MEAYERS EDWARDS, NATIONAL GEOGRAPHIC STAFF

By Colin Fletcher

PACK ON HIS BACK, PEACE IN HIS SOUL,

A HIKER SEEKS SOLITUDE AND SPLENDOR

On the Crest of the West

From 8,894-foot Sahale Mountain, climbers survey North Cascades National Park, newest of those coursed by the Mexico-to-Canada Pacific Crest Trail; James P. Blair, National Geographic photographer

JAMES P. BLAIR AND (OPPOSITE) BATES LITTLEHALES, NATIONAL GEOGRAPHIC PHOTOGRAPHERS

The warmth woke me. I opened one eye. The sun, barely broken free from the snowcapped peaks, had already evicted the chill of night from my bedroom—a granite niche. I loosened the drawstring of my mummy bag hood, slid my down jacket from under me, and put it on. Leaning against my pack, I lit the pressure stove and soon was eating breakfast and watching fingers of sunlight grip the green meadow below. An hour later I was walking south again on the Pacific Crest Trail.

Designated a national scenic trail by Congress in 1968, the route does not yet form a continuous line. When completed it will run for 2,350 miles from Canada to Mexico, following fairly closely the mountain backbone of the Pacific states. Mostly it winds through forest or across the open world of rock and snow that begins where the trees end. In the south, though, it drops down into desert. Occasionally it passes through country that man has dominated. But eighty percent of the Pacific Crest Trail lies within the protecting boundaries of national parks and forests, so the wilderness that you and I find along it should be there for our children, and for their children too.

To walk down the trail, border to border, takes more than a summer. Along most of those two thousand miles the season is short. Mountain snow lies deep and long; some years, the highest passes never open up to horse travel. And by June the low desert is a furnace. But, as a good substitute for a summer-long trek, make the complete trail a continuing project, even a lifetime one, for yourself or your family. Attack each leg at its best season. Keep the daily mileage modest. And take side trips. In a sense, they are the whole point of the trail.

CASCADES CAVALRY FORDS A FROTHY STREAM on the Park Creek horse trail in North Cascades National Park. Nearby, the Pacific Crest Trail winds along the backbone of Washington from Canada to the Columbia River. In the wild northern reaches of the highland path, mounted mountain buffs often deploy with the infantry. Pack trains must carry a week's worth of grub, and trail map symbols not only mark campsites but include an "F" where equestrian campers can get feed for their steeds.

As if poured from the heavens, Oregon's 620-foot Multnomah Falls (opposite) ricochets from rock to rock as it rushes to the Columbia. Here the Crest route makes a highway detour, crossing state border and river gorge on the Bridge of the Gods, named for a legendary natural span destroyed by a god of the Indians. Following Indian paths, the trail traces the skyline of Oregon's Cascades. Amid the lava fields of McKenzie Pass hikers pause at an observatory where each of 11 windows cut in lava walls frames a different peak. Farther south, side trails lead to Crater Lake, blue gem set amid the volcanic scars of its namesake national park.

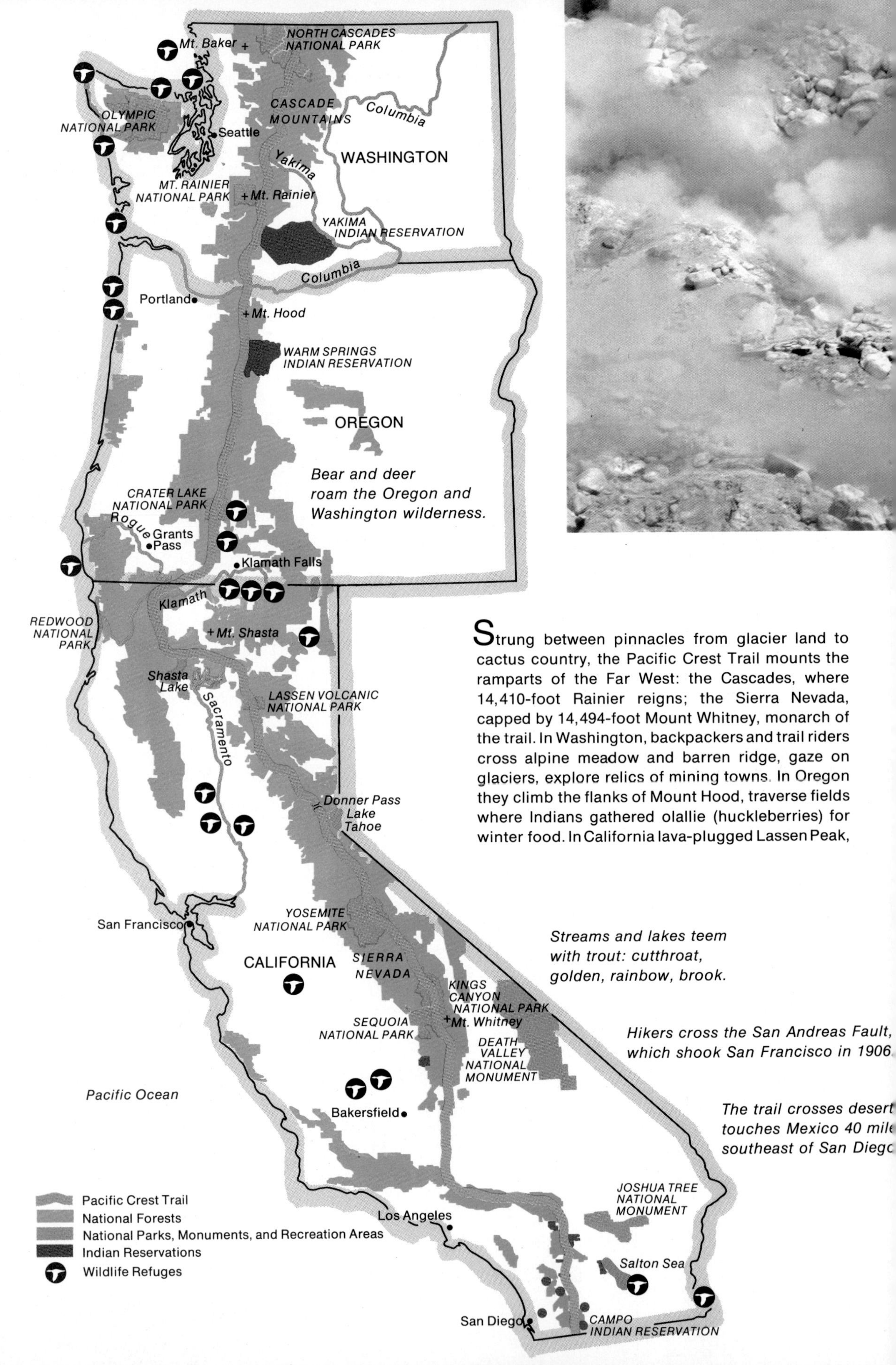

Bear and deer roam the Oregon and Washington wilderness.

Strung between pinnacles from glacier land to cactus country, the Pacific Crest Trail mounts the ramparts of the Far West: the Cascades, where 14,410-foot Rainier reigns; the Sierra Nevada, capped by 14,494-foot Mount Whitney, monarch of the trail. In Washington, backpackers and trail riders cross alpine meadow and barren ridge, gaze on glaciers, explore relics of mining towns. In Oregon they climb the flanks of Mount Hood, traverse fields where Indians gathered olallie (huckleberries) for winter food. In California lava-plugged Lassen Peak,

Streams and lakes teem with trout: cutthroat, golden, rainbow, brook.

Hikers cross the San Andreas Fault, which shook San Francisco in 1906.

The trail crosses desert, touches Mexico 40 miles southeast of San Diego.

torn by eruptions early in this century, ends the march of the Cascades. At Lassen Volcanic National Park, campers canoe near Cinder Cone (below) and climb past steaming fumaroles (above).

Starving pioneers, trapped by Sierra snows, turned cannibal at Donner Pass in 1846. Trail hounds today feast eyes on Lake Tahoe beauty. Here's a chance to swim and boat, and at nearby Squaw Valley (right), a chance to ski even in spring—reminder that the high country requires dress for all seasons. "Trail travelers must depend entirely on their own resources," warns the U. S. Forest Service, whose lore-filled maps (page 421) lead vacationists to high adventure.

B. ANTHONY STEWART AND (ABOVE RIGHT) JAMES P. BLAIR, BOTH NATIONAL GEOGRAPHIC STAFF. MAP BY VIRGINIA BAZA AND ISKANDAR BADAY, GEOGRAPHIC ART DIVISION

I go up into the high country at least once a year. And always I bring back memories: scarlet columbines nodding in a shaft of sunlight; a marmot whistle-warning from his rocky home; a coyote hunting in a meadow, quartering across the wind as he works the gopher holes.

I remember a morning during the summer I walked from Mexico to Oregon (though only occasionally, as that day, along the Pacific Crest Trail). Beside a lake in Desolation Valley I chatted with a father and son who wore identical caps, each half-hidden under a thicket of impaled trout flies. As I walked on up the trail, I looked back. They were fishing side by side under huge snowbanks. They looked very much alone, very much together.

On another day, south of Mount Whitney, I spread groundsheet and mummy bag beside a juniper log and set out the stove and pots and food bags and other items that build a backpacker's house wherever he stops. Then I sat and waited. And soon, far below, the sunset ignited a line of dark desert hills into fiery incandescence.

Mile after mile, day after day, in solitude or quiet companionship, I travel free from the crush and clash and scurry of our man-dominated world. For the world around me rests in harmony. Everything fits in with everything else, stone with soil, bird with branch, coyote with highland meadow. And in the end, when my mind is quiet enough, and ready, I find that I have fitted in too.

"CLIMB THE MOUNTAINS AND GET THEIR GOOD TIDINGS," urged wilderness evangelist John Muir. "Nature's peace will flow into you as sunshine flows into trees." In his beloved High Sierra country, Pacific Crest hikers find those good tidings: 306 peaks that top 12,000 feet, a 200-mile stretch of trail that never dips below 10,000.

In Yosemite, Sequoia, and Kings Canyon national parks, sunshine flows into temple groves of giant sequoias that "press close together in beautiful lines." Near Crescent Meadow in Sequoia (opposite) awed visitors find nature's peace among the thick-barked big trees; some have stood 3,500 years.

From Yosemite, with its "songful streams . . . granite domes" and ever-swelling tide of campers (below), the John Muir Trail winds southward along the Pacific Crest "through the wild untrampled kingdoms of the Sierra." Fittingly, Muir's memorial trail ends on the great flat dome of Mount Whitney, where the view sweeps from groves thick with sequoias eastward toward the searing sink of Death Valley.

B. ANTHONY STEWART, NATIONAL GEOGRAPHIC STAFF. OPPOSITE: JOE MUNROE

 Mountain-walled range beckons white-faced cattle and white-stetsoned guests on a Wyoming ranch

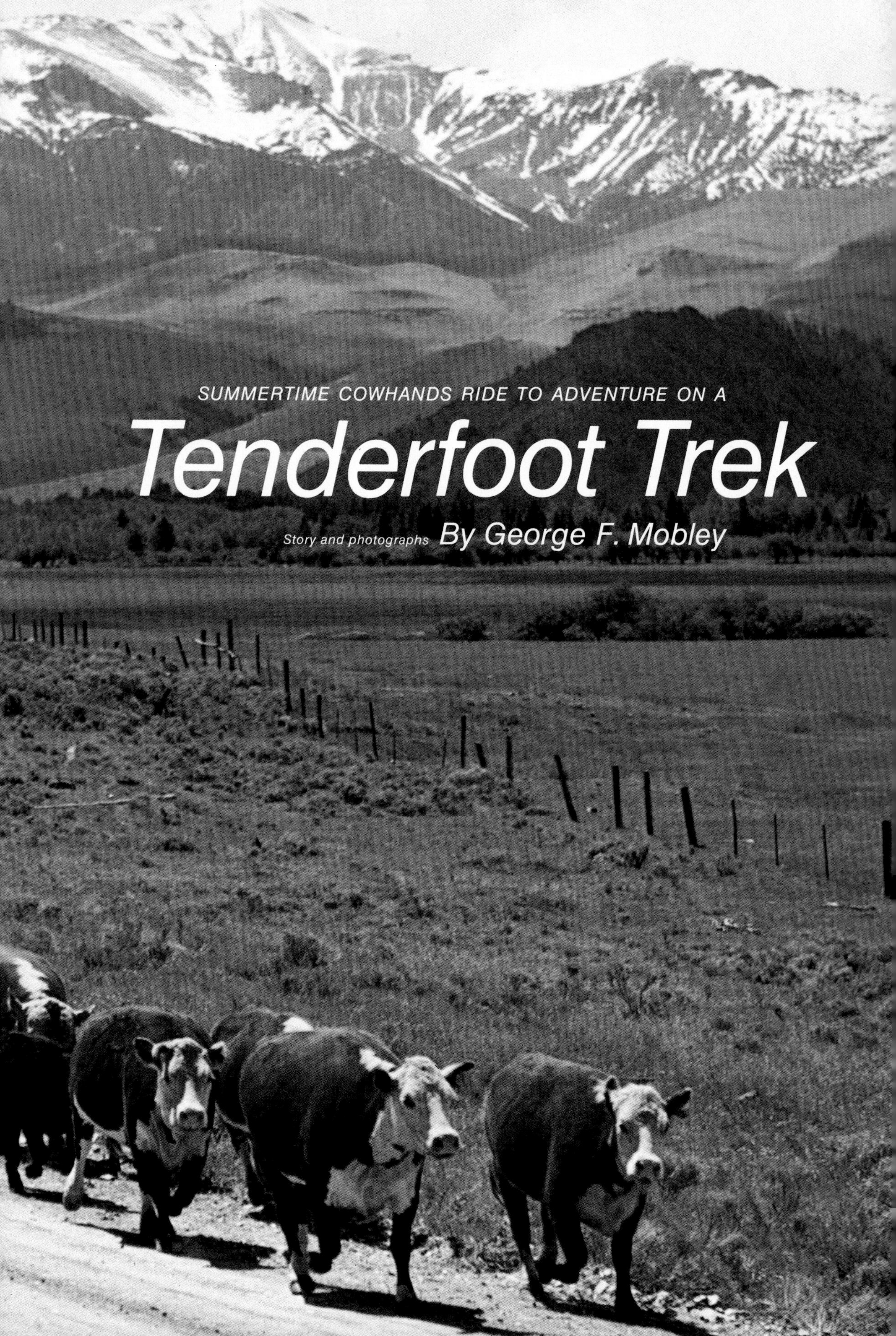

SUMMERTIME COWHANDS RIDE TO ADVENTURE ON A

Tenderfoot Trek

Story and photographs By George F. Mobley

WHEN IT'S ROUNDUP TIME at the ranch house, saddle-stiff vacationists ease onto sofas. The Seven D spread, near Cody, Wyoming, raises cattle and horses, and stirs dreams of the Old West. Pitching horseshoes, driving stock, loping along trails, grownup greenhorns play cowboy roles. Young'uns raised on TV westerns tune in on the real thing down at the old corral. Ranch lingo calls their style "Bill-show cowboy," after the dressy getups worn in Buffalo Bill's Wild West Show. Scout and hunter turned showman, he named Cody for himself, helped make it a town where Easterners—their city duds marked them as dudes—could relive frontier days. And dudes never stopped heading west.

For nearly an hour we had combed the dense pines and willow thickets along Sunlight Creek without a sign of the missing cattle. Then the whistling of a playful pair of mink caught our attention. We reined our horses out of the woods and splashed across the creek to have a look.

It was almost as if the mink had signaled to us. There in a stand of pine, beyond the quiet pool where the whistlers frolicked, stood our quarry—two cows and their calves. Ralph Newell, head wrangler of the Seven D Ranch, circled around behind the pines while I waited, ready to cut off the strays if they broke.

"Yi! Yi! Yi!" Ralph hollered. As the cows burst from the thicket, we headed them off and steered them down a dusty road toward greener pastures.

Thinking back on it at the ranch house that night, I realized it was just the kind of day I'd hoped for back East when Sunlight Basin was only a gleam in our summer

HOME ON THE ABSAROKA RANGE, WHERE THE ELK and the visitor play, the Seven D nestles in a forested valley once roved by Indian hunters—the Absaroka, or Crow people, who wandered to the Rockies from the plains; the Shoshone, whose horses bore Lewis and Clark across the Continental Divide. Shoshone National Forest surrounds the ranch, its wild solitude beckoning the hordes that crowd around Old Faithful in Yellowstone National Park, just over the horizon.

In the forest's 2,500,000 acres, hikers and horsemen trek to campsites amid mountains two miles high. Elk (below), deer, mountain sheep, grizzly and black bears roam a land still a hunting ground. Buffalo Bill guided royal gunners here; Camp Monaco marks the site where a prince roughed it. Through South Pass, at the edge of neighboring Wind River Range, climbed Mormons and '49ers on the Oregon Trail.

thoughts. My wife Marilyn and I had grown up in the big-sky country but 11-year-old Tim and 8-year-old Tammy, children of suburbia, knew the West only from textbooks and television. They had a lot of learning to do, about the way of wild things, the majesty of mountains, the wonder of a star-spattered sky, and—well, yes, about saddle sores, pesky strays, the stink of cowhide at branding time.

Our eager young dudes began learning before they ever got close to a corral. Dr. Dewey (Doc) Dominick, a retired physician who owns the Seven D, met our jet in Billings, Montana, eyed us critically, and ushered us into the nearest Western outfitter. "You can't work a ranch dressed in city duds," he explained. Laden with stetsons and riding boots, we headed south to Sunlight Basin deep in the Absaroka Range of the Wyoming Rockies.

Here amid Shoshone National Forest lay Doc's 255-acre spread, some 20 miles east of Yellowstone National Park and 50 miles northwest of Cody. We had barely settled into our three-room log cabin when the dinner bell summoned us to a meal that would awe a range-starved wrangler—elk steak, homemade bread, country butter.

Tim caught the hang of things right off. At home we often have to drag him out of bed. First morning on the ranch he

came up with the dawn and had a roaring fire going before the rest of us stirred. Decked out in our new outfits, we wandered out to the corral, leaned over the fence, and watched the ranch hands bring in a dozen horses.

Tammy quickly discovered Pedro, a mischievous little donkey who kept nudging past the corral turnstile and munching the roses that rambled round the ranch house. He was more Tammy's size than the saddle horses, and for a time he showed her a gentle side. But she discovered another donkey trait when she tried to lead him around with a rope. "He won't move!" she complained.

The rhythm of ranch life fascinated the children. Routine chores? To Tim and Tammy nothing was routine, and each chore a challenge. Tammy gathered eggs; Tim helped Doc dam the irrigation ditches that watered the hayfield. They gathered round for the horseshoeing and branding, and welcomed neighboring ranchers at the Saturday night square dances. And we all dreamed of the Cody Stampede with its rodeo coming up on the Fourth of July.

One day Ralph Newell offered to show me a beauty spot at the headwaters of Gravelbar Creek. As we saddled up, a crack thundered out of the sky and made the earth tremble. "Sonic boom," Ralph said. "The Old West is gone forever."

GUESTS IN THE WEST: THEY CAN SIT ON THE FENCE —OR EARN THEIR SPURS AT COWBOY CHORES

Rassling Pedro, a mulish donkey, or watching cowhands brand a horse, Tim and Tammy Mobley see, hear—and smell—a working ranch. "Hot iron!" yells a brander. Smoke and sizzle. "Does it hurt?" "Sure, son. But we do it fast and clean." From irons (opposite) they learn that brands, not owner names, still label ranches of the West.

Lessons in rural lore await city folk on thousands of ranches and farms in every state (page 421). Farmers harvest a new cash crop with such ads as "Restful and quiet here" or "Cookie jar always full." Lured to a 9,000-acre spread in Alaska or a dairy farm in Ohio, families discover another America that stretches beyond the suburbs. Kids gather eggs, bring home the cows, help dad coax a combine through a field of grain. Mother cans fruit or bakes pies for a social down at the Grange. Guests often live and eat with their hosts, rising and sleeping by farm time. Farmers learn to rouse visitors for the predawn birth of a calf; some welcome guests who spend the day skiing, touring, or fishing, then hurry "home" to farm-size suppers.

One city boy summed up his summer: "Everything grows! Trees, corn, beans, everything!"

We squeezed through a narrow portal of towering limestone cliffs and picked our way across several miles of fallen timber. High above the valley we spied two cow elk leading three calves downslope to our right. We watched silently as they sloshed across a creek up ahead, sunshine sparkling in the spray and glistening in the new, soft hair of the prancing calves. Suddenly the warning trumpet of a sentry elk blared forth. The woods on both sides of us exploded as spooked elk clattered up the canyon slopes and ran off. We had ridden right into the center of a herd of about 200 of them without realizing it. For 20 minutes the whistling of cows calling their calves echoed above us. Then the shrill notes died away and all was silent except for the music of tumbling water.

At the end of a hard day like that, weary of the saddle, I always looked for a plume of smoke rising through the trees beside Sunlight Creek. It signaled sauna, Indian style. Hot stones from the fire were placed in a pit in a wickiup. We crowded around, splashed water on the stones, and reveled in the clouds of steam. Then we plunged into the icy creek and emerged clean and exuberantly refreshed.

The day that we packed off into the wilderness broke warm and clear, marred only by cottony tufts clinging to the peaks. Tim and Tammy fidgeted on their horses, eager to have a go at those looming mountains. When the last pack animals were tied into line, Doc's son John led out and we began a steady climb toward the crest of the Absaroka Range. A brace of grouse, feathers ruffled, darted out to protest our intrusion into their domain, but with scarcely a pause we pushed on.

Soon the high white puffs boiled into swirling black clouds. Pines creaked eerily as a biting wind swept down

Beckoned by fingers of snow, the Seven D's pack train toils into the Absaroka wilderness. Ropes tied to tails keep skittish horses in line; on their backs rides the camp, complete with a treat of oats to top off their grazing. A frigid day's ride ends in warmth two miles up, at a site campers will leave unspoiled. Ranch rule for riding: never on Sunday, horses' day of rest. Then restless guests walk, or shatter the stillness with skeet shots.

our canyon. Thunder crackled above the crags and grumbled back and forth between the canyon walls. Last year's snowdrifts fouled our switchback trail; above timberline, fresh snow and freezing rain flailed us.

When we reached the sheltering pocket of Hoodoo Basin in late afternoon, everyone pitched in to help set up camp. Chilled and damp, I nursed the fire so that Glen Smith, our camp cook, could get the coffee started.

"You know how the old chuck wagon cooks knew when the coffee was strong enough?" asked Glen, who has roamed these mountains for most of his 60 years. "They said you could drop a horseshoe in the pot, and if the coffee was ready, the shoe would float."

Soon the tents were up, the horses staked out, and the steaks sizzling in Glen's huge iron skillet. Well-filled, warmed and dried by the fire, we crawled into sleeping bags. We awoke to a gray day sprinkled with snow. White puffs blew off the slopes in fitful squalls and churned around the evergreens. Since wet gear greatly increases the burden of breaking camp, we decided to sit out the storm.

Next morning a chorus of cheers echoed through Hoodoo Basin. Sunshine flooded our campsite and warmed our spirits. We packed up and moved on. The wilderness

__BUCKSKINS AND BRONCOS, RIDIN' AND ROPIN'__ keep the Old West alive—and kicking—at the Cody Stampede. For two July days the town corrals aficionados from horse country and horseless city, including Timberjack Joe who traps for a living and wears what he traps. Another rugged breed—the rodeo professional—rides the 500-show circuit for cash and glory; losers leave broke, sometimes broken.

Saddle-bronc contestant (below) grabs sky to prove he rides with one hand. To qualify, he must stay on 10 seconds, boots in stirrups. Fine form earns points and prizes. Unbreakable bronc bucks against rider's weight and flank cinch.

Rodeo events date from days of the trail-end roundup, when proud range riders talked big and backed their brag with payday bets.

teemed with life. We saw deer everywhere, met herds of elk, stared down porcupines, even spotted a grizzly and a pair of coyotes. When Marilyn and I returned to camp one evening and told of watching a buffalo graze, Tim protested, "I thought buffalo were extinct." The next day he saw one himself, and another Wild West fable bit the dust.

Tall tales—and true ones—went the rounds as we huddled in the fireglow under a canopy of stars. Buffalo Bill had known the solitude of these mountains; explorer John Colter had trapped beaver through here. And Sunlight Basin had sheltered rebellious Chief Joseph and his tattered band of Nez Percé Indians during their courageous 1,000-mile march in 1877. Pursuing cavalrymen laid a trap, but Joseph outfoxed them and led his tribe safely out of the valley to continue his futile bid for freedom.

Tim's fishing, not much to write home about near the ranch, picked up on the pack trip. One day he hit a hot spot at Cold Creek, reeled in his limit of cutthroat trout in short order, and scurried back to the tents with the biggest catch of our entire camp-out. Glen fried the trout for dinner,

LIKE GHOSTS GALLOPING OUT OF A VANISHED WEST, cowboys, horses, and desperate steer sweep across the night. Lassos fly, then pull tight. A crowd whoops—the show goes on. For it is only a show. The past lies buried on the plains, on a prairie no longer lone. The heritage, portrayed in a rodeo's dust, survives.

baked fresh cornbread to go with them, and, as a special treat, whipped up a chocolate frosted cake.

So it went for 10 days. We came to know the living harmony of the unspoiled wilderness, basked in its peace, and felt very close to one another. But the trip was not without its mishaps, and Tim experienced more than his share. While cutting wood one evening he sliced off the tip of a thumb. We rushed about pumping up the gasoline lantern and boiling instruments from Doc's first-aid kit. But when all was ready Marilyn, a nurse, simply clamped the tip in place with three Band-Aids. Surprisingly, the thumb healed perfectly.

Tim and Tammy grew to love the land of the cowboy and to understand his life. They learned that cowboys were real—men who worked for a living on the ranch and rode for a precarious living at rodeos.

The Seven D—as well as just about every other spread in the area—emptied for the annual Cody Stampede to watch some of the top riders of the West pit skill, stamina, and raw courage against the rage and power of beasts determined to resist man's yoke.

Glen Smith, who had worked the circuit for eight years, told us how it is with rodeo riders. "I doubt there were 10 days all told during those eight years when I wasn't black or blue or lame," he recalled. We could see why. Often Marilyn and the children hid their eyes as contestants raced and wrestled in the calf-roping and bulldogging events, hung on for dear life in saddle bronc, bareback, and bull riding. They cheered one of Glen's sons who doggedly stuck to the saddle through some fearful bucking. Just a wink before his 10-second ordeal was up, the bronc reared, forelegs kicking, butted him in the head, and flung him off. But it had been a beautiful ride.

On our last morning at the Seven D I got up at 5 a.m., saddled my palomino, and headed out with Ralph to bring in the horses. Fog lay low in the valley over Sunlight Creek, and the muted grays of twilight draped the silent woods and meadows. We climbed through sagebrush into the rolling hills and paused atop a ridge to listen to the lonely wail of a coyote defying the dawn. My horse shook his head impatiently but I lingered, watching the stars fade, witnessing the slow birth of a new day. Then, certain that memory would preserve the moment, I rode on.

By David F. Robinson

"Glory hole" of Treasure Hill, Nevada, once disgorged silver. Today it gapes at diggers hunting history in bottles—gems like those opposite that held the miners' mineral water, medicine, brandy, pickles, and stout; C. David Hiser

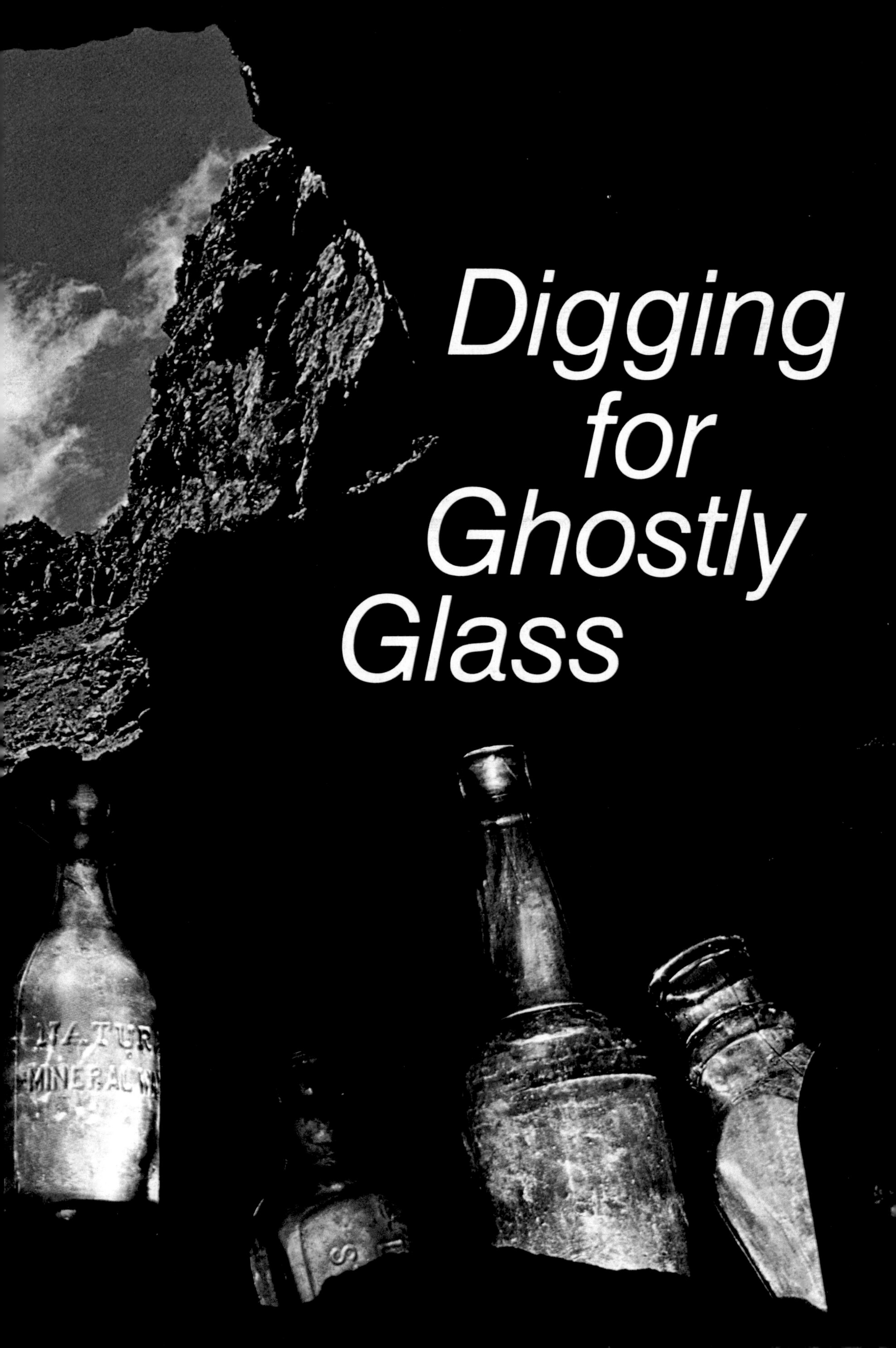
Digging
for
Ghostly
Glass

"Charlie?" I yelled. There was no reply. Moments ago he had stood behind me as I scanned the gaunt bones of miners' shanties, general stores, and saloons dotting the barren shoulder of Treasure Hill. Now only the yawning mine shafts answered the whispery breeze in eerie moans. Charlie Frates, the sun-browned Nevadan who had guided me to this haunted height, had disappeared. Funny.

No, I realized, not so funny. Some of those shafts sink only a few feet, but others will swallow a dropped boulder and you won't hear a thud for three seconds.

Suddenly a shovelful of Nevada erupted from the maw of a nearby shaft. Not the merciless rock some silver-seeker of the 1870's had blasted and pickaxed, but the soft dirt that time had tamped into the hole he left. I inched to the edge and peered over. Six feet down I saw plaid.

"She goes down at least three more feet," Charlie huffed, sweat-dappled shirt pasted to his back as he drove a yard-long iron probe into the earth. "But chances are pretty good there's bottles at the bottom. Shafts that didn't pay off at least made good dump holes." Then the probe rested while the shovel rained more of Nevada on my shoes.

We sought a treasure the old miners threw away: the heavy handmade bottles that once held cures for their ills, treats for their tables, and red-eye for their Saturday nights. As Charlie strained at the shovel—he wears out five a year prospecting for bottles—I strained for that satisfying squeak of metal against glass.

"Course you never know about bottles." His *bawtles* betrayed a New Bedford, Massachusetts, boyhood. "Once I went down 16 feet and got nothin' but a medicine vial!"

It will take more than a "dead hole" to cool Charlie's ardor for antique bottle collecting. Part detective, part historian, part gopher, Charlie began digging old glass from the ghost towns of Nevada in 1960. Friends who snickered then are shoveling now, dirt-smirched devotees of an infectious treasure hunt that some rank third behind stamps and coins in the Nation's hobby hierarchy.

Yes, I'm hooked too; I've been digging for years. At first every find was a prize—until I learned how a bottle tells you its age. Ripples, bubbles, an uneven lip, once-clear glass turned purple by the sun, a crooked neck, a seam running up to the shoulder, a ragged scar called a "pontil mark" on the base—these whisper, "Keep me, I'm handmade." But threads for a screw-on cap, a top-to-bottom hairline seam, a look of perfection mark the 20th-century bottle, a tribute to the machine, a bother to the collector.

My spade has coaxed out "keepers" from a New Hampshire cellar hole, a Michigan hedgerow, a retired Indiana

"THIS IS WHAT I CALL A LIVE TOWN . . . EVERYONE IS EXCITED." *Faded phrases from a prospector's 1869 diary haunt Nevada's White Pine Mountains where Hamilton boomed in a frantic, short-lived silver rush. Miners sank shafts, investors as far away as London sank fortunes; one syndicate raised $10 million to back a seeress whose visions never paid off. Tired of hacking rock, men filed claims for snowbanks, charged more for water than saloons got for whiskey. Today bottle hunters rove such towns; some tote metal detectors (below) to sniff out long-lost dumps.*

Elvera Frates digs where a Hamiltonian stashed his trash, while up on Treasure Hill, stripped of pines for charcoal smelters, her husband Charlie sends dirt flying from a shallow shaft. Harsh toil in a hard land, but a lucky strike may bring to hand an opium vial, balm for the bottle buff as were its contents for the weary pick-wielder who emptied it.

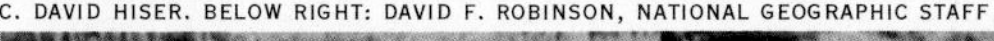

C. DAVID HISER. BELOW RIGHT: DAVID F. ROBINSON, NATIONAL GEOGRAPHIC STAFF

"THOU ART MISSED IN OUR CIRCLE. LEFT US FOR A BETTER PLACE." Deserted by flood-plagued farmers, the church in Grafton, Utah, seems to echo an epitaph from its graveyard. Whiskey flask makes a fit memorial for Hamilton, Nevada (below); its first frame business building housed a saloon. Standing relics, like buried bottles, preserve precious clues to the folkways of the early West.

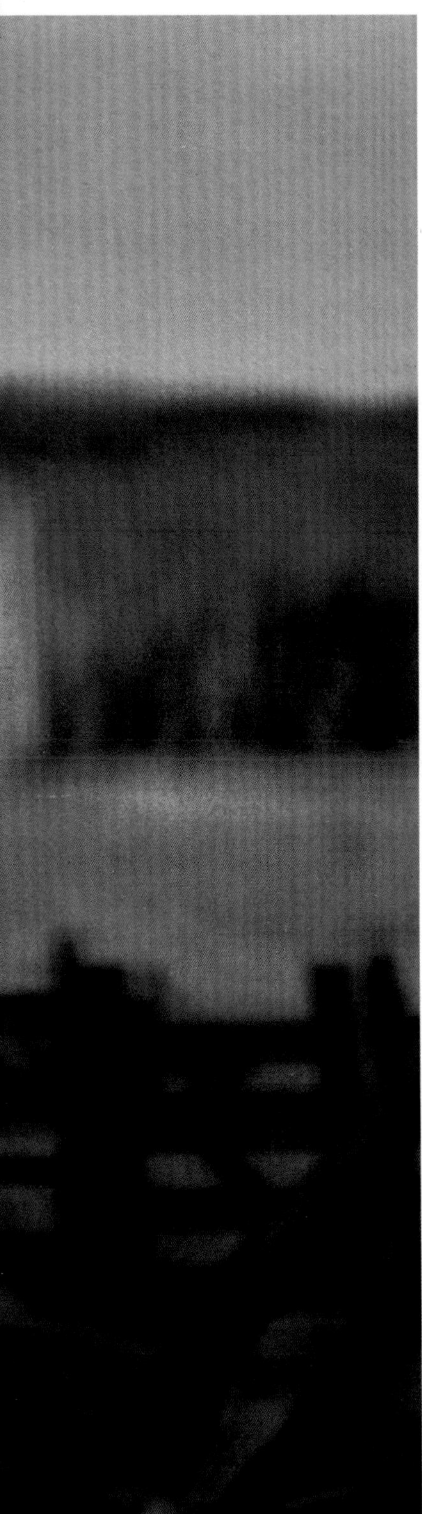

dump, a tumbledown New Jersey stable, a Virginia highway project. Now I had ventured out to the Old West, where boom and bust had left deserted cabins, sometimes whole towns beside dry gulch and rutted trail.

My quest in eastern Nevada began at the Frates home in East Ely, a near-museum where rainbows of antique glass sparkle on shelves and sills while Charlie and his wife Elvera live in the space that's left. There I laid reverent hands on a bubbly brown flask embossed with a horse and cart and the words "Success to the Railroad"; a blue ink bottle shaped like a schoolhouse; a tall blue-green jar with Gothic arches in relief on its sides. In bottle-hound jargon these were an "amber historical," a "cobalt schoolhouse," and an "aqua cathedral pickle."

I admired ironstone dishes that had survived nearly a hundred winters underground, and hefted an 1860 Colt cap-and-ball revolver that once—who knows?—held up the stage to Eureka, barked out a few salutes on the hundredth Fourth of July, maybe marched a desperado into the Cherry Creek jail. What wouldn't a prisoner have given for the huge old key that Elvera had unearthed beside that jail and now placed in my hand as a gift!

We loaded shovels, gloves, snake-bite kit, and a hamper full of Elvera's kitchen wizardry into my mini-bus. An hour of highway through sage-dotted desert led to the dirt road to Hamilton, a ruin hard by Treasure Hill. For another hour the game little bus groaned out of gullies, clawed gravel on steep upgrades, jounced over rocks scarred with metal scraped from lower-slung sedans. Here and there, mufflers and tortured tires poked from graves of drifted sand. Maybe the old miners had struggled up this track, prodding their

C. DAVID HISER

C. DAVID HISER

burros and wincing at whitened bones or broken wagon wheels along the way. Already the ghosts were stirring.

They leaped to life as we rounded a high mountain bend and dragged a tail of dust down the ruts of Hamilton. Proud arches of the Wells Fargo depot stared at our new-fangled stagecoach as we reined up. Those arches had watched prospectors, gamblers, painted ladies, and fortune hunters of every stripe pile off the stages to swell this town to 15,000 in 1869. They heard the stiff cussing of drivers whose loads had been lightened by gunslingers along the way. And after the ore petered out and a cigar-store merchant decided to collect his fire insurance, those old portals survived the flames that swallowed Hamilton.

In his 1869 diary, miner John McQuig wrote, "Buildings are going up with all possible haste"; two months later Hamilton had "grown so much . . . I hardly knew it." He would never know it now. Stone shells, a few wood shacks, and—somewhere—a trove or two of century-old bottles are all that's left of the boom town where 101 saloons made glad the night and the main street stretched a mile.

"TO CALICO . . . PURTY AS A GAL'S PETTYSKIRT"—*Thus the boys in Hank's Saloon toasted the mountain they mined, thus they named their California town that night in 1881. They dug $86 million in silver at Calico; when prices dropped, Calico shriveled. Now, in this grizzled ghost restored to life, visitors stroll where Wyatt Earp strode. They see bottles by the bushel make a little glass shack (opposite) glow in the desert sun.*

Hues highlight a fragile fortune in the Frates home in East Ely, Nevada (upper): top flasks, Wormsers of 1850's, held first of Western whiskeys; round medicinals at bottom offered a cure-all for everything but twisted tongues—"LaCour's Bitters Sarsapariphere."

TEETH
Welcome to North Calico

"Let's go up to Treasure City and dig," prodded Elvera. I spurred the bus up the steep trail where Hamiltonians hailed their first Fourth of July with all the parade they could muster: a two-man "band" whistling "Yankee Doodle" under a flag made of odds and ends, four Mormon girls in borrowed miners' boots, a boozy fiddler with an honor guard to keep him sober for the evening ball, and a worthy who orated atop a horse trough.

Treasure City, three miles from Hamilton and nearly 10,000 feet above sea level, was born when an Indian led three prospectors to a fabulous silver vein to atone for purloining a pot of beans. Motley hordes swarmed in like flies to honey. Swiftly a city rose, built partly from rock hauled out of shafts. Two autumn arrivals built a hut of stones picked up on their claim, then "mined" their home the following spring for $75,000 in silver!

The ore was incredibly rich—and tragically shallow. Maybe the bottles would assay the same, I mused, shuffling a foot through the shards left by previous diggers. Some were heartbreakers: the traceried arch of a cathedral pickle, the roof and spout of a log-cabin-shaped Plantation Bitters, and bottom after bottom with a raw pontil mark, the jagged navel where the finished bottle had been broken away from the rod that held it. On one base a name stood out: "J. Walker's V.B." Vintage Bottle? Very Busted?

"Vinegar Bitters," Elvera explained. I thought of the teetotalers of yesteryear swilling bitters in myriad variations, blithely unaware that these cure-alls often packed a wallop that put whiskey to shame. No wonder they felt better.

"What a find a whole one like that would be," I said. While Charlie dug in his rock-walled wishing well, Elvera and I staked a claim by the corner of a fallen shanty. We rolled away surface rock, shoveled down a foot, troweled a bit farther, and—*squeak*. Gingerly, Elvera freed a thumb-sized cylinder from its tomb. "D[r] Thompson's Eye Water New London Conn[t]," the little bottle proclaimed.

"Wow!" I crowed.

Without a sound Elvera casually laid the find aside and kept troweling. "Don't let on," she murmured, though I couldn't see another soul on Treasure Hill. "If another digger hears, he might move in on your spot when you leave for lunch. Some even watch with binoculars."

Blasé outside, butterflies inside, we coolly mined our tiny lode. Day's end found us gloating over a two-inch "Dr Sages Catarrh Remedy," an aqua Helmbold Extracts, a leaning liquor bottle so dark it made the sun a tiny olive, and a little clay crucible that once told a miner the

"WE'VE STRUCK 'ER BOYS! . . . SILVER GALORE!" Iron monsters heard the yells and snorted to the sites. Today scenic riches of crag and canyon keep old rails throbbing. On narrow-gauge track laid in 1882, the Durango-to-Silverton coal burner chugs through San Juan National Forest in Colorado (below).

Passengers at Calico (opposite) ride in style old-timers never knew. There burros hauled ore, on rare holidays bore picnickers to nearby moonscapes in Odessa Canyon, today a rock hound's rugged Eden.

C. DAVID HISER. BELOW: JAMES L. AMOS, NATIONAL GEOGRAPHIC PHOTOGRAPHER

"HERE'S A DANDY ROCK!"

Like any other rock hound, the collector exulted: "A grapefruit-sized dandy!" And the world exulted with him. For this was Astronaut Pete Conrad adding a chunk of the moon to the priceless collection of Apollo 12.

America's million other rock hunters can only gaze on a moon rock in a museum (page 120) and yearn for such a prize. But give them a weekend and off they go, eager as any bottle digger—which many of them are—in quest of down-to-earth prizes of their own: jade from a Wyoming riverbank, gold from an Indiana stream, topaz from a Colorado mountain.

With chisels and picks they nibble at cliff and highway cut. With crowbar and car jack they leave no stone unturned in the search for specimens, some with names only a rock hound could love: manganotantalite, granodiorite, pahoehoe, clinozoisite.

With magnifiers they peer at anthills; a bright speck may signal gemstones. Some gem hunters pack an empty bottle and discard any stone too soft to scratch it. One test of how a rock will look when polished: lick it.

Some explore with Geiger counters, metal detectors, ultraviolet lamps that find brilliance in drab-looking "fluorescent" rocks. Most try simpler tests. Scratching with thumbnail, penny, knife, or file gauges hardness; pouring vinegar on a rock detects calcite content (limestone fizzes merrily). Iron pyrite (left) may look like gold; dreams fade when "fool's gold" draws a black line on a "streak plate" of unglazed tile.

Thousands of varieties await collectors, many only a stone's throw from home, others far afield. Only the West yields obsidian; Franklin, New Jersey, boasts franklinite, found nowhere else. Agate-filled thunder eggs can be picked up around Prineville, Oregon, and in New Mexico's Rock Hound State Park. Visitors to Inyo National Forest in California may keep bits of rock containing fossilized creatures 400 million years old.

Rock hounds often grow from "pebble pups," youngsters awed simply by "pretty stones." In New York's Adirondacks a lad fishes from a pothole a rounded rock that helped grind it (opposite). In such humble stones—granite from magma, shale that once was mud, slate that once was clay—collectors read earth's biography. Since life wrote the latest chapter, many collections include fossils, artifacts of early man, Indian, and colonist—and even bottles.

Petrified wood, green malachite on blue azurite, and amethyst in brownish matrix; Victor R. Boswell. Above, James P. Blair, and opposite, David F. Robinson. All National Geographic staff

quality of his ore. Charlie had burrowed nine feet without a squeak—but who could say what waited at twelve?

Though we hadn't hit a bonanza, our little strike was reward enough for one day. For some it wouldn't be. They build collections with dollars instead of sweat, paying hundreds in shops or at auctions for something I might one day dig up. But maybe they miss the time-mellowed elixir of history that pours from a new-dug bottle, that tells you what its owner drank or suffered from, that makes holding it like shaking hands across a fence of years.

I shook across that fence many times in ghost towns all over the West. Some slumber in ruin, others cling doggedly to life, a few lure tourists with restorations of "the way it used to be." But for me, the Old West came in bottles. "Shake, podner," I could say across the decades, "I got a hankerin' for buried treasure myself."

Several days and hundreds of miles after I had bidden goodbye to Charlie and Elvera, I discovered in the luggage deck a beautiful old bottle, a rippled cylinder of deep aqua topped by a bubbly neck and a crude handmade lip. Inside was a note: "I was lying peacefully for 100 years on Treasure Hill until a couple of nuts from East Ely dug me up."

I turned the prize over and read "J. Walker's V.B."

Back home in Virginia I watch a dying sun do wondrous things to a windowful of bottles. I glance at my treasure from Treasure Hill, the ghosts begin to stir again, and I'm ready to start packing. That's the way it is with bottle hounds, never happy unless they're down in the dumps.

*"**PROSPECTS... WERE NEVER MORE ENCOURAGING**," wrote a visitor to Eureka, Nevada, in 1872. He was right: In the next quarter century Eureka poured out gold and silver, led the world in lead. In 1879 the elegant Opera House (opposite) rang up the curtain. Here crowds cheered the era's brightest stars. Vaudeville, movies, even billiards in time played brief roles. Now only a curio shop holds the spotlight.*

Graves in nine cemeteries mirror Eureka's rise and fall, from stone mounds of a mining camp to fenced and sculptured monuments of a city of wealth, finally to warped wooden slabs of a hard-times hamlet.

Men of Eureka drive 150 miles for a haircut; Belmont boasts but a single resident; a sign in Nipton, California, notes a population of three, then adds "Town for Sale." One Nevadan, shamed by the rotting bonanza towns, once proposed plowing them under. But the skeletons still stand, delighting bottle hunters and nostalgic roamers, remembering past glories, dreaming impossible dreams. Somethin' might pan out. Around Eureka there's talk of oil.

C. DAVID HISER. OPPOSITE: DAVID F. ROBINSON, NATIONAL GEOGRAPHIC STAFF

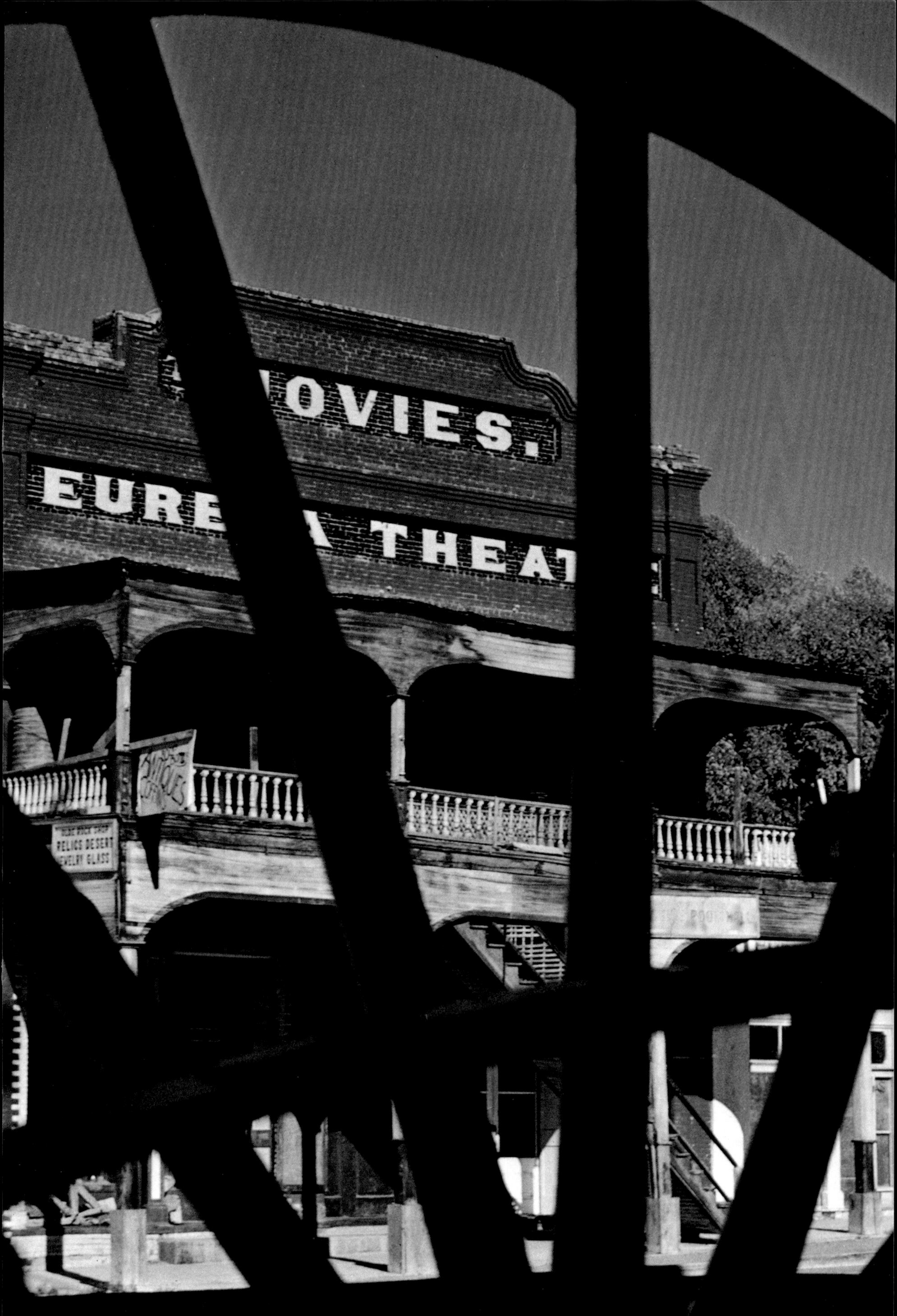
OVIES.
EURE
A THEA
RELICS DESERT

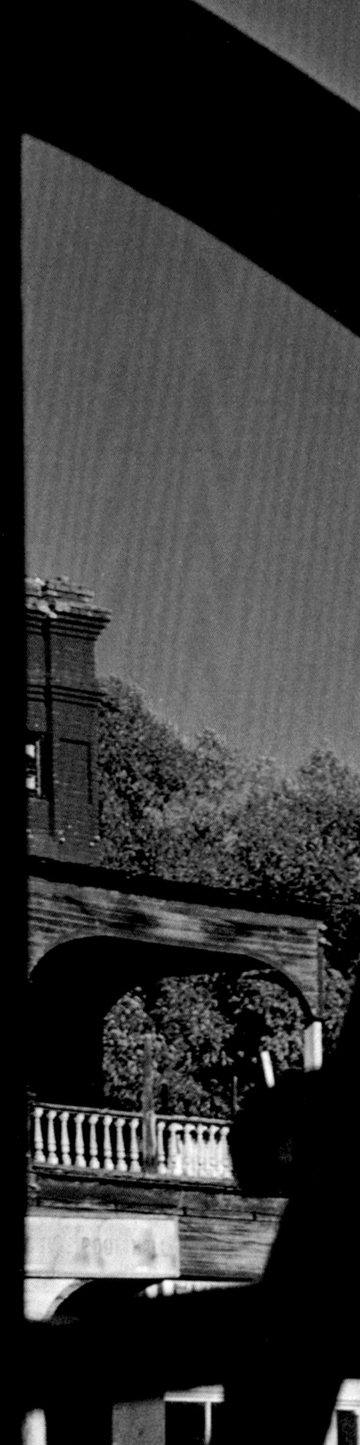

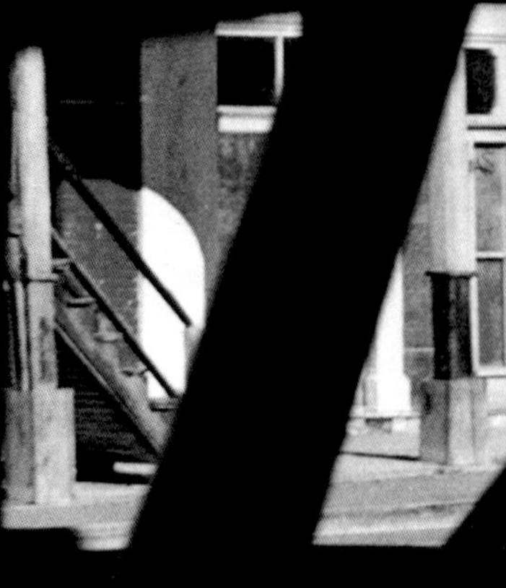

ON POWDERED PEAKS ROUND ASPEN
WINTER WANDERERS REAP NEW SKILLS AS

Skifarers in the Rockies

In flawless form, instructors furrow fresh snow at Aspen; Dick Durrance II, National Geographic photographer

By Samuel W. Matthews

DICK DURRANCE II, NATIONAL GEOGRAPHIC PHOTOGRAPHER

Down the Big Burn she came, her blond hair streaming in the sunlight, singing at the top of her lungs, "This . . . is . . . MY-Y-Y-Y . . . mountain!"

That can't be Katy, I thought. Nine years old and skiing the highest slope of Snowmass-at-Aspen? But it was. Legs apart, arms outstretched, pure joy untouched by fear.

Behind her, skis carving fresh powder, swooped our three other *Wunderkinder:* Mary, 16, all elbows and stately snowplow; David, two days before his 15th birthday, parallel-turning as if born to it; and Tom, 11, spraying snow, poles flashing as he swung in sheer exuberance.

This was Aspen, Colorado, in late February, and a long winter's dream had come to life. From the brown, snow-bare hills around Washington we had flown to this skyline of white-crowned peaks marching rank on rank across the horizon: the Rockies, courtyard of heaven for skiers.

We were, and are, a typical Eastern ski family. We spend precious weekend hours driving to the machine-made snow and traffic-jam slopes of the mid-Appalachians, from Virginia's Blue Ridge to Pennsylvania's Alleghenies and Poconos. We have sampled New England's bustling ski-grounds, where David and I, on another birthday, threaded

BENDING TO THE WILL of their instructor (opposite), Sam Matthews and children Katy, Tom, David, and Mary shift weight, flex knees, tilt torsos—building balance and timing that leads, one expert says, to "the real joy . . . the lightness, the floating" on Aspen's feathery runs. Ski school split the author's family into classes where members could progress with peers. Preschoolers, like the hapless lass on her knees, flop and flounder until true grit and sturdy poles hoist her erect on rubbery legs. Many a first-timer's "real joy" is simply standing up.

Sun-swathed snow bowl lulls skiers at a rest stop on Aspen Mountain (above) deep in Colorado's rocky heart Tourtelotte Park here honors the memory of a silver prospector of the 1880's, when unschooled skiers barreled down the slopes on hefty planks called "snow shoes" and steered with long wooden staves.

the tree-walled trails of Mount Mansfield in Vermont. And one mid-July, on a camping trip, we paused at 12,000-foot Independence Pass in Colorado, pelting one another with summer snowballs. Then we drove down to Aspen and saw soaring slopes awaiting winter's touch. Someday, we vowed, we would return in snow time. And now we had.

The snow hissed under my skis, pluming upward on the turns like dust tossed into the sun. It was unlike anything we had known in the East—lighter, drier, free of ruts or ice, on a firm base six feet deep. Next day, almost surely, there would be more of it, a fresh new counterpane.

Down I rocketed—for I was far behind the children now—past the lift-top restaurant on Sam's Knob, through the Banzai Cutoff to West Village, amber-shingled, bright flags fluttering amid silvery aspens. My legs ached, my lungs gulped. Katy was just leaning her skis into a rack.

"Where've *you* been, in a snowbank?" she wanted to know. "It's time for a hot chocolate." Aspen, cradled in its high, white, breathtaking world, does that to you.

It is a town reborn from the past. In the bonanza days of the 1880's, Aspen reigned as queen of Colorado's silver-rich Western Slope. It boasted an opera house and brick hotel, handsome Victorian homes, 10 churches, and a "fancy ladies" district. Some 15,000 fortune hunters worked and wrangled and rollicked there, and ore poured from the mountains. Then came the Panic of 1893; silver prices fell, and Aspen withered.

Only a few hundred residents remained by the winter of 1936-37, when André Roch, a Swiss engineer and skier, blazed the first ski trail on Aspen Mountain. World War II interrupted, but Roch's vision lived on and snow proved a bonanza richer than silver.

Today not one but four of Aspen's surrounding mountains are crisscrossed by some 30 lifts and more than 200 miles of manicured slopes and trails: Aspen Mountain, now called Ajax by many to distinguish it from nearby Aspen Highlands; Buttermilk, across the scenic Maroon Creek Valley, specially designed for beginning and intermediate skiers; and Snowmass, seven miles west, the highest and largest ski development in Colorado.

Most skiers go to Aspen, as we did, for at least a week. Its distance from any major city discourages weekenders. Its pace is thus more leisurely, and though 15,000 skiers may be in town, it seldom seems crowded.

Veteran Aspen-goers advise new arrivals to avoid headaches by spending a day letting lungs adjust to the 8,000-foot altitude. But few can long resist putting on skis. We began, as most do, at Buttermilk. There the Aspen Ski School, with as many as 200 instructors at peak of season,

DICK DURRANCE II, NATIONAL GEOGRAPHIC PHOTOGRAPHER. OPPOSITE: TONY GAUBA

ASPEN EXPLODES FOR THE WINTERSKOL FESTIVAL. Salutes shred the night as torch-bearing skiers sizzle down Little Nell, one of 47 runs that rise above the town; float parade, dances, ski races add sparkle to the season's crescendo in late January.

Off the beaten tracks, Aspen-goers don light skis for a cross-country glide capped by a cookout (above), peak-hop by helicopter, and swim in heated pools rimmed by snow. Stiff limbs limber up après-ski; *food (and prices) run the gamut—pizza,* haute cuisine *in high style, or steak in a barn reached by sleigh (left).*

In summer Aspen welcomes a famed music festival and the Institute for Humanistic Studies, where scholars and business executives trade ideas and volleyball shots amid the mind-opening beauty of the green-walled valley.

teaches both neophyte and expert. Grouped by ability, students form classes of up to 10 each.

Katy, who could do creditable snowplow turns, queued up in the chair-lift line behind a smiling girl in the blue parka of Aspen instructors. Tom, a level higher in skill, was assigned to a group his own age. David, the best of us all, found himself the only teen-ager in a class labeled "Advanced," meeting a sunburned, skeptical instructor named Bob Kesselring. For the next few days I was to struggle simply to keep up. Meanwhile, gentler, more forgiving teachers took charge of Mary and her mother.

Gliding successfully downhill on a pair of supple, willful boards longer than you are demands balance, coordination—and sheer gall. A slight shift of weight from ski to ski, a flexing of knees at just the right moment, and amazingly the skis will turn. How they turn is up to you, a matter of practice until controlling them becomes all but unconscious. Then skiing comes close to natural flight—an ultimate exultation, a "fierce euphoria."

"Kess" began with basics—how to drop knee and shoulder and shift weight in a parallel turn. He had us finish by plunging a pole into the snow and punctuating the move with bloodcurdling shouts. All day passing skiers stared at an apparently peaceful class bellowing "Kill! Kill!"

Finally he was satisfied. "Keep it up," he said, "and you can try the Aspen Standard Race on Friday." That was enough. David had his goal.

With our class we practiced new skills on Aspen's other mountains. At Snowmass we ran the spectacular, spruce-dotted swath of Big Burn, a mile wide and a mile long. On Ajax, gazing down at Aspen as if on a street map, we skied the giant chute-the-chute of Spar Gulch, which can be taken straight and fast or in a series of roller-coaster swoops from wall to wall.

It was at Snowmass that we heard of the skier on the Last Great Chair Lift in the Sky who saw a figure speeding downhill with form too perfect for any mortal. "Who's that?" the skier asked his accompanying angel. "That's St. Peter," came the reply, "but he thinks he's Stein Eriksen."

Eriksen, the Norwegian Olympic champion who formerly directed the ski school, is widely regarded as the most graceful man ever to don skis. Riding the Campground lift one day, we spotted him leading a conga line of off-duty instructors. As they shot over a knoll they extended their arms, caught the air with gaudy kite sails, and soared into space. Seconds later, they were lost in a cloud of powder.

The week flew by, and suddenly it was David's birthday

NORM CLASEN. UPPER: DICK DURRANCE II, NATIONAL GEOGRAPHIC PHOTOGRAPHER. OPPOSITE: C. DAVID HISER

THE SKY'S THE LIMIT FOR SOARING SNOWBIRDS *who once toiled "upski" on a wheezy rope tow rigged from old mining gear. Speedy chair lift (above) shuttles 1,200 skiers an hour to the "Sundeck" atop Aspen Mountain. Copter hauls fewer but ranges farther and higher; passengers (upper) alight on 13,561-foot Mt. Hayden, to cleave its deep powder in splendid solitude.*

Daredevil at Aspen Highlands (opposite) blasts off in a crouching Geländesprung *(field jump) contest. Skiing migrated to America with Scandinavians; daring "yoompers" got the sport off the ground.*

—and the day of the standard race as well. In this event a champion runs a giant slalom course, with its zigzag, pole-marked gates, to set a standard time. Contestants race against that time; any who come close enough win a coveted Aspen skier's pin—gold, silver, or bronze.

As we donned bibs with numerals front and back, the forerunner flashed down the half-mile course on Buttermilk at 42.2 seconds, nearly 45 miles an hour.

At the sound of the starter's "Go!" David catapulted from the gate, swung through three hard turns, and disappeared. We could hear the timer at the foot of the run by walkie-talkie: "He's in sight . . . holding the gates well . . . here he comes. . . ."

And after a pause: "Fifty-seven seconds flat."

Tom started off like a commando, fast and recklessly. Halfway down his feet came apart, a ski caught an edge, and he fell, wiping out a gate. He scrambled back on course and finished gamely, but he had lost precious time.

When my own turn came, I suddenly found that all I had learned from Bob Kesselring had vanished. I lurched through the turns; yet, I almost outlasted the run. Then breath, balance, and control went simultaneously, a ski shot out from under, a boot snapped free, and Walter Mitty ended in a shower of snow.

But David's time had won him a bronze pin. His grin as he received the award at day's end was as wide as all Buttermilk Mountain. Months later, that pin still glints on his sweater. Aspen lies half a continent away. But the memory of it is as close as the next snowfall, as shining as the years of skiing still to come.

GLIDING DOWN TRACKLESS SLOPES,
VROOMING *OVER FROZEN HILL AND DALE,*
INDOORSMEN BREAK OUT TO FROLIC IN

WILD WINTER

In mountains that even Indians abandoned to the cold, a flight of snowbirds swoops and schusses down spruce-shaded slopes. It's Vail, Colorado, a winter paradise—with an instant Swiss village—that sprouted out of the Rockies' thin air in White River National Forest.

In the Great Smokies, North Carolina drawls mingle with Alpine accents as imported experts coach native novices through snowplow turns and stops. It's a booming "banana belt" ski resort, where snow guns spew out a blizzard every

SKIERS TRAIL ROOSTERTAILS AT VAIL; DEAN CONGER, NATIONAL GEOGRAPHIC STAFF

BOBSLEDDERS HIT A CURVE AT LAKE PLACID; B. ANTHONY STEWART, NATIONAL GEOGRAPHIC STAFF. LOWER: ICEBOATS SKIM ACROSS LAKE CHAMPLAIN, VERMONT, AT UP TO 80 MPH; ERNEST GAY. LOWER RIGHT: HUSKIES AND THEIR LADIES RACE AT WAITSFIELD, VERMONT; B. ANTHONY STEWART. RIGHT: SNOWMOBILER GETS A BOUNCE FROM HIS BRONCO DURING AN OBSTACLE-COURSE RACE AT LACONIA, NEW HAMPSHIRE; DICK DURRANCE II, NATIONAL GEOGRAPHIC PHOTOGRAPHER

Friday—or any other day cold enough to keep the powder dry. North and South, frost-smitten Americans respond as gleefully as schoolboys let out for a snowball fight. Today nearly one out of every three people vacation in the cold. Hibernation is for the bears.

Snowmobilers invade white wonderlands to gaze on snowscapes few men have seen. Big, open-roofed tractors clank sightseers along once impenetrable trails in Yellowstone National Park. Why roar into the frozen wilds? "When the store or the family crowd too much," says a Maine druggist, "I take to the deep woods in my snowmobile, shut off the engine, and sit alone in a beautiful, silent world. It's better medicine than anything in my pharmacy."

Younger snowmobilers crisscross the countryside to explore, to socialize, some to race at speeds up to 100 miles an hour. Grandsons of sleigh drivers, forsaking the family car, go courting in snug snowmobiles where three's a crowd. But there's no romance in running out of gas in the snow.

Some people sputter at "motorcycles on skis"; industry codes and state laws keep them in check, channel them into

a network of trails and old logging roads—2,000 miles of them in New England alone. In the Arctic, Eskimos trade in their dogsleds for motorized huskies.

But dogsledding thrives. At Laconia, New Hampshire, some 30,000 people crowd in to watch hundreds of huskies, some driven by lady mushers, compete in championship races; in Alaska, purses may reach $50,000. On frozen lakes fleets of brightly colored fiberglass boats sail across the ice, replacing the heavy wooden ice yachts of yesteryear. And bobsledding, a popular Olympic spectator sport, offers the thrill of participation at the run near Lake Placid in the Adirondacks, where pros steer tourists down the mile-long

SKIERS STEP LIVELY THROUGH A FROSTED WOODLAND ON CANNON MOUNTAIN, NEW HAMPSHIRE; B. ANTHONY STEWART, NATIONAL GEOGRAPHIC STAFF

trough. Sledding took a new twist when collegians imported the flexible little *luge* (French for sled). To steer, you lie back, press toes against the runners' tips, pull reins, and apply body English. Basic gear includes helmet and goggles, for luges careen down icy runs at speeds up to 60 miles an hour.

Sleek garb and safer equipment have lured the timid onto ice and snow. Artificial-ice rinks blossom even in magnolia country; from Palm Springs, California, to Central Park, New York, millions of skaters spin and spill. Winter, once a delight only to small boys and fuel dealers, is now open to all—those who want to speed through it, as well as those who would pause to relish its lonely majesty (page 421).

UPPER: SPEED SKATERS RACE AT LAKE PLACID; JAMES L. AMOS, NATIONAL GEOGRAPHIC PHOTOGRAPHER

Ghostly Spanish riders in a Navajo pictograph, perhaps cavalrymen in a bloody 1805 invasion, haunt the walls of the "Canyon of the Dead" in Canyon de Chelly National Monument, Arizona; Ernst Haas

By Arthur P. Miller, Jr.

PROUD DWELLERS OF PUEBLO AND PLATEAU WELCOME A FAMILY

Exploring a Cherished Past

Like figures from a canyon wall painting come to life, corn dancers of Santo Domingo Pueblo fill the plaza. Juniper bough in one hand, gourd rattle in the other, tribesmen in deerskin kilts stomp, sway, pivot, and stomp again. Black-garbed women step softly in place, caressing the brown earth with bare feet.

The drummer picks up the tempo, pounding on his hide-topped hollow log. Rattles quiver in reply. Bells clink. A priest holds aloft his prayer wand to bless the dancers as a chorus of elders adds a moaning chant to this plea for rain.

Villagers and relatives from nearby pueblos take in the tableau from flat rooftops or from the shade of adobe dwellings that frame the plaza. As outsiders, we swelter in the August sun of New Mexico. Silently, I second the priest's prayers.

Now a black-kilted figure, face and body painted a ghostly white, darts through the rows of dancers. "Who's that?" whispers 11-year-old Kathryn, second oldest of my four daughters. A *Koshare*—a clownish master of ceremonies, I explain. As he cavorts, he corrects the dancers to assure a flawless performance. Through the long day the ritual continues, 600 Indians in two groups repeating their entreaties for a good crop, for harmony among all mankind, but most of all for rain.

I do not know how Santo Domingo's crops fared. Harmony among men remains a distant hope. But late in the afternoon of that day cumulus clouds piled high, blotting out the sun. A breeze brushed by, rain at its heels. Yet no dancer missed a step, no drummer a beat. The dampened chorus chanted on. When the cooling drops

IN INDIAN COUNTRY THE VISITOR VENTURES INTO OTHER WORLDS, *where strange speech strikes his ear, sweeping vistas steal his breath. Vestiges of ancient ways open his eye to the original Americans whose forebears trekked from Asia to tame two continents. The author's daughters clamber in a cleft of time in Monument Valley (opposite upper), red-rock showplace of Navajoland.*

To moderns daring its heights, New Mexico's Puye Cliffs (lower) whispers of men tilling mesa tops centuries ago. From thousands of rooms in this cliff city archeologists have dug weapons, utensils, and pottery depicting the Plumed Serpent, preserver of life-giving springs and streams.

The splendid ruin belongs to the living Santa Clara Pueblo, where a villager (left) cooks "fry bread" over open flame. Here men sway to the rhythm of the rain dance—some just home from their jobs at Los Alamos, birthplace of the atomic bomb.

TERRY EILER

turned to a downpour, I shepherded my wife Marge and the girls to the shelter of an overhang.

You can read in books about the Pueblo people—how they believe themselves a part of nature, not masters of it; how their ceremonies encourage the seasons to come in proper order. But you will not see those raindrops bless the arid earth unless you are there. The best way is to see for yourself, as we did.

For five weeks we roamed the bleak beauty of the sculptured southwestern landscape. We strolled dusty Pueblo villages little changed from days when Spanish conquistadors marched into them. In the vast realm of the Navajos—inheritors of a nomadic tradition, unlike the Pueblo townsfolk—we watched free-spirited shepherds guide their flocks across the red rangelands.

Everywhere we encountered people with leather-tan faces and jet-black hair who spoke a strange language. Among the Pueblos you will hear Northern Tiwa and Southern Tiwa, Tewa and Towa—with dialect variations in each. Sometimes people of neighboring villages cannot understand each other unless they speak Spanish or English.

"It's almost like being in a foreign country," remarked 13-year-old Susan. "Yes, except here we're the foreigners in our own country," I reminded her. Our country? How easily we forget that the predecessors of today's Pueblo Indians probably inhabited the Southwest at least 6,000 years before our own ancestors crossed the Atlantic.

To follow the Indian trail and learn the ancient ways of folk who trace their ancestry not to Europe but to Asia, my tribe chose a late-model prairie schooner. Our rented motor home slept six snugly and charmed my squaw with its refrigerator, sink, and stove. Hopefully, we named our covered wagon *Pay-e-tha*—"Friend" in Tiwa.

We began where the old Santa Fe Trail ended. At the Museum of New Mexico in Santa Fe we studied the story of the Anasazi, the "Old Ones" of prehistory, who learned to cultivate corn ("Pueblo gold") and settled down in villages; of Navajo and Apache raiders ravaging the peaceful farmland; of conquistadors singlemindedly searching for gold. Across the museum's sunlit patio the girls peered into full-scale replicas of an early Apache wickiup, a traditional Navajo hogan of mud and logs, and a Pueblo adobe.

Next day we stepped into a living, multi-tiered pueblo at Taos, one of the Indian villages strung like brown beads along the brown Rio Grande. Past blended with present as shawled women and blanketed men of the mountain town trod the picture-postcard plaza.

TERRY EILER. FAR RIGHT: ERNST HAAS

FAITH OF THEIR FATHERS STILL STIRS INDIAN HEARTS, *still draws tribesmen together for timeless rites to ancestral gods. Though youngsters—like Navajos at an Arizona tribal festival (far right)—may liven a lull with a giggle, their elders keep traditional ceremonies solemn. Outsiders may not photograph or take notes at some dances, may not even witness others. Some they do see may honor only the tourist, bringer of dollars to reservations that admit him (page 421).*

Drummers (above) set the tempo for dancers (opposite lower) in an annual ritual at Puye Cliffs. Outfits hark back to hunters who honored the spirits of beasts they slew and danced to ensure a successful hunt.

"Behold us maned with buffaloes' dead manes," droned chanters in one Zuni rite. Many chants made no sense; meaningless syllables made them easily borrowed by tribes of a different tongue. Dress, too, spread from tribe to tribe as celebrants donned finery to please themselves and visitors. Now garb of the Plains enriches Eastern powwows, and a daughter of the Crows from Montana (opposite) joins a New Mexico ceremonial with a jaunty feather in her hair, badge of manhood among her ancestors.

TERRY EILER. OPPOSITE: JOERN GERDTS, PHOTO RESEARCHERS, INC.

"I smell something baking," sniffed Kathy, suddenly aware of how long it had been since breakfast. Near Hlaukwima (South House) we found Ann Romero baking yeasty loaves in a thick-walled oven, a giant beehive of adobe. She told us how her brother early that morning had built a fire of cedar logs inside the oven, let the logs burn to ash, then scraped the interior clean. Into the still-hot oven Ann set 20 loaves of dough. Fifteen minutes later, out came fragrant, golden-crusted bread—gobbled up by hungry tourists like the Millers at 50 cents a loaf.

Fascinated by pottery, Marge soon learned to recognize each pueblo's style—the geometric patterns of Santo Domingo, the round bean pots of Picuris, the animal motifs of Zia, the polished redware of Santa Clara. And the beautiful "black-on-black"—designs in dull black on a burnished background—fashioned by famed Maria Martinez.

"UP THE LADDER AND DOWN THE LADDER" went pueblo dwellers, scaling first-floor adobe walls, then entering by hatches the rooms within; there village life pulsed. In time of danger ladders went up and enemies faced a blank wall. Doors and windows now hole houses; but at Taos (above) and 18 other pueblos, life cleaves to old ways. In beehive ovens women still bake bread; on overhead racks they dry the family's winter meat.

Navajos shunned villages; many still do. Like the pattern on a Navajo loom (opposite), the ancient design is passed along.

IN CRAFTS THAT SPAN THE CENTURIES, THE ART OF THE INDIAN SHINES. A skin becomes a moccasin in the patient fingers of a Taos artisan (opposite). Pueblo men hunted the animals, dressed and sewed the skins, proved their skill by crafting knee-high moccasins for their betrothed. From the pueblos comes most Indian pottery, shaped from clay coils and fired on a bed of coals. Steady hand of a San Ildefonso potter (bottom) adds a finishing touch; tribal symbols—even a pot's shape—tell which pueblo produced it. Design marks a girl's silver finery as Navajo (below); her forebears learned this craft in the 1850's.

TERRY EILER

Acclaimed for innovations which stirred a renaissance in the Indian potter's craft half a century ago, once a guest at the White House, Maria lives and works in the tiny pueblo of San Ildefonso, 20 miles north of Santa Fe.

Her son Popovi Da—Red Fox in the Tewa tongue—led us up a hill to Maria's adobe home. Reading my wife's mind, he asked, "Would you like to try a pot?"

Pueblo potters use no wheel, only their hands. Deftly kneading the red-brown clay, Popovi showed Marge how to roll a "sausage" between her palms, then carefully coil it around the edge of the *puki,* or base, to build the wall.

"Keep the wall thick so you have something to shape," he said. "Hold it up once in a while. See if it's even all around. Smooth the outside with the gourd scraper."

Just then Maria herself slipped in, a slight figure whose sparkling eyes belied her eighty-odd years. She and her son talked in Tewa as Marge proudly put the finishing touches to "her" pot. Now the vessel would dry in the sun, bake over a fire, and then. . . . Maria pointed outside to a waist-high bush with a lavender blossom: "You cut it, boil it, use it for black dye. Very good."

This is the way of the Pueblo craftsman: He takes gifts of the earth and with his art and his skill transforms them into things of beauty and utility.

Indian jewelry, too, tugged Marge like a magnet to trading post and shop window. Santo Domingo takes pride in its shell-and-turquoise necklaces, as do the Hopis in their overlay silverwork and the Navajos in their concha belts of hammered silver. But the clever fingers of the Zuni create the Southwest's most intricate lapidary work. Even other Indians buy Zuni jewelry.

On the Zuni reservation south of Gallup we stood on heaps of rubble, the remains of the ancient town of Hawikuh, where Coronado discovered with dismay that the pueblos of the Southwest were not paved with gold. Today silver, not gold, brings outsiders to Zuni—and purchase orders for jewelry from San Francisco and New York. I spent a morning watching master silversmith Horace Iule create a turquoise-studded necklace. Later, in Gallup, I spotted another example of Horace's artistry—a magnificent concha belt with price tag to match: $3,500.

"With beauty before me, I walk. With beauty behind me, I walk." The words of the old Navajo chant ring true. The Navajos walk with beauty, 16 million acres of it, a richly painted desertland that sprawls across northeastern Arizona, spills into New Mexico and Utah, and surrounds the mesa-top homeland of some 6,000 Hopis.

On an arrow-straight road, as we sped into the "51st State," eight-year-old Janet poured out guidebook statistics while seven-year-old Nancy kept a lookout for animals that wandered freely across our path. In this fenceless domain live the adaptable people whose tribe has increased more than ten-fold in the last century to 120,000, making the Navajo the largest Indian tribe in the Nation.

Here shepherd families shift with the seasons from mud-chinked hogan to breezy brush shelter, and women weave bright rugs on timeworn upright looms. Here, too, Navajo rangers welcome tourists to seven tribal parks complete with campgrounds. And at the bustling capital of Window Rock, Arizona, Navajo leaders negotiate leases for the oil and gas beneath this red-rock realm, while data processing machines grind out the tribal payroll.

"You should see the arts and crafts center we built at Monument Valley in the Four Corners region—and the view from the observatory," Navajo parks director Sam Day III told us at Window Rock.

Everyone should. The picture window at the Monument Valley Visitor Center frames a scene of incomparable grandeur—red sandstone slabs marching across the burnished desert beneath a turquoise sky. In these majestic monuments geologists read the story of a great plateau wracked by ancient upheaval, scarred by storm, chiseled and honed by wind and rain.

To get a closer look, we signed up for a jeep trip at the trading post and lodge built here 45 years ago by Harry Goulding and his wife Mike. Whom should we find at the counter but Sam Day, confirming reservations for a tour.

"The tribe's latest venture," Sam smiled. "We take sightseers on a five-day bus tour around the reservation, stopping each night at a motel or lodge. Navajo students serve as driver-guides, Navajo co-eds as hostesses. This way visitors see our land through Navajo eyes."

Fortified by a family-style breakfast of flapjacks and eggs, we piled into four-wheel-drive vehicles for an all-day ride with Harry Goulding. I felt lucky to be able to hit the trail with this remarkable frontiersman. He has made his life among the Navajos, and has quietly given profits from his trading post for scholarships to educate their children and for a hospital to heal their sick.

A jounce through the valley with Harry brings insights into both nature and Navajos. He called by name each massive monument, each Navajo family whose hogan we passed. Clumps of juniper, salt sage, and rabbit brush sprinkled the stark landscape with green as we gawked at monoliths, soaring pinnacles, gaping arches.

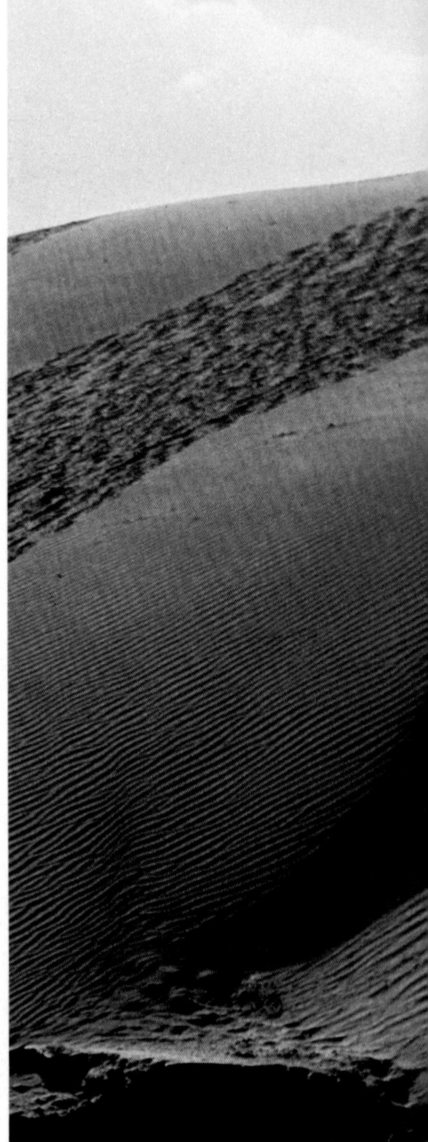

WOOLLY FLOTSAM ON A SEA OF SAND, A HERD DRIFTS OVER *Monument Valley dunes swept by the winds that carved the valley's magnificent buttes and mesas. In desert country where 65 acres grew only enough shrubs to feed a single sheep, the Navajos spent bitter years scraping a living from the meat, hides, and wool of their hardy flocks. Today they thrive in harmony with nature, their birth rate twice that of the Nation.*

Many still tend herds; others turn to newer pursuits. The girl who teaches a visitor to card wool may go to college on tribal profits from coal, oil, and uranium. The young shepherd may one day guide his brothers as Tribal Council delegate at Window Rock, Arizona, a booming capital aglow with murals of a proud past and aclatter with payroll computers and the presses of The Navajo Times.

TERRY EILER (ALSO OPPOSITE). UPPER: ROBERT F. SISSON, NATIONAL GEOGRAPHIC PHOTOGRAPHER

TERRY EILER

"WITH BEAUTY ALL AROUND ME, I WALK. IT IS FINISHED IN BEAUTY." Like the haunting Night Way chant, night ends in a benediction over Monument Valley, where a pool mirrors massive Brigham's Tomb and lonely King on His Throne. From hogan and pueblo men turn proud faces to a new dawn.

Around a twist in the trail we came face-to-face with a broad-shouldered butte whose stone folds harbored a small cliff dwelling, haven for a family of Anasazi some 800 years ago. "There are hundreds of prehistoric dwellings in the valley," Harry told us. "The Navajos say there are cliff houses back in these canyons no white man has ever seen."

We lunched in the shade of a canyon wall, entertained by a pair of goats stretching hind legs as they browsed on the branches of a juniper tree. As afternoon shadowed the valley floor, Harry hailed a lone Navajo horseman garbed in red shirt and yellow headband. They chatted softly in the Navajo manner. Then Harry motioned me over.

"Like for you to meet John Cly. He's lived in the valley man and boy. Raises sheep and a few cows. He wants to know where you're from."

"Way east," I replied as Harry translated. "Close to the ocean. Where we don't have scenery like this."

John Cly smiled broadly, displaying a gap in his front teeth. "He wishes he could give you some of it to take back," Harry laughed. "He says he has a whole lot of it."

By Seymour L. Fishbein

FROM A SUMMER SCHOOL IN THE SNOW
NEW-MADE MOUNTAINEERS STRUGGLE

To the Top of Rainier

Summit-bound above the clouds, climbers mount crevasse-scarred Ingraham Glacier, heads down, hopes high, hands full; C. David Hiser

A mile above Paradise, on a fringe of volcanic scree barren as moonsoil, I fidget through another night at Camp Muir. I dream, wide-eyed, of the golden days I left behind a week ago and a world away, where spring blooms had already withered and streams had slowed to summer's cadence. But Muir on its two-mile-high perch still sleeps in winter's trance. And here we lie, my sons and I and a score of other four-day-old snow climbers, swaddled in damp down bags, packed hip to hip in a drafty hut, yearning for the white crown of Mount Rainier.

Through gray days of snowfall we had fueled our bodies on thin air and the canned austerity of high-camp cuisine. We shivered in clothes that never dried, and trudged out across rock ridge and fractured glacier to learn the climber's skills, climber's hazards—and climber's fatigue. Now, on the last night of our mountain seminar, I roll restlessly with the thought that another storm, another whiteout could abort our hopes for a try at the 14,410-foot summit.

Moonbeams sifting through a frozen pane promise a sky at least partly uncluttered. Then, at 3:17, the door rasps open and the ringing mountain voice of big Lou Whittaker confirms a clear dawning: "Good morning. It's a beautiful day. The temperature is 16 degrees. We'll have breakfast in 30 minutes. Please be ready to go with crampons on. The ropes are laid out by the guide hut."

Head lamps slash the gloom; hands grope for socks, boots, sweaters, parkas, goggles, wool hats, mittens, pack frames. My teen-agers Joe and Jeff mumble the morning litany: "Boots frozen" . . . "Socks wet." Clothed at last, we wander out to taste the icy air. Down mountain, a quilt of cloud shrouds green Paradise Valley. Upslope? All clear.

Before this day ebbs we will take the measure of our desire—and of our bodies, my sons' limber though barely tested, mine stiffened by deskbound decades. And we will know for sure how wise we were to forgo the familiar delights of lakeside cottage and trout stream in New Hampshire or the bracing knobs of Virginia's Blue Ridge.

"It's a happy mountain, a magnificent mountain—but it's out to get you," a ranger had told us as we checked into the national park that enshrines Rainier in the heart of Washington State. An odd greeting, I thought. But as we

FLAUNTING FINE FORM, A CLIMBER RAPPELS DOWN *the jagged face of 6,562-foot Pinnacle Peak in Washington's Cascades. To brake the dangling descent, her lower hand pulls tight, forcing friction on rope that threads the carabiner's eye and curves around her back. Beyond, veiled by cloud, cloaked by ice, Rainer rises more than twice as high.*

BOB AND IRA SPRING

talked the picture became clear. A shining summer day draws thousands from the Seattle area two hours away. Lightly garbed, they fairly leap up the mountain. The air's warm, the snowfields unbelievable. Why not try it to Muir? Then Rainier whips up a storm. Skill shortens the odds but does not guarantee success. Even as we spoke to the ranger, Lou Whittaker was retrieving five veterans hit by a rockfall on the treacherous north face. Four survived.

So people die on this ice-clad volcano—people who know the mountain and the art and get trapped at the wrong place at the wrong time when only luck can save them; and people who know nothing except that it's there and they must have it now, and that may take too much luck.

Properly equipped and shepherded by guides on time-tested routes, people in climbing school do not die. They dehydrate, they may heave with nausea, their knees turn to rubber—but they survive. Some quit; but most struggle, step by brutal step, all the way.

The day smiled, a come-hither, go-higher smile, as our car left the ranger station and snaked up the 12-mile road to the Rainier Guide Service. Douglas firs, hemlocks, red cedars, patriarchs of the rain forest, sentineled our path. The sun turned on a hundred faucets, sending snowmelt grooving down the slopes. We spun around a rising curve and found ourselves in the visitor complex called Paradise.

On his way to the summit in 1888, naturalist John Muir paused near this spot and, as we did now, looked up: "Out of the forest at last there stood the mountain . . . awful in bulk and majesty, filling all the view like a separate, new-born world . . . so fine and so beautiful."

Inside the visitor center Lou Whittaker, twin of "Big Jim" the Everest conqueror, looked us over—Joe and Jeff up and down and me around the middle—and assembled our rented gear. Next morning, as Rainer's crest disappeared in a blustery drizzle, we met our classmates: college students, a globe-girdling airline pilot, a symphony cellist, a Japanese engineer, a lady schoolteacher.

Packs snug, luminous parkas pulled tight, we stepped off the asphalt onto the snow, a platoon of psychedelic ants bent under their burdens, toiling up into the mists. Around 7,000 feet, trees and heather disappeared. The rain turned climbing boots into cisterns, mittens into water bags. Discomfort sapped common sense. Time and again I lifted a hand to adjust the pack. Each time water poured out of the mitten, down the arm, into the armpit.

Camp Muir. Double-decker shelving for bunks, one tired lantern, no heat. Canned stew, mashed potatoes, Jell-O,

A "BOTANIZING EXCURSION" LED PUGET SOUND PIONEERS *to the slopes of Rainier; its "sublime form" first drove men to its frosty dome in 1870, undaunted by an Indian's warning: "No one can do it and live. A mighty chief dwells upon the summit in a lake of fire."*

Greenery and grandeur still charm excursionists in the 378 square miles of Mount Rainier National Park, where avalanche fawn lilies (above) spring up as snow recedes, harbingers of midsummer's riot on the alpine meadows. Here hardy hikers test nature's bridge across a misty gorge, explore a frozen fairyland in the Paradise Ice Caves, shaped by water and air and tinted by filtered sunlight. Newly discovered passageways may rank these grottoes as earth's largest ice caverns.

From water-laden westerlies Rainier each year wrings rain and some 50 feet of snow to nourish 700 kinds of flowering plants, cathedral forests with 200-foot spires, and 26 glaciers, most on any U. S. peak outside Alaska. Deer and bear, mountain goat, marmot, and man find sanctuary in the shadow of a volcano created in cataclysm hundreds of thousands of years ago.

BARRY C. BISHOP, NATIONAL GEOGRAPHIC STAFF. BELOW: BOB AND IRA SPRING. OPPOSITE: C. DAVID HISER

GO TELL IT ON THE MOUNTAIN: OLD HANDS GUIDE GREEN ONES IN SURVIVAL ON SLIPPERY SLOPES

Glissading on his backside ("Great fun—but you get wet pants"), 14-year-old Jeff Fishbein starts a self-arrest drill: As he rams the ax head into the snow, he will roll over to press his chest against the shaft and dig his toes in—ending a slide that could otherwise end in a crevasse. Spike-studded crampon (below) can stop a slide before it starts.

Lou Whittaker, chief guide of the Rainier Guide Service and Mountaineering School, shows how a boot-ax belay (left) feeds a lifeline to a partner on thin ice. If he breaks through, belay brakes his fall, and crevasse rescue (opposite) brings him up. Foot slings hitch to rope with the ingenious Prusik knot. Without tension, it slides up; under body weight, it holds. Climber shifts weight to one sling, inches up the other—and slowly hoists himself from the pit.

C. DAVID HISER. OPPOSITE: BARRY C. BISHOP, NATIONAL GEOGRAPHIC STAFF

and Lou Whittaker—feeding, teaching, recounting the triumphs and tragedies of more than a quarter of a century of climbing. "I'd go through this just to listen to him," said a graduate student flushed with mountain fever.

We learned to climb with crampons, to stop a slide with the ice ax, to tie in with nylon rope that could save our lives if the ice ax failed, to belay our ropemates over snow or ice bridges. On the crest of a cornice the guides introduced us to the delights of the free rappel.

We practiced on pitches that verged on the vertical. Surmounting one of these, I shook my head. Surely climbers must have some kind of deep-seated death wish. "Not at all," countered the lady teacher. "We're constantly defying death here. This is an affirmation of life."

Summit morning. At daybreak in subfreezing weather, it is the same with middle-agers as with teen-agers. Ice axes turn up missing; crampons don't snap on. We are late tying in. As I fumble, I glance at the six other four-man lines. There they stand, the college bucks, shoulders a yard wide, hot to go. Their sideburns seem to bristle.

"Let's go for it!" Lou's cry rings out, and we step out behind him. On our route, across Cowlitz Glacier, over a gap in the spires of Cathedral Rocks, and up Ingraham Glacier, we will need no expertise, no Batman tricks with rope and pitons—only endurance, will, and the caution the guides have drilled into us.

But the first hard slog empties the mind of everything except doubt and fear of embarrassment. You forget to take that full breath with every step, grumble at Lou's reminder:

CLIMBING CLASSMATES CROWD CAMP MUIR'S ROCK-WALLED GUIDE HUT *to prepare for a breathtaking graduation. They pack extra clothes, sandwiches, sweets for quick energy, melted snow in plastic bottles (opposite). Ahead lies the fearsome chop of Ingraham Glacier, so none neglects the posted caution—better phrased by a wag with a Dantean flair: "Abandon hope, without three on a rope, all ye who enter here."*

Some 2,000 a year enter here, in guided groups and private parties whose equipment, fitness, and skill park rangers have checked. Some, veteran rock climbers dreaming of McKinley or Andean peaks four miles high, tackle Rainier to master mountaineering on ice and snow. American conquerors of Everest trained here, but a storm packing a Himalayan punch denied them the summit.

Coached by friends, guides, climbing clubs (page 421), a growing army swarms to mountains from Sierras to Appalachians. Its members seek not ease but freedom, the hard-won "freedom of the hills." They share the spirit of Prof. Olof Bull who hauled his violin to the crest of Rainier in 1896 and there gave a concert, ending with—what else?—"Nearer, My God, to Thee."

C. DAVID HISER

SUNGLOW DYES A CARPET OF CLOUD AT THE DAWNING OF A SUMMIT DAY

"Ventilate your lungs—hoooo—get rid of the stale air." You stumble, and dig a crampon tooth into slack rope. "That's like stepping on your neck," a guide scolds.

You banish doubt and forget fatigue long enough to drink in the blue-white wonder of Ingraham Glacier, cleft by those deadly crevasses; the enchanted-castle look of Little Tahoma Peak, its pinnacle ablaze in the morning sun.

We cannot see our goal; a mass of rock and Ingraham's headwall hide it. Old-time climbers thought they could see it, until they topped the rock and looked up. That rock is called Disappointment Cleaver. On it we pause for lunch, at 8 a.m. Two thousand feet to go.

Now the air is thinner, the pitch steeper (about 40 degrees), the climber's rhythm ever more crucial: step . . . breathe . . . step . . . breathe. The boys and I follow in Lou's footsteps; then a step collapses and I sink hip-deep into the snow, huffing, puffing, squandering precious energy, finally churning myself onto firm footing. But I have nothing left!

Nothing? There stand my sons and Lou, waiting. I gulp once, twice, three times, plod on. Now I begin to scheme. How much longer before I can ask for a breather? We start up the headwall. It seems like hardly a minute goes by now before I call for a rest. Why don't Jeff and Joe ask? Probably because they know I will. Who cares? We're not racing anyone. "Hey Lou, how about a break?"

At the top of the headwall the punishing pitch flattens. There up ahead, surely within range now, a fringe of black rocks curves away—the crater rim! The pace picks up. Desire drives me along with it for a few steps. But only a few. We soon slow down. A rope of four passes ours. No

Fourteen thousand feet and climbing: Five hours from Camp Muir and a somber daybreak (opposite), a string of novices, tethered to Lou Whittaker in the lead, slowly traverses the last and steepest leg, the headwall of Ingraham Glacier. Uncertain footing trips them, ice axes sink hilt-deep, but soon there's only sky above! Joe Fishbein registers the triumph at Columbia Crest, high point of the summit cone. Though Rainier hasn't blown its top in more than a century, fumaroles still warm climbers and geologists monitor the mountain for new signs of restlessness.

C. DAVID HISER

matter. It is no longer a climb, only a walk—or, if need be, a crawl. I will get there.

Incredible scene. A shallow, dark-rimmed bowl of ice, tiny puffs of steam belched up from the volcano's innards. Men shed packs, laugh and joke, slap each other on the back. Joe and Jeff, faces flushed and crinkled, shout, "Hooray! We did it!" Lou Whittaker shakes hands with each of his graduates: "Congratulations. That was great." And I am draped across an ice-gripped boulder, body drained, spirit soaring.

Have we conquered Rainier? Hardly. But it didn't conquer us. We have slithered

Splendid and harsh and guarded by rivers of ice, the mountain rises in challenge, and man responds.

in its snowfields, stumbled over its ridges, groaned up its mighty shoulders, dodged its jumble of gaping chasms. The mountain has taken from us more than we ever dreamed we had. Now we reap the reward: unbounded delight and a sharpened self-awareness we could have won no other way.

Best of all, for this one week, this priceless moment in our lives, the boys and I have reached across the perilous chasm between our generations and found ourselves together. What more can a summer do?

The tortuous way steepens, and man endures, reaching for the heights, growing taller as he goes.

11,117-FOOT LITTLE TAHOMA PEAK SHADES A FLANK OF RAINIER; C. DAVID HISER

INDEX

Text references appear in roman type; illustrations and illustrated text in boldface. *Designates map.

Where to Get Vacationland Information

The excellent "Guides to Outdoor Recreation Areas and Facilities" lists federal, state, and private publications on camping, canoeing, fishing, hiking, and ghost towns. To get it, send 40 cents to Supt. of Documents, Government Printing Office, Washington, D. C. 20402. Other sources:

Campsites await in most national and state parks. Write to National Park Service, Interior Bldg., Washington, D. C. 20240, and state agencies (page 422). National Geographic's America's Wonderlands *guides you to 90 national park areas;* America's Historylands *visits historical sites.*

Where are the big ones? State information agencies (page 422) will give you tips on spots and licenses. National Geographic's Wondrous World of Fishes *describes North American species, tells how to catch and cook game fish.*

American Alpine Club, 113 E. 90th St., New York, N.Y. 10028, leads you to regional mountaineering groups. Sierra Club, 1050 Mills Tower, San Francisco, Calif. 94104, sponsors high-country treks. For caving, the National Speleological Society, Inc., 2318 N. Kenmore St., Arlington, Va. 22201, will tell you where to find the nearest grotto (chapter).

Navajos in Arizona, Sioux in South Dakota, Seminoles in Florida—most tribes welcome visitors. Bureau of Indian Affairs, 1951 Constitution Ave. N.W., Washington, D. C. 20242, can help you find the trail.

American Youth Hostels, Inc., 20 W. 17th St., New York, N.Y. 10011, opens doors to members from "4 to 94." Annual fees range from $5 for under-18'ers to $12 for families. AYH Bicycle Atlas maps 150 bike routes.

The annual guide of Farm & Ranch Vacations, Inc., 36 E. 57th St., New York, N.Y. 10022, describes U. S. spreads. Or get list of agencies that provide names of vacation farms from U. S. Dept. of Agriculture, Office of Information, Special Reports Div., Washington, D. C. 20250.

Skis. Skates. Snowmobiles. Sleds. Whatever your wintry wants, get tips from snowy states (page 422). Check national parks for winter programs. More than 200 ski areas mantle national forests; write Forest Service, U. S. Dept. of Agriculture, Washington, D. C. 20250, for skiing sites.

Do go near the water—and under: Learn how to learn from Underwater Society of America, 427 Chestnut St., Philadelphia, Pa. 19106. For river fun ideas: American White Water Affiliation, 2019 Addison St., Chicago, Ill. 60618. For national seashores, scenic rivers, reclamation lakes: Bureau of Outdoor Recreation, 18th and C Sts. N.W., Washington, D. C. 20240. For pleasure-boating rules and equipment hints: U. S. Coast Guard Hdqrs., Comdt. (B), Washington, D. C. 20591.

For Appalachian Trail guides: The Appalachian Trail Conference, Inc., 1718 N St. N.W., Washington, D. C. 20036. For Pacific Crest Trail maps: Regional Forester, 630 Sansome St., San Francisco, Calif. 94111 (California stretch); Regional Forester, Box 3623, Portland, Oreg. 97208 (Washington and Oregon). Tips on backpacking in national forests: Forest Service, U. S. Dept. of Agriculture, Washington, D. C. 20250.

National wildlife refuges dot the map (pages 100, 276; Vacationland U.S.A. *map supplement). Get state-by-state list, leaflets on specific refuges from the Director, Bureau of Sport Fisheries and Wildlife, Washington, D. C. 20240.*

State Vacation Information

Time your vacation to events (Happenings, pages 99, 275) by getting dates from these state agencies. They'll also supply specific information on such activities as camping and fishing.

Alabama Bureau of Publicity & Information, Montgomery 36104

Alaska Dept. of Economic Development, Travel Division, Pouch E, Juneau 99801

Arizona Dept. of Economic Planning & Development, Suite 1704, 3003 N. Central Ave., Phoenix 85012

Arkansas Parks, Recreation & Travel Commission, 149 State Capitol Building, Little Rock 72201

California Office of Tourism & Visitor Services, 1400 10th St., Sacramento 95814

Colorado Division of Commerce & Development, 602 State Capitol Annex, Denver 80203

Connecticut Development Commission, State Office Bldg., Hartford 06115

Delaware State Development Dept., Travel Division, 45 The Green, Dover 19901

District of Columbia Washington Convention & Visitors Bureau, 1129 20th St. N.W., Washington, D. C. 20036

Florida Dept. of Commerce, 107 West Gaines St., Tallahassee 32304

Georgia Dept. of Industry & Trade, Box 38097, Atlanta 30334

Hawaii Visitors Bureau, 2270 Kalakaua Ave., Honolulu 96815

Idaho Dept. of Commerce & Development, Rm. 108, State House, Boise 83707

Illinois Tourism Division, 222 South College, Springfield 62706

Indiana Dept. of Commerce, Division of Tourism, State Capitol, Rm. 336 MO, Indianapolis 46204

Iowa Tourism and Travel Division, Development Commission, 250 Jewett Bldg., Des Moines 50309

Kansas Dept. of Economic Development, State Office Bldg., Rm. 122-S, Topeka 66612

Kentucky Dept. of Public Information, Capitol Annex, Frankfort 40601

Louisiana Tourist Development Commission, Box 44291, Baton Rouge 70804

Maine Dept. of Economic Development, State Office Bldg., Augusta 04330

Maryland Travel Development Division, Dept. of Economic Development, State Office Bldg., Annapolis 21401

Massachusetts Dept. of Commerce & Development, 100 Cambridge St., Boston 02202

Michigan Tourist Council, Stevens T. Mason Bldg., Lansing 48926

Minnesota Dept. of Economic Development, 57 West 7th St., St. Paul 55102

Mississippi Park System, 502 Milner Building, Jackson 39201

Missouri Tourism Commission, 308 East High St., Box 1055, Jefferson City 65101

Montana Advertising Dept., Highway Commission, Helena 59601

Nebraska Information & Tourism Division, Game & Park Commission, State Capitol, Lincoln 68509

Nevada Tourism-Travel Division, Dept. of Economic Development, Carson City 89701

New Hampshire Division of Economic Development, Box 856, Concord 03301

New Jersey Dept. of Conservation & Economic Development, Box 1889, Trenton 08625

New Mexico Tourist Division, Dept. of Development, 113 Washington Ave., Santa Fe 87501

New York Dept. of Commerce, Travel Bureau, 112 State St., Albany 12207

North Carolina Travel & Promotion Division, Dept. of Conservation & Development, Raleigh 27602

North Dakota Travel Dept., State Highway Dept., Bismarck 58501

Ohio Travel Division, Development Dept., 65 S. Front St., Columbus 43215

Oklahoma Industrial Development & Park Dept., Will Rogers Memorial Bldg., Oklahoma City 73105

Oregon State Highway Dept., Travel Information Div., 101 Highway Bldg., Salem 97310

Pennsylvania Bureau of Travel Development, Dept. of Commerce, Rm. 402 South Office Bldg., Harrisburg 17120

Rhode Island Development Council, Roger Williams Bldg., Hayes St., Providence 02908

South Carolina Travel Division, Dept. of Parks, Recreation & Tourism, Box 1358, Columbia 29202

South Dakota Travel Division, Dept. of Highways, Pierre 57501

Tennessee Dept. of Conservation, Division of Tourist Information & Promotion, 2611 West End Ave., Nashville 37203

Texas Tourist Development Agency, Box TT Capitol Station, Austin 78711

Utah Travel Council, Council Hall, Capitol Hill, Salt Lake City 84114

Vermont Development Dept., Montpelier 05602

Virginia Dept. of Conservation & Economic Development, Travel Service, 911 East Broad St., Richmond 23219

Washington Dept. of Commerce & Economic Development, Tourist Promotion Division, General Admin. Bldg., Olympia 98501

West Virginia Dept. of Commerce, Travel Development Division, State Capitol, Charleston 25305

Wisconsin Vacation & Travel Service, Dept. of Natural Resources, Box 450, Madison 53701

Wyoming Travel Commission, 2320 Capitol Ave., Cheyenne 82001

Composition by National Geographic's Phototypographic Division, HERMAN J.A.C. ARENS, Director; JOHN E. McCONNELL, Manager. Color separations by Beck Engraving Company, Philadelphia, Pa., Graphic Color Plate, Inc., Stamford, Conn., and Charlotte, N.C., The Lanman Company, Alexandria, Va., Lebanon Valley Offset, Inc., Cleona, Pa., Progressive Color Corporation, Rockville, Md., Stevenson Photo Color Company, Cincinnati, Ohio. Printed and bound by Fawcett-Haynes Corporation, Rockville, Md. Paper by Oxford Paper Company, New York.

NATIONAL GEOGRAPHIC SOCIETY

WASHINGTON, D. C.

Organized "for the increase and diffusion of geographic knowledge"

GILBERT HOVEY GROSVENOR

Editor, 1899-1954; President, 1920-1954
Chairman of the Board, 1954-1966

THE NATIONAL GEOGRAPHIC SOCIETY is chartered in Washington, D. C., in accordance with the laws of the United States, as a nonprofit scientific and educational organization for increasing and diffusing geographic knowledge and promoting research and exploration. Since 1890 the Society has supported 573 explorations and research projects, adding immeasurably to man's knowledge of earth, sea, and sky. It diffuses this knowledge through its monthly journal, NATIONAL GEOGRAPHIC; more than 27 million maps distributed each year; its books, globes, atlases, and filmstrips; 30 School Bulletins a year in color; information services to press, radio, and television; technical reports; exhibits from around the world in Explorers Hall; and a nationwide series of programs on television.

NATIONAL GEOGRAPHIC MAGAZINE

MELVILLE BELL GROSVENOR
Editor-in-Chief and Board Chairman

MELVIN M. PAYNE
President of the Society

FREDERICK G. VOSBURGH, Editor

Associate Editors
GILBERT M. GROSVENOR, FRANC SHOR, JOHN SCOFIELD

Senior Assistant Editors
Allan C. Fisher, Jr., Kenneth MacLeish, Robert L. Conly

Assistant Editors: Andrew H. Brown, James Cerruti, W. E. Garrett, Edward J. Linehan, Carolyn Bennett Patterson, Howell Walker, Kenneth F. Weaver

Senior Editorial Staff: Lonnelle Aikman, Jules B. Billard, Rowe Findley, William Graves, Jay Johnston, Stuart E. Jones, Robert P. Jordan, Joseph Judge, Nathaniel T. Kenney, Samuel W. Matthews, Bart McDowell; Senior Natural Scientist: Paul A. Zahl

Foreign Editorial Staff: Luis Marden (Chief); Thomas J. Abercrombie, Howard La Fay, Volkmar Wentzel, Peter T. White

Editorial Staff: Harvey Arden, Thomas Y. Canby, Louis de la Haba, William S. Ellis, Alice J. Hall, Werner Janney, Jerry Kline, Elizabeth A. Moize, Ethel A. Starbird, Gordon Young

Editorial Layout: Howard E. Paine (Chief); Charles C. Uhl, John M. Lavery

Geographic Art: William N. Palmstrom (Chief). *Artists:* Lisa Biganzoli, William H. Bond, John W. Lothers, Robert C. Magis, Robert W. Nicholson, Ned M. Seidler. *Cartographic Artists:* Victor J. Kelley, Snejinka Stefanoff. *Research:* Walter Q. Crowe (Supervisor), Virginia L. Baza, George W. Beatty, John D. Garst, Jean B. McConville, Dorothy A. Nicholson, Isaac Ortiz (Production). Marie L. Barnes (Administrative Assistant)

Editorial Research: Margaret G. Bledsoe (Chief); Ann K. Wendt (Associate Chief), Jan Holderness, Levenia Loder, Frances H. Parker, Patricia Rosenborg, Elizabeth C. Wagner

Geographic Research: George Crossette (Chief); Newton V. Blakeslee (Assistant Chief), Leon J. Canova, Bette Joan Goss, Lesley B. Lane, John A. Weeks

Phototypography: John E. McConnell (Chief); Lawrence F. Ludwig (Assistant Chief)

Library: Virginia Carter Hills (Librarian); Margery K. Barkdull (Assistant Librarian), Melba Barnes, Vera Cassilly, Louise A. Robinson, Esther Ann Manion (Librarian Emeritus)

Administration: Betty T. Sanborne, Administrative Assistant to the Editor; Harriet Carey, Virginia H. Finnegan, Joyce W. McKean, Winifred M. Myers, Shirley Neff, Inez D. Wilkinson (Editorial Assistants); Dorothy M. Corson (Indexes); Rosalie K. Millerd, Lorine Wendling (Files); Evelyn Fox (Transportation); Carolyn F. Clewell (Correspondence); Jeanne S. Duiker (Archives)

ILLUSTRATIONS STAFF: *Illustrations Editor:* Herbert S. Wilburn, Jr. *Associate Illustrations Editor:* Thomas R. Smith. *Art Editor:* Andrew Poggenpohl. *Assistant Illustrations Editors:* Mary S. Griswold, O. Louis Mazzatenta. *Layout and Production:* H. Edward Kim (Chief). *Senior Picture Editors:* Charlene Murphy, Robert S. Patton. *Picture Editors:* David L. Arnold, William C. Latham, Michael E. Long, W. Allan Royce, Jon Schneeberger. *Research:* Paula C. Simmons. Barbara A. Shattuck (Asst.). *Librarian:* L. Fern Dame

Artists: Walter A. Weber (Naturalist), Peter V. Bianchi

Engraving and Printing: Dee J. Andella (Chief); Raymond B. Benzinger, William W. Smith, James R. Whitney

PHOTOGRAPHIC STAFF: *Director of Photography:* Robert E. Gilka. *Assistant Director:* Dean Conger. *Film Review:* Albert Moldvay (Chief); Guy W. Starling (Assistant Chief). *Photographic Equipment:* John E. Fletcher (Chief). *Pictorial Research:* Walter Meayers Edwards (Chief). *Photographers:* James L. Amos, James P. Blair, Bruce Dale, Dick Durrance II, Otis Imboden, Emory Kristof, Bates Littlehales, George F. Mobley, Robert S. Oakes, Winfield Parks, Joseph J. Scherschel, Robert F. Sisson, James L. Stanfield. Lilian Davidson (Administration). *Photographic Laboratories:* Carl M. Shrader (Chief); Milton A. Ford (Associate Chief); Herbert Altemus, Jr., Donald McBain, Claude E. Petrone, Donald E. Stemper. Edwin L. Wisherd (Consultant)

RELATED EDUCATIONAL SERVICES OF THE SOCIETY

Cartography—Maps, atlases, and globes: Chief Cartographer: Wellman Chamberlin; *Associate Chief Cartographer:* Athos D. Grazzini; *Assistant Chief:* William T. Peele. *Base Compilation:* Charles L. Stern (Supervisor), Charles F. Case, James W. Killion. *Name Compilation:* Donald A. Jaeger (Supervisor), Charles W. Gotthardt, Jr., Manuela G. Kogutowicz, David L. Moore, George E. Stuart. *Map Drawings:* Douglas A. Strobel (Supervisor), Robert W. Northrop, Thomas A. Wall. *Map Editing:* Ted Dachtera (Supervisor), Russel G. Fritz, Richard K. Rogers, Thomas A. Walsh. *Projections:* David W. Cook. *Layout and Design:* John F. Dorr, Harry C. Siddeley. *Revisions:* Richard J. Darley. *Administrative Assistant:* Catherine M. Hart

Books: Merle Severy (Chief); Seymour L. Fishbein (Assistant Chief), Thomas B. Allen, Ross Bennett, Charles O. Hyman, Anne Dirkes Kobor, John J. Putman, David F. Robinson

Special Publications: Robert L. Breeden (Chief); Donald J. Crump (Assistant Chief), Josephine B. Bolt, David R. Bridge, Margery G. Dunn, Johanna G. Farren, Ronald M. Fisher, Mary Ann Harrell, Bryan Hodgson, Geraldine Linder, Philip B. Silcott, Joseph A. Taney

School Service: Ralph Gray (Chief and Editor of National Geographic School Bulletin); Arthur P. Miller, Jr. (Assistant Chief and Associate Editor of School Bulletin), Jeanne A. Davis, Joseph B. Goodwin, Paul F. Moize, Charles H. Sloan, Janis Knudsen Wheat. *Educational Filmstrips:* David S. Boyer (Chief); Ledlie L. Dinsmore, Margaret McKelway Johnson, Bonnie S. Lawrence.

News Service: Windsor P. Booth (Chief); Paul Sampson (Assistant Chief), Donald J. Frederick; Isabel Clarke (Assistant)

Television: Robert C. Doyle (Chief); David Cooper, Carl W. Harmon, Jr., Sidney Platt, Patricia F. Northrop (Administrative Assistant)

Lectures: Joanne M. Hess (Chief); Robert G. Fleegal, Mary W. McKinney, Gerald L. Wiley

Explorers Hall: T. Keilor Bentley (Curator-Director)

EUROPEAN OFFICES: W. Edward Roscher (Associate Secretary and Director), 4 Curzon Place, Mayfair, London, W1Y 8EN, England; Jacques Ostier, 6 rue des Petits-Pères, 75-Paris 2e, France

ADVERTISING: *Director:* William A. Boeger, Jr. *National Advertising Manager:* William Turgeon; *Executive Director of Advertising Relations:* Harley L. McDevitt, 630 Fifth Ave., New York, N.Y. 10020. *Regional managers—Eastern:* George W. Kellner, New York. *Midwestern:* Robert R. Henn, Chicago. *Western:* Thomas Martz, San Francisco. *Los Angeles:* Jack Wallace. *Automotive:* John F. Grant, New York. *Travel:* Gerald A. Van Splinter, New York. *International:* James L. Till, New York. *European:* Richard V. Macy, Paris